How to Build & Modify GM
PRO-TOURING
Street Machines
Classic Looks with Modern Performance!

TONY E. HUNTIMER

Copyright © 2004 by Tony E. Huntimer

All rights reserved. All text and photographs in this publication are the property of the author, unless otherwise noted or credited. It is unlawful to reproduce – or copy in any way – resell, or redistribute this information without the express written permission of the publisher.

All text, photographs, drawings, and other artwork (hereafter referred to as information) contained in this publication is sold without any warranty as to its usability or performance. In all cases, original manufacturer's recommendations, procedures, and instructions supersede and take precedence over descriptions herein. Specific component design and mechanical procedures—and the qualifications of individual readers—are beyond the control of the publisher, therefore the publisher disclaims all liability, either expressed or implied, for use of the information in this publication. All risk for its use is entirely assumed by the purchaser/user. In no event will CarTech®, Inc., or the author be liable for any indirect, special, or consequential damages, including but not limited to personal injury or any other damages, arising out of the use or misuse of any information in this publication.

This book is an independent publication, and the author(s) and/or publisher thereof are not in any way associated with, and are not authorized to act on behalf of any of the manufacturers included in this book. All registered trademarks are the property of their owners. The publisher reserves the right to revise this publication or change its content from time to time without obligation to notify any persons of such revisions or changes.

Edited By: Travis Thompson

Layout By: Joshua Limbaugh

ISBN-13 978-1-61325-003-7

Order No. SA81P

Printed in the USA

CarTech®, Inc.,
39966 Grand Avenue
North Branch, MN 55056
Telephone (651) 277-1200 • (800) 551-4754 • Fax: (651) 277-1203
www.cartechbooks.com

OVERSEAS DISTRIBUTION BY:

Brooklands Books Ltd.
P.O. Box 146, Cobham, Surrey, KT11 1LG, England
Telephone 01932 865051 • Fax 01932 868803
www.brooklands-books.com

Brooklands Books Aus.
3/37-39 Green Street, Banksmeadow, NSW 2109, Australia
Telephone 2 9695 7055 • Fax 2 9695 7355

Front Cover, Main: **Tony Huntimer's big-block powered '68 Camaro is a perfect example of a Pro-Touring machine, with major upgrades to the powertrain, chassis, suspension, and interior. The body's classic styling, though, remains largely intact.**

Front Cover, Left Inset: **Kyle Tucker welds a custom tubular control arm in a special fixture.**

Front Cover, Middle Inset: **DSE's display frame is fitted with their high-performance suspension components and Baer brakes.**

Front Cover, Right Inset: **Jeff Hyosaka's fuel-injected small-block Chevy.**

Back Cover, Left: **It's not everyday (for most people) that you see a full-tilt turbocharged Buick V-6 like this one. This engine produces a 925 hp on 24 lbs of boost and has motivated the car to over 208 mph! On asphalt!** (Photo courtesy Joe Pettitt)

Back Cover, Right: **This El Camino is an engineering marvel. You can see the large custom fuel cell and some of the cage tubing. Not as visible are the rocker-arm actuated Koni coil-overs. The exhaust exits unconventionally, from under the rear wing.**

Back Cover, Lower: **MAD Ink made a concept rendering before spending any money on their '65 Malibu SS. It gave them an idea of how it might look when it was done, using the same color, stance, and chosen parts. The finished product looks very close to the way MAD envisioned it; in fact, I would say they nailed it. It's a well-executed project.** (Photo courtesy MAD Ink)

Title Page: **Andrew Borodin's big block Chevy powered '70 GTO sees frequent track time, and took first place in Car Craft Magazines Real Street Eliminator 14.** (Photo credit Jim McIlvaine)

TABLE OF CONTENTS

	About the Author	5
	Introduction: An Introduction to Pro-Touring	6
	The Term	7
	Roots	7
	What is Pro-Touring?	8
Chapter 1	**General Suspension, Brakes, and Tires and Wheels**	**13**
	Shock Absorbers	13
	Sway Bars	14
	Bushings	16
	Handling – Understeer and Oversteer	17
	Why Upgrade Brakes?	17
	Brake Parts	18
	Brake Cooling	19
	Boosting Brakes	19
	Balancing a Braking System	19
	Brake Master Install	21
	Tires	24
	Wheels	24
	Fitting Tires and Wheels	25
Chapter 2	**Front Suspension and Steering**	**28**
	Alignment	28
	Control Arms	32
	Springs	34
	Spindles and Brakes	35
	Ball Joints	36
	Aftermarket Subframes (20 Questions)	37
	DSE Coil-Over Kit	39
	Steering	41
	Steeroids Rack-and-Pinion Conversion	43
Chapter 3	**Rear Suspension**	**50**
	Pinion Angle	50
	Universal Joints	53
	Leaf Springs	54
	Coil Springs	60
	Live Axle Rear Suspension	60
	Independent Rear Suspension	61

Table of Contents

Chapter 4 **Frames** **64**
- Frame Types 64
- Frame and Subframe Bushings 66
- Subframe Connectors 67
- Front Support Systems 68
- Frame Boxing 70
- Tubbing 70
- Rear Frame Rail Tricks 71
- Roll Bars and Roll Cages 72

Chapter 5 **Engines** **77**
- Engine Swaps 77
- Engine Parts 80
- Cooling System 81
- Oiling System 87
- Induction and Fuel Systems 91

Chapter 6 **Drivetrain** **98**
- Manual Transmissions 98
- Automatics 102
- Rear Ends 105
- Limited-Slip Differentials 105
- Gear Ratios 105
- So What Rear End to Use? 105

Chapter 7 **Body and Electrical** **108**
- Stock Body 108
- Custom Bodywork 109
- Fiberglass 111
- Spoilers, Air dams, and Body Mods 112
- Aerodynamics 114
- Safety Upgrades 117
- Charging System 120
- Basic Electrical and Wiring 121
- Interior 122
- Air Conditioning 124

Chapter 8 **Buying Parts and Finding Information** **131**
- Purchasing Parts 131
- Purchasing Cars 133
- Getting Information 135

Appendix A Source Guide 140

Appendix B **General Motors Body Designations** 143

ABOUT THE AUTHOR

Tony Huntimer has been into hot rodding since he was old enough to build model cars. In high school, his friends, Chris Mead, Ed Matthews, and Chris Fogarty, were driving hot rodded American Iron while he was interested in VWs. He periodically assisted on Super Gas racer, Doug Bracey's pit crew. Finally, at the age of 19 he purchased his first V8 powered car, a 1973 Camaro with a small block. He's been sold on V8s ever since.

Tony then worked for a General Motors contractor, spending five years performing mechanic's duties; disassembling, reassembling, and repairing brand new General Motors vehicles. In that time, he was able to take a good look at how GM designed and engineered their chassis, bodies, and interiors. This was a big influence on how he builds his own cars, and how he wrote this book.

By 1996, Tony had owned seven Camaros and had finished a budget Pro-Touring buildup on a 1968 Camaro. The Camaro was raced around Sears Point Raceway, and taped for audio included in Sony Playstation's Gran Turismo video game. In 1999, he navigated for Karl Chicca, while racing his 1969 Pro-Touring Camaro in the Pony Express open-road race. The following year, Karl and Tony took first place in the Pony Express 140 MPH class with an average speed of 139.985 MPH. It wasn't long before Tony was racing his Camaro in open track events alongside Karl Chicca. In 2001, Tony got back into automotive related work when Speed Merchant in San Jose, California, hired him. The shop has given him access to a ton of information, parts, and Pro-Touring project cars.

Acknowledgments

For some extra technical help, I enlisted a few professionals (and friends) as contributing editors. Vince Asaro is a professional builder, fabricator, and racer. Paul Caselas is a fuel system specialist, engine specialist/builder, and racer. Kevin Long is a builder, tire and wheel specialist, and racer. Kyle Tucker is an ex-GM suspension engineer, builder/fabricator, designer, racer, and holds a Mechanical Engineering degree from University of Missouri-Rolla. Thanks guys!

Special thanks (in no particular order) goes out to my wife, Vikki Huntimer for the support and sticking by me, Steve Hendrickson, Maureen Huntimer, Robert Cera, Randy Oldham, Steve D'Aurora, Mark Schwartz, Wayne Due, Kyle and Stacy Tucker, Mark Deshetler, Charley Lillard, Mark Stielow, Lindsay Jones, Bob Spears, Vic DeLeon, Kevin Stearns, Ray Barney, Nick Kikes, Anders Odeholm, Joe Pettitt, Dan Gottlieb, John Parsons, Larry Callahan, Chris Kerr, Ken Sink, Lee Grimes, Cam Douglass, Scott Parkhurst, Rick Love, David Barker, Thomas Read, David Pozzi, Andrew Borodin, Steve Chryssos, Tyler Beauregard, Britt Guerlain, Jim McIlvaine, Tiffany Cline, and Steve Nestlerode Jr.

INTRODUCTION

AN INTRODUCTION TO PRO-TOURING

When did Pro-Touring start? That is a hard question to answer. Nobody really knows how or when it started. Its lineage is broad. One thing is for sure — Pro-Touring has been alive and well since the mid to late 1990s.

Some other people think that the Pro-Touring style started in 1988 when Dan and R.J. Gottlieb's '69 Camaro hit the pages of *Car Craft*. The car's name was *Big Red*. It was called "The Baddest Camaro Ever Built," and it was. How else would you describe a 200-plus mph '69 Camaro? It was basically a NASCAR chassis with a '69 Camaro body welded onto it. In the middle of the Pro-Street revolution, it stood out in the crowd and left us wanting more. But Pro-Street kept getting stronger, and we were going to have to wait a while longer for high-tech, corner-carving Pro-Touring cars.

Some people think this style was started by Mark Stielow's first famous white '69 Camaro. It was called *Tri-Tip*. It showed up in the magazines when it competed in the '93 One Lap of America. It was the first time I saw an older street car built to handle well in the corners, with new technology widely used throughout.

Like many other people, I was watching the tire and brake technologies advancing rapidly from 1985 to 1995. I was building a '68 Camaro to race in high-speed open-road racing, just like *Big Red* had done. I even chose a big block to motivate my Camaro, just like *Big Red*. I decided to make it faster in the corners than GM had intended, and have better stopping power too. I was going to need more than 15-inch diameter radial tires to get the cornering ability I was searching for. The four-wheel drum brakes had to go too. Some 16-inch wheels and tires from a '95 Z28 and

Big Red *hit the pages of* Car Craft *magazine in October 1988. It was right in the middle of Pro-Street's prime. With its production-car body on a NASCAR-style chassis, it caught many eyes. People were left wanting more, but they were still caught up in the Pro-Street era.* (Dan Gottlieb)

This car hit the magazines in 1994. It was known as "Mark Stielow's white car," but it was later named Tri-Tip. The name Pro-Touring was still years away, but it fueled the fire. Mark is known as the person responsible for starting the build style, since Tri-Tip was the first well-publicized Pro-Touring car. Other people were building cars with this style, but this car was making waves. (Mark Stielow)

An Introduction to Pro-Touring

some factory disc brakes on all four corners did the job. In 1996 I sent a photo into *Popular Hot Rodding* magazine and they put my retro/road racer in the readers-rides section in the October issue. They mentioned that I wrote I was looking for a "different look." They also wrote, "it won't be (different) for long." And they were right. Like me, many other people have had the desire to build older muscle cars that could beat the pants off the newest Corvette in the corners and in a straight line, while still being mild mannered enough to comfortably drive across the country.

Pro-Touring may have started even earlier than Gottlieb's Camaro in 1988, but there will always be people who dispute the person who started it all.

The Term

It was 1998. Pro-Street was getting tiring. People still wanted cars that were powerful, but they wanted to be able to drive powerful muscle cars in more than a straight line or around the fairgrounds. Then came the term "Pro-Touring." Mark Stielow coined the name, using it in reference to the latest automotive building style. Mark went on the *Hot Rod* Magazine Power Tour with Jeff Smith, editor of *Chevy High Performance* magazine at that time. On the tour, they were talking about giving the style a name. After they returned home, Mark called Jeff and suggested "Pro-Touring." The rest is history.

Roots

Many forms of racing are incorporated into Pro-Touring. You will find hints of NASCAR, Formula-1, Trans-Am, open-road racing, and drag racing to name a few. Many ideas have come from automotive manufacturers too. American automotive manufacturers have been turning out serious performance cars since the mid 1980s, after taking a long hiatus since the early 1970s. New Camaros and Corvettes have been a great place to get ideas and parts. European automotive manufacturers have been consistently producing great performers for many years. You might not see many

Some Pro-Touring cars incorporate great ideas from NASCAR. The cars you see here were set up for Sears Point Raceway road course. Unlike their high-speed oval twins, they turn left **and** *right.*

Probably the most influential racing cars for Pro-Touring builders have been early Trans Am series cars. This is a restored '69 Trans Am series Camaro. It's run in the historic races on a regular basis. (Photo courtesy of Chad Raynal)

Introduction

Styling and engineering ideas come from supercars like this Ferrari Enzo. It has the best of both worlds: competition suspension and some luxury items.

people transplanting Ferrari engines or Lamborghini transaxles into older American muscle cars, but you will notice people incorporating ideas from them. There is quite a bit of race proven technology from many manufacturers turning up on Pro-Touring cars.

What *is* Pro-Touring?

"By improving your car's ability to handle, brake, and accelerate with the best of them, you have just stepped on board with the Pro-Touring movement. Pro-Touring is a genre like no other, it brings qualities and performance minded ideas from all areas of racing, as well as all areas of the car enthusiasm movement. Pro-Touring *is* carving up your nearest canyon road or road course with an older piece of Detroit iron that handles like it is on rails, due to the suspension modifications you made to it." - Ralph LoGrasso

The following question and answer section should explain Pro-Touring a little more in depth. For all intents and purposes, the following answers are based on the collective views and opinions of the author and some others in the Pro-Touring circle.

Q. Is there a cut-off year that a car must fall before or after to be considered Pro-Touring?

A. This has been the most controversial issue of Pro-Touring. Taking a car with ill handling and inferior brakes and modifying it with better brakes and chassis dynamics is what makes it a Pro-Touring car. A car like Ben Chase's street/autocross '96 Camaro would be considered Pro-Touring. It came from the factory handling better than most production cars of its time, but it has a wheel and tire combo that has been upgraded from the factory offerings. It's equipped with upgraded Baer brakes, larger sway bars, weld-in subframe connectors, upgraded shocks and struts, and a strut-tower brace. Although this Camaro came factory equipped with good-handling suspension, it has been highly modified to improve the all-around driving experience. That's what makes it a Pro-Touring car.

Tony Laruffa's '81 Malibu is a late model car that didn't handle or brake well from the factory. It is definitely considered a Pro-Touring car, with its upgraded engine, front and rear suspension, brakes, transmission, tires, and wheels. Pro-Touring also spans many years earlier, due to the inferior engineering (compared to nowadays) that went into cars like '74 Chevrolet Novas, '64 Oldsmobile 442s, and '71 Pontiac GTOs. Even cars like Brent Jackson's '57 Chevy and Summit Racing's small-block-

Pro-Touring car builders get ideas from drag racing too. The drag cars do not handle well around corners, but they do have serious power and have some chassis stiffening that should be looked at for ideas.

An Introduction to Pro-Touring

Compared to a '69 Camaro, Ben Chase's '96 Camaro handled great when it rolled off the assembly line. With the extent of the modifications done to this car, it crosses over the fine line into Pro-Touring status for newer cars.

Tony Laruffa's '81 Chevy Malibu is a prime example of a Pro-Touring machine. It came from the factory with less-than-stellar power and handling abilities. It now has fully upgraded suspension and a supercharged big-block Chevy.

Chevy-powered '32 Ford *QuadraDuece* are considered Pro-Touring. So no, there isn't really a limit by year.

Q. Can an import car be considered Pro-Touring?

A. Yes. Cars from Australia, such as the Holden, are cousins of the American auto manufacturers. And I've seen some early 1970s Datsun 240Zs that are Pro-Touring. Cars like Lamborghini and Ferrari would be hard to improve to Pro-Touring status, since they have been advanced in their designs for so long. For the most part, Pro-Touring is limited to American auto manufacturers. But as with most trends, Pro-Touring will bleed over into other markets.

Q. Does the car need to be lowered?

A. Part of the Pro-Touring look is the lowered stance. Stance is everything! Usually lowering your car gives you a lower center of gravity and helps your car handle better. In most cases, if you made all the improvements to your car and left it stock height, the higher center of gravity would decrease the effectiveness of the other modifications. However, you don't have to be scraping on every dip in the road or speed bump. A car that is too low is defeating one of the main purposes of building a Pro-Touring car: They are meant to be driven on the street, and hopefully on a road course. A car with extremely low stance looks great, but it's not always practical, safe, or good handling. A car can be so low that its suspension geometry is adversely affected.

Q. Is there a minimum wheel and tire size?

A. Like all the other aspects of Pro-Touring, it's a complete package, not just big wheels and tires. Pro-Touring is about appearance and the pursuit of better handling. Most people would think it is necessary to have at least a 16-inch wheel and tire combination, but for some cars, 15-inch wheels are an

This '57 Chevy belongs to Gilbert Lindley. It shows that Pro-Touring is not restricted to 1970s and newer cars. It features '94 Corvette front and rear suspension and an LT1 powerplant.

Introduction

The QuadraDuece is a Chevy-powered, all-wheel-drive '32 Ford. It was the brainchild of Mark Stielow. It shows that all years, makes, and models can be Pro-Touring. (Photo courtesy of Anders Odeholm)

An Introduction to Pro-Touring

This '70 Chevelle (above) looks great slammed down. This is a great example of a car that has been lowered too much for its own good. The right photo shows that the exhaust is about two inches off the ground. This makes the car hard to drive on the street, and even on a track.

upgrade. Technology has come so far in the last 15 years. Tire and wheel manufacturers are focusing on larger diameter tires and the growing market for them. As of writing of this book, 22-inch wheels and tires are readily available, and 26-inch wheels and tires are starting to show up for SUVs. Who knows if they will start showing up on Pro-Touring cars. A larger-diameter wheel and tire package not only gives the illusion of a smaller car, but it also allows for the lowered look without drastically lowering the car past the effectiveness of the suspension geometry. Smaller diameter wheels will not fit over the calipers of larger than stock disk-brake packages. Larger diameter wheels are necessary when 12-inch (or larger) rotors are installed on older cars.

Q. Is there a braking system requirement?

A. Yes. Disc brakes are part of the Pro-Touring image. Front drum brakes are outdated. If you have 4-wheel disc brakes, then that's even better. Drum brakes are not as safe or effective on cars that are built to travel at high speeds around a road course. If you are going to have a lot of power under the hood of your car, you need to invest in stopping your car quicker than the factory intended. You can use aftermarket brake packages, or upgrade to factory disc brakes.

Q. Is the car required to have electronic fuel injection?

A. No. Fuel injection is nice, but it isn't a requirement. Carburetors work very well, but in most cases will not give you the fuel efficiency and power that fuel injection can.

Q. Does the car need to have a 6-speed or an overdrive transmission?

A. No. Most Pro-Touring cars have 5- or 6-speed manual transmissions. Some of them have automatic overdrive transmissions. Having overdrive will get you better driveability and fuel mileage out of your car, but it's not a requirement.

Introduction

Here are some different examples of brakes. The far left picture shows a front drum brake. Drum brakes are ineffective for the purpose of stopping a car with added horsepower. They fade fast when used on a road course, especially on the front of a car. Front drum brakes are considered old technology. The middle photo is of a stock disc brake. This is more than adequate for most Pro-Touring applications. The far right photo shows a Brembo caliper and slotted rotor. Aftermarket parts like these are necessary on aggressive cars that have extreme power-to-weight ratios. The faster a car can go from zero to 100, the faster it should go from 100 to zero.

Q. Does it need to be a streetable car?

A. Yes. There are different opinions on what "streetable" means. Some people have full roll cages with large obtrusive door bars in their cars. Some people have their car so low that the exhaust scrapes on every little bump. These things make the cars less streetable. For the most part, if the car has a license plate and current registration, it is still legally considered a street car.

Q. Do you have to modify the suspension?

A. Yes. Pro-Touring cars should have at least two of the following items: larger sway bars, upgraded control arms, performance shocks, and high-rate springs. The original suspension installed on production cars is designed to have a fairly docile ride. Upgrading these items is necessary to get better handling out of your car.

Q. Is there a minimum engine size or performance requirement?

A. No. Some guys are running stock engines in their cars. Most cars have V-8s in them. Some cars are running Buick V-6s or high-output Cosworth 4-cylinder engines. Upgrading the performance of your engine is a positive move, but stock engines are not frowned upon.

That should answer some of your questions about what makes a Pro-Touring car. Read the rest of the book for more information on how to build these cars and what makes Pro-Touring practical, and most of all — fun!

Fuel injection and supercharging like this setup on Rick Bernetti's Corvette is nice, but it's not necessary for Pro-Touring. A stock engine with a carburetor is just as acceptable as a fuel-injection system.

Some Pro-Touring cars push the envelope. Karl Chicca's '69 Camaro is shown in progress. This car was built to open-road race at speeds reaching 180 mph, so class rules make the NASCAR-style door bars necessary. They look cool and make the car fun to enter and exit Dukes-of-Hazzard style. This would be considered an extreme Pro-Touring car due to its extensive race-car construction. A less obtrusive 4- or 6-point roll bar would be more practical for the street, but a cage is not a necessity for being considered a Pro-Touring car.

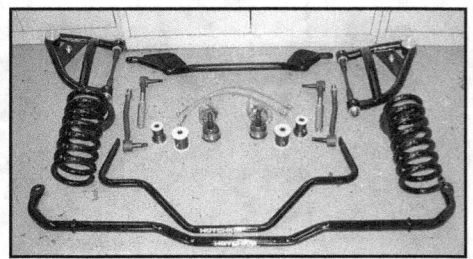

There are many parts coming from the aftermarket industry that you can use to increase the handling abilities of your car. Larger sway bars, redesigned upper control arms, stiffer springs, stiffer control-arm bushings, and a few other items are pictured here. This pile of parts includes Hotchkis sway bars and a Global West Category 5 suspension kit (minus the taller spindles and Wilwood brakes pictured in the suspension chapter) waiting to be installed on a '69 Camaro.

This turbocharged and nitrous-assisted Buick V-6 packs a serious punch with its small package. There are no limitations to the size or power output of an engine in a Pro-Touring car. Of course, if you are going to have a good-handling car, it makes sense to put more power under the hood for the purpose of pushing the limits of those suspension parts.

Chapter 1

General Suspension, Brakes, and Tires and Wheels

Shock Absorbers

The basic job of the shock absorber is to control or dampen the movement of the springs. A shock absorber that is too soft will have a hard time controlling the suspension, causing the ride to be bouncy and inefficient while cornering. If the shock is too stiff, the ride will be harsh and cause the vehicle to slide too easily.

The shock absorbers have two functions: compression and rebound. Most factory replacement shocks do not have adjustable compression or rebound. Some aftermarket performance shocks are available with internal valves that are serviceable for preferred compression and rebound. Those two settings are different for each application, due to many factors, including vehicle weight, tires, and spring rates. A drag car will use a pair of 90/10 shocks in the front. That means the shock will be valved 90 percent compression and 10 percent rebound. This allows the front to lift easily during acceleration, which transfers more weight to the rear wheels for off-the-line traction. Shock valving closer to that of a road-racing car would be more suited for Pro-Touring applications, since there is less emphasis on straight-line acceleration.

Compression describes the collapsing of the shock absorber. This occurs when the car hits a bump and the suspension moves upward, pushing the piston rod into the shock body. Rebound is described as extension of the shock absorber. Most people associate this with their car hitting a dip in the road, causing the suspension to drop and the shock to extend. Rebound does much more than that. When you drive your car into a hard left turn, the right front (outside) shock compresses, the left front (inside) shock extends. If you have the right shock valving, and the inside shock will resist extending (rebound), and the outside shock will resist compression. The shocks assist the springs and sway bar to limit body roll and increase cornering (lateral) traction.

Most conventional shocks are not rebuildable. The more expensive race shocks are rebuildable and can also be revalved for fine-tuning your suspension. These shocks are usually adjustable in some way. Some shocks have a knob at the bottom or top to adjust from soft to firm. Other shocks have to be compressed in order to adjust the firmness of ride.

Mono-Tube Shocks

The mono-tube shock has a single chamber inside the body of the shock. A single valve at the end of the piston modulates dampening of the shock. Mono-tube shocks are typically of high-pressure gas design. They range from

A mono-tube shock has a piston with a valve on the tip. This valve controls the rate of the shock. The small stack of discs partially blocking the flow passages limits the speed of the fluid flowing through the valve. The discs are swapped to change bump and rebound.

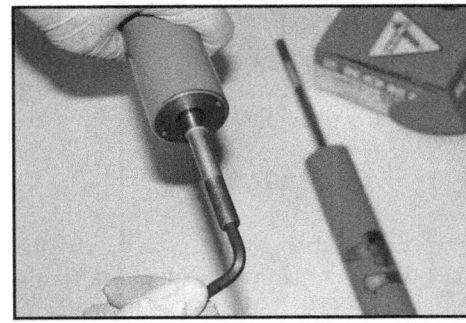

To adjust the firmness of a Koni Classic, you compress the shock to engage the valve in the shock. Turn it clockwise to increase firmness, and counterclockwise for a softer ride. You are never stuck with a setting, if you don't like the ride — adjust it.

Chapter 1

250 to 400 psi. The pressure inhibits cavitation caused by foaming or aeration if air gets drawn through the valve. Due to the single chamber, the mono-tube shock dissipates heat faster than twin-tube designs. Mono-tube shocks can be mounted upright or upside down.

Twin-Tube Shocks

A twin-tube shock has two chambers inside the body of the shock; an inner and outer chamber. The inner chamber contains the piston and the oil. On the end of the piston is a valve. There is also a valve at the bottom of the inner chamber, which modulates the amount of fluid forced into the outer chamber.

There are two different ways to build twin-tube shocks. The less inexpensive way is the use of a cellular bag (also known as a "gas bag"). Inside the bag is typically Freon gas at 10 to 20 psi. Some designs also include a foam material inside the gas bag. Some sources say non-gas bag designs are more efficient. Unlike high-pressure twin-tube shocks, twin-tube gas-bag shocks don't rely on gravity. They can be mounted upright, upside down, or even sideways.

Coil-Over Shocks

Coil-over shocks are the same as conventional shocks, except for the threaded body or threaded adapter collar. A coil-over shock replaces the factory shock and spring. The coil rate is chosen by the vehicle weight and ride quality intended. The coil is placed on the shock and allows vehicle height adjustment. Mono- and twin-tube shocks are available as coil-over shocks.

Sway Bars

A sway bar or anti-roll bar is one part of many that play a role in reducing *body roll*. The body-roll elements are: spring rate, wheel center rate, tire rate, ride rate, and roll rate. The springs, shocks, bushings, wheels, tires, chassis, and sway bars are all key parts in the car's ability to corner well. Obviously, a car would operate without a sway bar, but it would not be very safe or fun to drive.

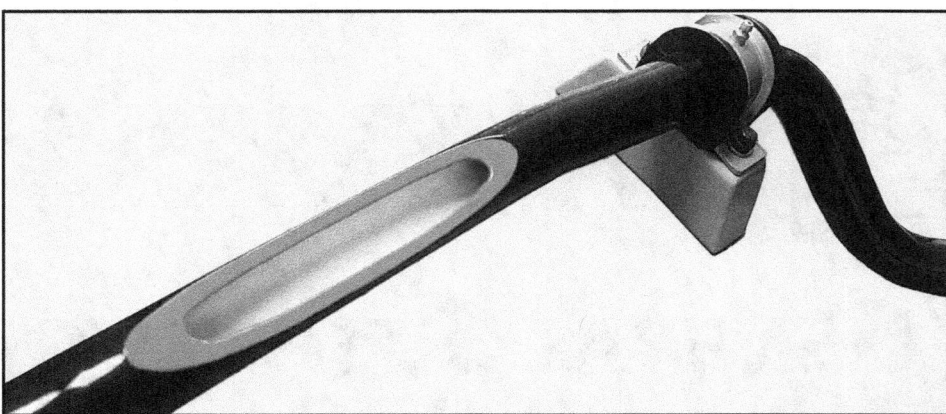

Until recently, if you had a conventional sway bar, you were stuck with the heavy solid version. Hotchkis has introduced a hollow sway bar that comes with all the strength and only a fraction of the weight. (Photo courtesy Hotchkis Performance)

A front sway bar increases the lateral traction of the front tires, and a rear sway bar increases the lateral traction of the rear tires. A rule of thumb: If your car has understeer, you can decrease the diameter of the front bar and increase the size of the rear bar. If your car suffers from oversteer, you should increase the size of the front bar and decrease or remove the rear sway bar. Some body roll is necessary to increase the traction of the outside tire. If the suspension does not have any body roll, the tires will tend to slide, instead of biting for traction.

Aftermarket Sway Bars and Accessories

There are two types of aftermarket sway bars — conventional and racing. Conventional bars typically resemble the shape of a stock bar, with the exception of the diameter. They usually bolt into the stock bar locations. Conventional aftermarket sway bars were only offered as solid units until 2000. In 2000, Hotchkis Performance started processing hollow bars. These units are hollow large diameter bars that are as strong as their solid counterparts, but have only a fraction of the weight.

Gun-drilled racing sway bars are completely different than conventional sway bars in appearance, but do the same job. These bars are used on circle-

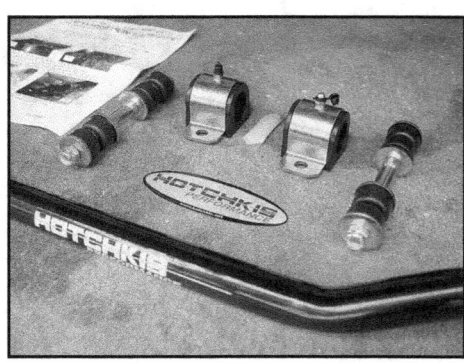

This is a kit for installing a Hotchkis hollow front sway bar on a '68 Camaro. The kit comes with the bar, polyurethane frame mount bushings with straps, polyurethane end-link hardware, lubricant, instructions, and a sticker for extra horsepower. The frame-mount bushing straps are equipped with a zerk fitting so they can be serviced on a regular basis.

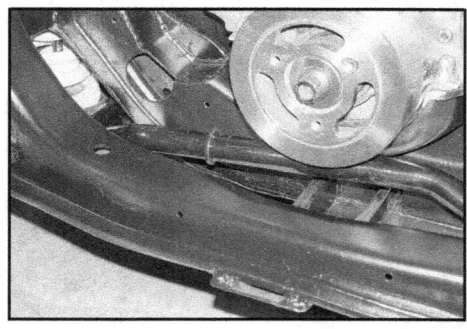

Before pushing the sway bar any further, it was necessary to turn it over, so the end of the sway bar was pointing towards the ground. After fishing the bar under the harmonic balancer, I was able to slide the bar all the way over until it hit the lower control arm. I was able to feed the bar over the top of the lower arm and slide it about two inches, and then BAM...

The sway bar hit the rotor on the driver's side. I steered the rotor to the full-locked position, but to no avail, the sway bar would still not clear the rotor. If you have large rotors like these, they will need to be removed in order to get the sway bar installed all the way.

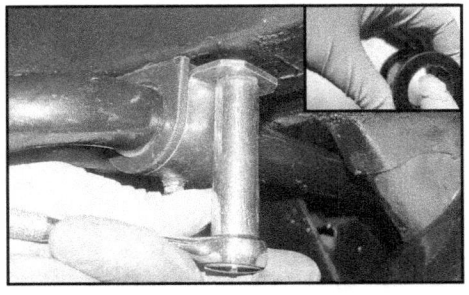

Lubricate the sway bar mount bushing by using a liberal amount of the lubricant from the little tube included with the kit. Install the polyurethane bushings over the sway bar on the outsides of the collars integrated into the bar. Install the bushing straps, but be careful, the threads in the frame can strip out fairly easy. I had to put a nut inside the frame to get one of my bolts tight.

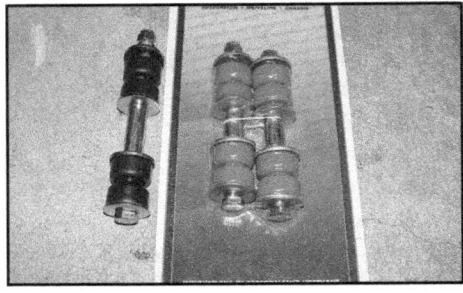

End-link bushing kits come in different lengths. They are available with 6 inches between connecting points, and some with only two inches. A shorter end-link set was installed after the previous picture was taken, but the bar was still not level. Installing a bushing that is too short will introduce more bind during suspension articulation, so a compromise was made.

The end links were installed hand-tight for test fitting. With the wheels, tires, and other parts installed, the car was safely put back on the ground. With the chassis loaded, you can see the sway bar kicks up to reach the end link. The sway bar should be as level with the ground as possible to eliminate bind during suspension compression.

and dirt-track racing cars, and they have also been showing up on extreme Pro-Touring cars. At the time of this book's publication, these types of bars were only available on aftermarket front clips as a bolt-on unit. They consist of a straight splined solid or gun-drilled (hollow) bar with aluminum or steel arms. They are mounted with solid bearings or Delrin inserts. These parts are available at many racing supply shops. The aluminum or steel arms are available in many shapes and lengths.

Sway bar bushings and end-links come in a few different types. The bushings are available in rubber and polyurethane. The end-links are available in the standard rubber and polyurethane through-bolt type, the solid rod-end type, or with stud-type rod ends.

The standard through-bolt end-links are the most common way to attach your sway bar to the control arms. These end-links come in different lengths. To determine the length you will need for your application, the car will need to be sitting at rest with the sway bar installed (with the exception of the end links. If you pivot the sway bar so the ends are parallel to the ground, there should be a gap between the end of your sway bar and the locating hole in the control arm. Measure that distance; it will be the length of the end-link that you will need.

The solid rod-end style end-links work well on the track because they offer non-binding, fluid motion. On the street, most car builders prefer the longer life of bolt-through types over the solid rod-ends. Once they wear, they will start making noise. As with any rod ends, installing safety washers will

Stock-car style splined sway bars are available in different lengths. Some are hollow, and some are solid. The sway bar arms come in different lengths and shapes, or you can get some custom made.

Chapter 1

This stud-type end link came off of a 2002 Corvette. It's a light, weatherproof unit that would work well in the right application.

Solid or polyurethane bushings do not distort like rubber bushings, so the suspension geometry stays in its originally designed location. Harder bushings transfer more road feel to the chassis. Detroit Speed & Engineering's version of the solid control-arm bushing has a zinc-coated outer steel casing. The casing can be welded to the control arm, so it can't move around in the bushing hole.

ensure the rod ends will not totally separate if the ball wears out. GM has introduced stud-type rod-ends on their C5 (1996 through 2003 Corvette). It is similar to a miniature tie-rod end, and is completely weatherproof. I'm sure Pro-Touring builders will start integrating them into their cars when possible.

Bushings

There are control arm and sway bar bushings in the front suspension systems of GM cars. They are usually made of rubber. Aftermarket companies offer bushings made from polyurethane, which is a stronger compound that offers performance benefits. For even more performance and more road feel, solid bushings are another option. Solids are either a combination of Delrin and metal, or metal and metal.

Keep in mind, the less flexible bushing used, the more precise your suspension geometry will be. Flexible bushings distort under load, altering your alignment to the point of reducing the effectiveness of your steering and suspension.

Read further to help make your decision on what is best for your application.

Rubber

Most stock front suspension bushings are rubber, especially in GM cars built before the late 1990s. The rubber bushings create a comfortable ride for the average driver by absorbing shock from imperfections in roads. Rubber bushings do have a drawback. They also flex and distort. When a car is driven hard in a corner, the control arm bushings distort enough to completely change the alignment settings. The changes in geometry can create unpredictable handling.

Urethane

There are benefits of using polyurethane over rubber bushings. Polyurethane has a higher load-bearing capacity, greater tear strength, and superior resistance to oils, depending on the formulation. Polyurethane bushings don't distort like rubber bushings. For instance, when the control arms are under load while cornering, the polyurethane bushings will keep more of a true alignment. This is a great advantage to creating a more predictable and controllable Pro-Touring car. Polyurethane bushings will also increase *road feel* compared to rubber bushings.

There an enduring myth about polyurethane: people say it squeaks. Polyurethane does not squeak. The squeak you hear is caused by the lack of proper lubrication between the bushings and the surface of the surrounding part. Not all polyurethane bushings are created equal. Each company has different theories, designs, and compounds to achieve their idea of a superior product. Each polyurethane manufacturer has its own blend of materials for their urethane and also for their lubricant. It is best to use the lubricant they supply, and fully clean the surrounding parts as they instruct.

Solids

Delrin and Aluminum

One of the companies offering Delrin and aluminum control-arm bushings is Global West. They call these bushings Del-a-lum (Delrin and aluminum). Since the materials don't flex, they offer precise suspension geometry. They are equipped with grease fittings so the moving surfaces can be kept lubricated.

Delrin and Steel

Many stock-car racing companies offer Delrin and steel control-arm bushings. Stock-car products are heavy-duty, but not always best for street use. I have seen Delrin and steel bushings with extremely loose tolerances, which work well, but they can generate some loud clunking in the front suspension when loaded and unloaded.

One company offering good street versions of the Delrin and steel lower control-arm bushings is Detroit Speed & Engineering. Their re-engineered Delrin and steel bushings have tighter tolerances, more Delrin on thrust surfaces, and offer a corrosion-resistant coating for increased lifespan. Since the outer bushing shell is steel, it can be tack-welded into place for a positive fit. This is a great feature for control arms that may have slightly worn bushing sockets.

Metal and Metal — Spherical Too

Stock-car racing companies offer bushings with steel housings and inserts. They are also available in aluminum versions. These are not forgiving. They transfer all road feel to the chassis and steering wheel. If you are building an extreme Pro-Touring car and plan to drive it on the street about 50 miles per year, you could get away with using these. They are equipped with grease fittings. It is necessary to keep solid bushings lubricated to minimize galling. You have to remember, the only thing keeping the two pieces of metal from binding, is a thin layer of grease.

General Suspension, Brakes, and Tires and Wheels

The other type of metal-to-metal bushing is the spherical aircraft bushing. Global West offers these for specific applications that require the movement offered by these bushings. Most applications are for rear suspension parts, but the fourth-generation F-body lower front control-arm bushings can be replaced with these inflexible, full-range of motion, spherical aircraft bushings. They will increase road feel, but also improve the handling with more precise suspension geometry.

Handling – Understeer and Oversteer

When I was at a driver meeting for a high-speed open-road racing event I was given a simple explanation for understeer and oversteer. Understeer is when your front end hits the wall. Oversteer is when your rear end hits the wall. That is about as simple as it gets. Understeer and oversteer can be caused by many things: weather, tire compounds, spring rates, alignment, acceleration, braking too hard, and much more.

Understeer condition is described as a loss of traction in the front tires, which in turn causes the front end to *push*. That push can be very dangerous since steering ability is usually non-existent. Not being able to control the direction that your car is traveling in can be dangerous.

Oversteer condition is described as a loss of traction in the rear tires during cornering, which in turn causes the rear end to slide. Many drivers prefer oversteer rather than understeer. At least in oversteer conditions, the car can be corrected by steering into the slide, unless extreme oversteer is experienced. Controlled oversteer can be helpful to get the car around a tight corner easier, but any loss of traction can be detrimental if you are shooting for fast laps on a track.

Drifting, or four-wheel drift, is caused when traction is lost in the front and rear tires. Both understeer and oversteer conditions are present. Experienced, highly skilled drivers pilot their cars in controlled drifting conditions in almost every corner. Having experience and knowing your car extremely well are important when pushing your car to the edge.

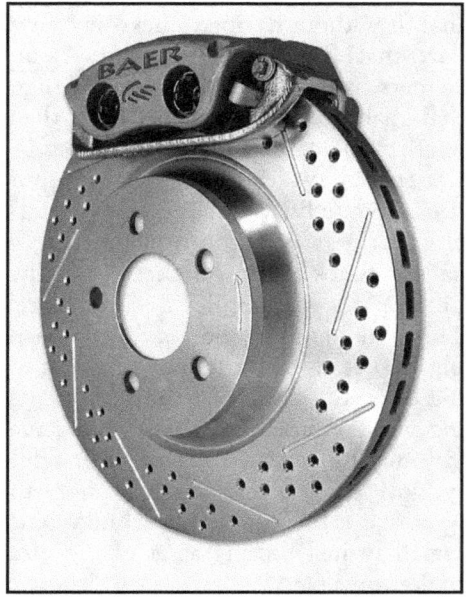

This is a Baer Brakes Track System rotor and caliper. The 13x1.1-inch rotors are a one-piece cast design that have been upgraded with cross drilling, slotting, and zinc-washing options. The caliper is a two-piston floating PBR unit. (Photo courtesy of Baer Brakes)

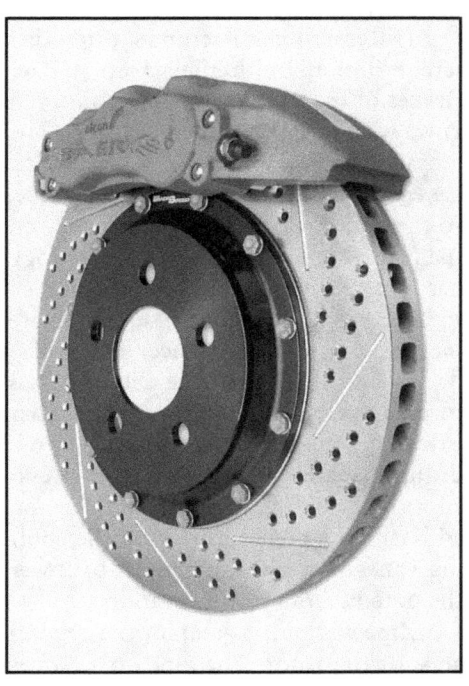

For the top of Baer's product line, this is the Extreme Plus System. The Plus automatically denotes the directional two-piece rotors with 6061-T6 billet hats and cast rotors. The caliper is a staggered-bore six-piston unit. (Photo courtesy of Baer Brakes)

Why Upgrade Brakes?

There are a few important items on every car. Probably the highest on the list is the brakes. Drum brakes operate by pushing brake shoes outward toward the brake drum. Disc brakes have a caliper that pinches the rotor with brake pads. Disc brakes are more efficient at dispersing heat than drum brakes, so they are better for repeated stops, which leads us to the hundred thousand dollar question — Why upgrade to better brakes if I already have front disc brakes?

If you plan on driving hard around corners and your engine is pumping out extra horsepower, you are going to need some more stopping power to be safe. If you are planning on ever driving on a road course, you will definitely need to upgrade to bigger rotors and better calipers. The stock drum and disc brakes are great for stopping a vehicle under normal driving conditions. On a road course, you are forced to use the brakes more than they were ever designed for — if you race the correct way, which is to slow your car down with the brakes, *not* the engine and transmission.

After a few hard stops, the stock brakes start to lose their effectiveness to heat caused by the excessive friction. Stock brakes don't cool off, and heat in the stock brake material starts causing outgassing. Outgassing causes gas pockets to form between the pad and rotor surface. This is even more pronounced with drum brakes, because the brake lining has even more surface area. When the lining doesn't completely contact the rotor surface, it cannot effectively slow or stop the vehicle. This is what's known as brake fade. Installing a brake cooling system (covered later in this chapter) is a way to combat brake fade, but it doesn't eliminate the problem. Aftermarket brake pads made for racing or high-performance driving use newer technology materials that minimize or eliminate outgassing problems. Look for pads that advertise with terms like "race ready," and "dynamic surface treatment."

The best improvement you can make to your braking system is to upgrade to larger diameter rotors that have more

Chapter 1

If you look closely, behind that nice 17-inch wheel, is a stock drum brake. This Pro-Touring '67 Camaro put the "Pro" in Pro-Touring when it was upgraded to four-wheel Wilwood disc brakes. (Photo courtesy Chris Flatmoe)

contact surface area for braking and for cooling. Upgrading to performance pads along with rotors and calipers will put the filling in the pie. With a properly balanced system (explained later in this chapter), the upgraded system will shorten your stopping distances and greatly improve the vehicle's ability to make repeated stops on a road course. Then you will be able to drive faster around the course, because you can drive deeper into a corner without braking, since you can wait longer before applying the brakes. You will leave lesser-equipped cars in the dust.

Brake Parts

A whole book could be written on performance brakes, so I will touch on the performance aspects of brake types, balancing your system, and brake cooling. To make things simple, only four-wheel disc brake systems will be covered in this chapter.

Most of the brakes I will be covering in this chapter are Baer Brakes. After experiences with brakes and kits from five different brake companies, I have found Baer Brakes kits to be the highest overall quality, the most likely to have all the parts that are supposed to be included, and most likely to have parts that fit without having to next-day-air a part that fits correctly. Their Alcon calipers have a superior internal design that makes them easier to bleed than another comparable big-name caliper.

Some guys have found ways to put C4 Corvette PBR brakes on early model cars, by way of custom building a caliper bracket and purchasing all the other parts at their local parts store. This brake modification is called cheap big brakes. I won't be covering cheap big brakes because of liability of writing about something that could have you buying parts that don't fit or safely work on your car. There is more to getting a safe and balanced brake system than just bolting a set of big disc brakes on a car.

Rotors

Performance rotors come in a few different types. They come machined from a single cast piece, a cast outer ring with an aluminum hat, or a carbon fiber outer ring (for racing only) with an aluminum hat.

Different manufacturers offer different options with their rotors. Baer Brakes offers cross drilling, slotting, and zinc washing with their rotors. The cross drilling was started for allowing gasses to disperse from the pad surface, so the pad could have better contact on the rotor surface. Brake pad technology has almost eliminated outgassing, so these days cross drilling and slotting are more for visual appearance. The cross-drilled and slotted surface allows gasses to disperse when they do occur under extreme racing conditions. Cross drilling creates the potential for stress-risers that can lead to cracks in the rotor, so Baer casts their rotors with the cooling vanes in a specific pattern to lower the potential of crack migration.

Zinc washing is great for the appearance of the rotor. The zinc coat comes off the rotor surface where the brake pad rides, but the coating stays on the rest of the rotor. If you coat the rotor, it protects all other surfaces from ugly rust that builds up on the part of the rotor surface that is visible through most aftermarket wheels.

Calipers

There are two types of calipers: floating and fixed. The floating caliper relies on pressure applied to the rotor from its single inboard piston to pull the outboard pad into the outside face of the rotor. This design is much more forgiving in production tolerances, and is used on almost all production vehicles on the market today. Fixed calipers are solidly mounted to the spindle or axle housing with opposing inner and outer pistons. When brake pressure is applied, the pistons squeeze the rotor equally and simultaneously for a better braking feel and faster response. Since the tolerances on mounting the fixed caliper over the rotor need to be precise, they are almost exclusively used on racing applications.

Fixed calipers are available in standard or staggered piston bore configurations. Standard bore calipers have symmetrical bore sizes from side to side and front to rear on each caliper. Staggered bore calipers have different size bores coinciding with the turning direction of the rotor. In the direction of rotation, the smaller bore is first in the rotation of the rotor. This applies the pad to the rotor more evenly. With standard bore calipers, the pistons are equally sized, so they push the pad against the rotor face at the same time. This causes the leading edge of the pad to dig in a fraction of a second sooner than the trailing edge of the pad, resulting in increased wear on the leading edge of the pad.

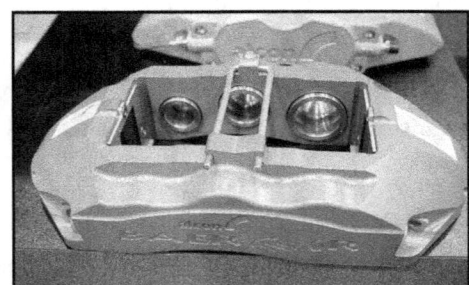

This is a mono-block Alcon with staggered bores. The term "mono-block," means that the caliper is a machined from a single cast unit. This makes the unit extremely rigid. The design eliminates the need for an external balance tube. The piston bores are staggered in size for better pad wear.

General Suspension, Brakes, and Tires and Wheels

This is a two-piece, fixed-caliper design. Two separate machined blocks are bolted together. This caliper requires an external balance tube to balance the left and right half of the caliper fluid pressure.

Notice anything strange about this picture? Some guys have found good success with a Corvette-specific kit from AO Engineering that provides the necessary brackets to bolt dual calipers to each front rotor.

Brake Cooling

Brakes don't like heat. Heat shortens the life and effectiveness of the pads. In racing and extreme driving conditions, the rotor can warp and/or crack from excessive heat. The key to running cool brakes is to have cooling ducts running to the center of the rotor, where the air can cool the internal rotor vanes and evenly cool the rotor. If you run the air duct to the inboard face of the rotor, you will be cooling the inboard face, but the outward face will run extremely hot. This will cause the inboard and outboard pads and rotor faces to wear unevenly.

Air intake ducts and hose can be purchased from racing supply stores. The heavy-duty plastic ducts come in different shapes and sizes. The intake duct should be placed in a high-pressure location, such as a front air dam or an opening in the front valance panel. It is a good idea to install wire mesh over the inlet to keep rocks and debris from entering the duct and hose. The brake duct hose comes in different diameters and temperature ranges. Typically, you have to fabricate your own duct/backing-plate to mount to the caliper bracket or spindle. You want to leave very little room for air to escape without going through the rotor vents. This will ensure that you are getting all the cooling possible. Attach the hose to the back of the intake duct, and attach the other end of the hose to the backing plate/duct on your rotor. A few plastic zip ties are good for affixing the duct hose to stationary items in the engine compartment. Be careful not to mount the hose where a tire or moving engine or suspension part will contact it. A spinning tire can rip the hose out of its position in a split second, and possibly damage the tire.

Boosting Brakes

If you don't want manual brakes, you will need to boost your brakes. There are two ways to boost your brakes. You can either install a vacuum- or hydro-style brake booster. Vacuum-assist brake boosters work great for stock to moderate applications. When increasing your engine's performance, you can adversely affect your engine's vacuum output, which can limit your brake boosting to an unsafe level. Large diameter vacuum-assist boosters can crowd engine accessories, like valve covers. They can also limit frame bracing. Small diameter vacuum boosters might give you more clearance, but they still rely on vacuum you may not be able to supply. You can try to hook up an electric vacuum pump for supply, but they rarely work as well as the installer hopes.

To increase braking on trucks, the manufacturers started offering hydro-boost braking systems. The booster bolts between the firewall and the brake master cylinder. The hydrobooster does not rely on vacuum. The boosting comes from fluid pressure that is plumbed in from the power steering pump. The pressure operates the brakes during any driving condition. This system is known to work better than any vacuum booster on the market. An aftermarket company named Hydratech Braking Systems offers complete kits that include the booster and hoses.

Balancing a Braking System

Standard brake systems are broken down into two separate systems that are joined by one link — the master cylinder. The front and rear systems need to be balanced. An average car needs about 70 percent of its braking ability in the front brakes and 30 percent in the rear. If you notice, cars with factory four-wheel disc brakes have smaller brake calipers in the rear than in the front. If the rear system had the same braking power that the front system, the car would have an unbalanced system. It would be very dangerous to drive. The rear brakes would lock up before the front brakes have a chance to slow the car down. When the rear brakes lock first, the car becomes unsafe to stop. The same goes for having too much braking in the front.

Having the correct caliper bore sizes in the front and rear is very important. To demonstrate this, I will write about my own experience with balancing the brake system.

I started with a generic six-cylinder '68 Camaro equipped with four-wheel drum brakes. I converted it to '74 Nova disc brakes in the front, and put a Ford nine-inch rear end from a '76 Lincoln MarkIV with the stock MarkIV rear disc brakes. I put a '79 Trans Am four-wheel disc brake master cylinder and brake booster on the firewall. It turns out I was extremely lucky, for my normal street driving, the system was well balanced from front to rear. Then I took the car out on Sears Point road course for a day. After a few laps, the brakes started to fade, so I would let them cool off in the pits and run again. When I upgraded my engine from 350 to 483 hp, I decided it was time to upgrade the brakes. I put money down on a Baer Brakes Track kit for the front. Due to some engine compartment constraint issues with my big-block Chevy, I removed the power brakes and converted back to a manual brake system. Against

Baer Brakes suggestions, I left the MarkIV disc brakes in the rear. What did they know? Disc brakes are disc brakes. They probably just want me to spend more money on their brakes. I showed them!

The Baer Track kit had some huge 13-inch rotors and two-piston PBR calipers. I installed a master cylinder with a 1-inch bore. The front brakes looked great, but it didn't work. The system was unbalanced. I had switched the large single piston calipers to the PBR calipers that had two much smaller pistons. Coupled with the large single piston MarkIV calipers in the rear, I could not push the brake pedal hard enough to actuate the master cylinder in order to the stop the car in a timely fashion. In fact, I could not get the front or rear brakes to lockup if I had pushed the pedal through the firewall. The amount of fluid it was taking the master cylinder to push the rear caliper pistons out was too much. The front brakes were doing all the work, but they were not doing their job either. The car was unsafe to drive. In relation to the rear brakes, the amount of fluid it took operate the front brakes was not enough. To band-aid the system into getting more fluid to the rear brakes, I would have to install a proportioning valve in the front brake system to restrict the fluid and force the rear system to operate sooner. This was not an option I was willing to take. I was already not getting enough braking force in the front, and there was no way I was going to limit it further. At this point, I tested my stopping distance from 60 to 0 mph. As hard as I tried, I could not lock the brakes. The stopping distance was 177 feet.

I called Baer to find out what to do. They told me to get smaller piston rear calipers. I figured, since I was going to change the brakes, I might as well get a system they suggested. I bought a Baer rear Touring kit with 12-inch rotors and single piston PBR calipers. They were equipped with parking brakes, which was a big plus, since I could never get the parking brake mechanism in the MarkIV calipers to work. I had Vic DeLeon at Speed Merchant install the kit, since the bearings had to be pressed off my axles to remove the Ford backing plates. The system worked great after that. The new caliper bore sizes were much smaller than the ones from the MarkIV. The front and rear brakes could safely stop my car, and the system was finally balanced. Baer had also suggested to switch my master cylinder to a 15/16-inch bore size for even better braking, but I had not done that yet. I tested the braking distance from 60 to 0 mph again. The car stopped in 148 feet — a huge improvement over the previous 177 feet.

I had a chance to pick up a used Baer Pro front kit from my friend, Karl Chicca. He was upgrading, and had these left over. I installed the four-piston fixed Alcon calipers onto my Track kit rotors. This further improved the brake feel and the balance of the system. The feel of a fixed caliper over a floating caliper was a night-and-day difference. The fixed calipers actually gave the brakes a power-brake feel at the pedal, since they react so much faster than the floating caliper. I ran one braking test from 60 to 0 mph. The distance was an improved 137 feet. On that one test, I was only five feet off of the ABS equipped '02 Camaro Z-28, which *Road & Track* tested in their November 2001 issue, at a stopping distance of 132 feet. Not bad for a '68 Chevy Camaro with an iron-headed Big Block. Just imagine what will happen when I change the master cylinder to a different bore size.

Since changing a standard dual-reservoir master cylinder to change the bore size affects both the front and rear brake system (except in rare occasions), you can either install a brake proportioning valve or change to a dual master cylinder setup.

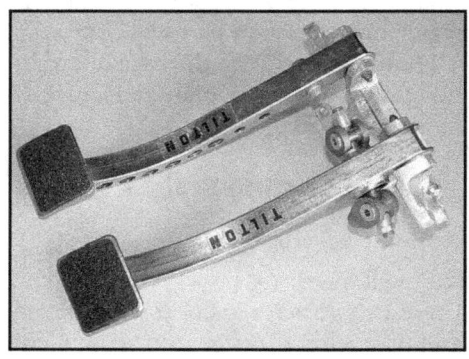

This is a Tilton brake- and clutch-pedal assembly. It utilizes dual master cylinders with a balance bar for brake bias tuning and a hydraulic clutch master cylinder.

This is a balance bar for the Tilton brake-pedal assembly. A spherical bearing is located in the pedal. The threaded rod moves the bearing from side to side for the correct amount of front and rear master cylinder actuation.

This is a lever-style Wilwood proportioning valve. It is within the drivers reach when he is strapped in his seat. The driver can adjust the front and rear brake bias on the fly. Other types of proportioning valves have a knob to turn for adjustment. (Photo courtesy Joe Pettitt)

General Suspension, Brakes, and Tires and Wheels

The proportioning valve is hooked inline between the master cylinder and the rear brakes to help balance the front and rear systems. If the rear brakes are locking before the front brakes, the proportioning valve restricts pressure to the rear brakes, which allows the front brakes to come on stronger before the rear brakes fully activate. Most street cars equipped with proportioning valves have them located in the engine compartment near the master cylinder. Some racing cars prefer to have the proportioning valve located within reach of the driver's seat, so the brake bias can be adjusted while on the track to adjust for tire, chassis, and track conditions.

The proportioning valve is less invasive than installing a dual master cylinder setup with a balance bar. A balance bar system allows you to custom tailor your master cylinder bore size for the front and rear brake circuits separately. The front and rear brake circuits become their own systems. If your front brakes would work best with a 7/8-inch bore master, and the rear brakes would work best with a 3/4-inch bore master cylinder, or any different combination, the balance bar system is for you. Putting in a balance bar system usually requires installing a new brake pedal assembly. Once you have installed both master cylinders and the balance bar system, you can make slight adjustments to the balance bar to change the front and rear brake bias. Most brake bias systems are available with an optional knob so you can adjust the bias on the fly. If you go through the trouble of installing the pedal assembly, it only makes sense to install the adjustable knob.

Brake Master Install

The following is a step-by-step installation of a Wilwood forward swing-mount brake pedal assembly with a balance bar, a front and rear master cylinder, and a remote balance bar adjustment cable kit. This was installed in a continued effort to fine-tune the brake system on my '68 Camaro. If you are going to attempt this installation and you have a manual transmission, you will need to get a pedal assembly with provisions to mount a clutch master cylinder or custom modify your clutch pedal to fit with the new pedal assembly.

The '68 Camaro used for this install was previously equipped with power brakes. When the big block required bigger valve covers, the brake booster was eliminated and the master cylinder was swapped. At the time, it was a concern that the brakes would be tough to operate. After upgrading the brakes and running a few "open track" days, it was decided the manual brakes did not require as much effort as originally thought, and the feedback was better as to the state of the condition of the brakes.

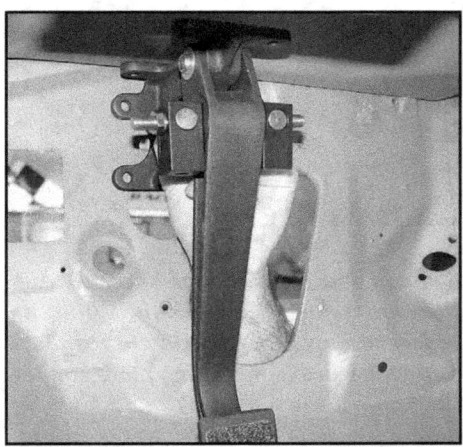

It is important to plan out the location of the pedal assembly. This picture shows it what it looks like pressed up against the firewall and moved as far as it will go upwards, where it hits the inner cowl panel. Mounting the assembly straight to the firewall will give very little strength. A lot of force is used to operate one of the most important parts on your car — your brakes. The strength of the mount is critical. A flat plate of aluminum to sandwich the firewall to the pedal-assembly bracket is in order. I had to take the steering column placement into consideration when placing the assembly.

To better balance the front and rear brakes without the use of an adjustable proportioning valve, it was necessary to swap over to a dual master cylinder setup. There are a few manufacturers offering these setups. The project Camaro has an automatic transmission, so a dual-pedal assembly with provision for a clutch pedal was not necessary. We chose to use a single-pedal operated dual master cylinder system that uses different bore sizes to balance the system.

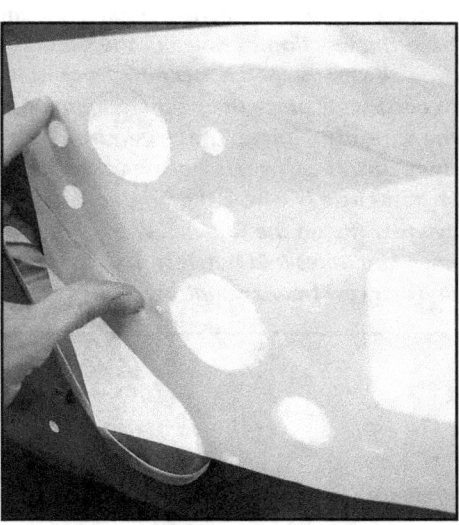

The first order of business was to start planning the overall project. I found another Camaro with a bare firewall, so I could start making templates for mounting the brake pedal assembly. I put a piece of paper up against the outside of the firewall and started marking where the factory holes for the master cylinder, wire harness, and steering column were located. The light shining from inside the car made it easy to make my marks on the paper.

Chapter 1

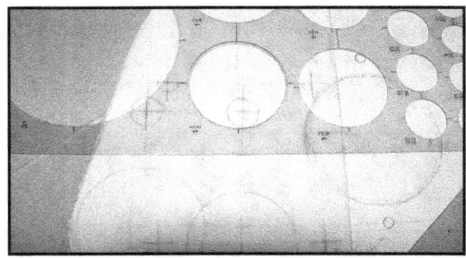

With the piece of paper, I was able to start transferring hole sizes and locations to another piece of paper to start making a template. I used an engineering circle template to make sure I was locating all the right size holes and their centerlines. Being more precise in the early steps will ensure better fitment later in the process.

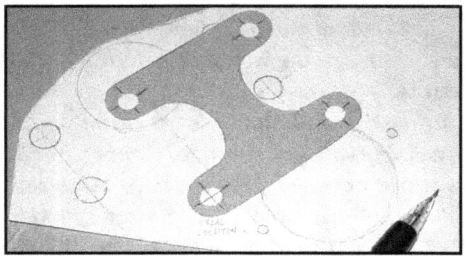

Using a couple of measurements taken from the location of holes in the Camaro firewall and the pedal location, I was able to accurately place the pedal template on the firewall template. The larger circle near the pencil is an access hole, and the next largest circle is where the original master cylinder fits on the firewall. With all these lines and holes laid out, it is time to make another cardboard template.

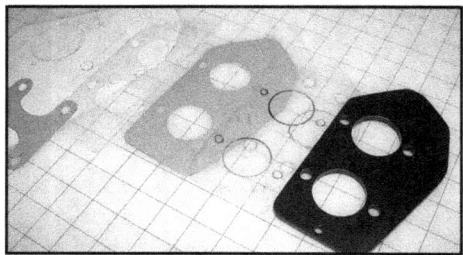

A cardboard template was made, so I could give my friend Dave Morin a solid piece he could transfer to a 3/16-inch plate of aluminum. Here you see the cardboard template with the aluminum plate. The aluminum plate was hard-anodized black for corrosion resistance. The two large holes are for the two master cylinders to mount through.

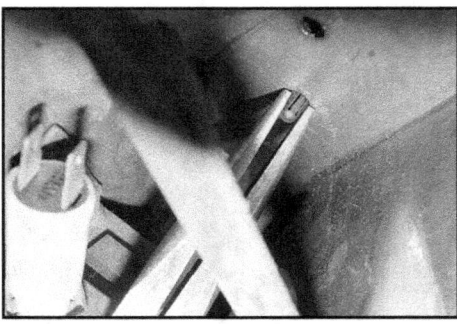

Before dropping the original pedal assembly from the car, there is a little plastic clip holding the gauge cluster wiring harness to the top of the assembly. It is located above the brake switch. If your car has this, it can cause major frustration, unless you follow this step: Using some needle-nose pliers, squeeze the little plastic tabs together and push it through the panel at the same time.

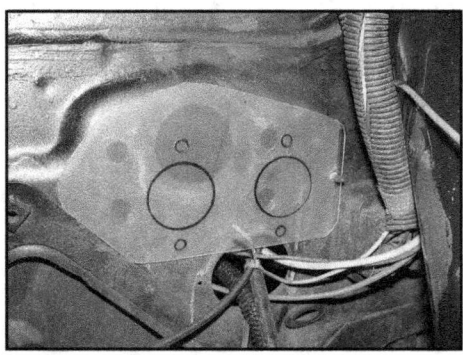

Remove the brake-pedal bracket from the underside of the dash. With the bracket removed, a transparent template of the new brake mounting plate can lay flat against the firewall. The dark circles on the template are the holes for mounting the new master cylinders. You can see the original holes behind the template.

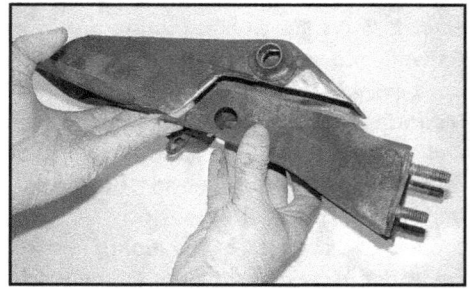

With the original bracket reinstalled, using the nuts that hold the steering column, the Wilwood pedal assembly is held in place by temporarily pushing the bolts through the firewall. A 1/8-inch steel plate is placed on top of the new pedal assembly, and the outline is marked. Now you can remove all the parts and finish mocking everything up out of the car.

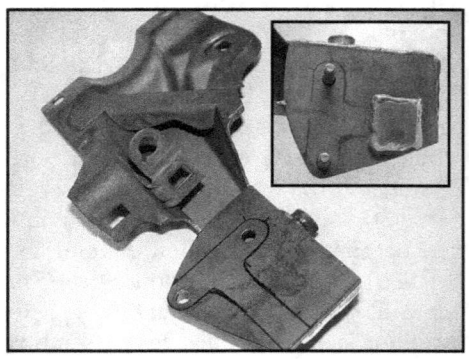

The steel plate is completely marked and laid out on the top of the old bracket. The mounting holes were also drilled in the plate. Once the plate is welded to the bracket, there won't be access to tighten the bolts, so they were welded in the holes from the backside. A small square plate was welded to keep the Wilwood assembly from rocking when it was installed.

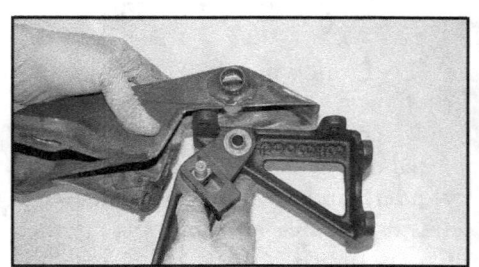

A cut was made along the lines drawn on the bracket. It was cut in two pieces. The half in the upper left will be used to mount the new pedal assembly. The other half will be discarded, because the new assembly will be mounted in that location (as shown in inset photo).

The stock brake-switch bracket was in the perfect spot. Wilwood suggests that you install a return spring if your pedal does not return to full extension. With a return spring, the pedal needs a stop to keep the master actuator rods from slamming against the internal snap rings. A nut was welded to the bracket so that a bolt and locking nut could be used to limit the return.

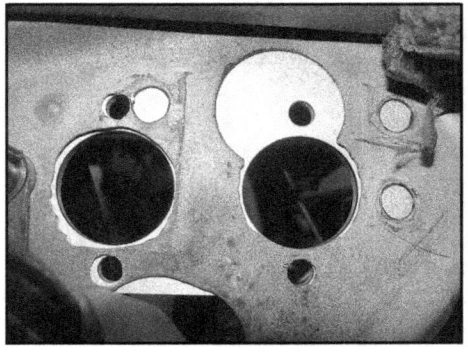

Place the new master cylinder plate up against the engine-side of the firewall, and use a scribe to mark the holes you will need to remove in order to mount the master cylinders. Using those marks, cut the holes in the firewall. The hole saw I needed was missing, and I wanted to finish the job, so I drilled and filed the holes. As you can see they are not perfect. Looking back, I should have driven to the store and purchased the right tool for the job.

The master cylinder rods were too short to properly place my pedal for correct operation. To get the pedal away from the floorboard, I had to extend the master cylinder pushrod. Then I cut the heads off of some grade 8 Allen bolts (grade 5 threaded stock is not safe for this application) and attached them with an extension nut and locking nuts to keep everything in place.

I ended up having to trim a little off the end of the pushrod to get the correct length, while still being able to use the proper locking nuts. For safety, after getting the correct pushrod length at the end of the project, I used thread locker on the extension nut. Don't add the thread locker until the project is almost finished, that way you'll ensure that you don't have to make any more adjustments. Do not use thread locker where the pushrod screws into the balance-bar lugs.

The pedal assembly has a balance bar with an adjustable spherical bearing that allows you to adjust the front/rear brake bias. The master cylinders mount to lugs on both sides of the pedal. There are little plates between the lugs and the pedal to keep the brake pedal actuation smooth. There is supposed to be .025 inch of clearance in the entire assembly for proper movement.

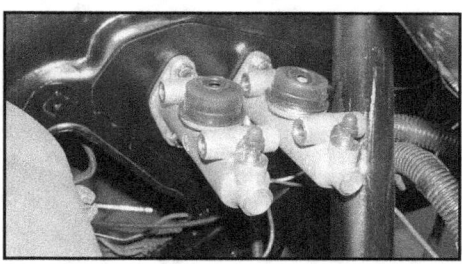

A little oil-resistant black RTV sealant was used to ensure a solid mount, but it also keeps oils and moisture out of the passenger compartment. The master cylinders were tightened while the sealant was fresh. The pedal assembly was also tightened up against the original pedal bracket.

The brake bias from front to rear is adjusted by positioning the master pushrod in the lug, and also by the adjustable bias rod on the pedal. For proper adjustment, read the pedal adjustment instructions that come with the assembly. If you cannot equalize the brake bias by adjustment, you may need a different size master cylinder bore on the front or rear brake circuit.

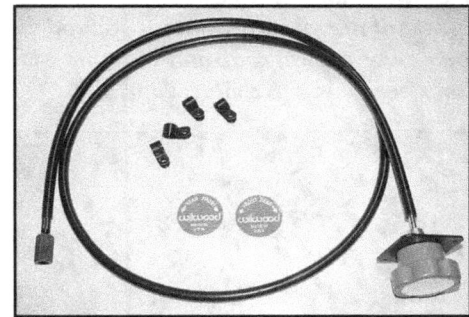

If you want fully adjustable brake bias that you can adjust while driving on the track, you can install a remote brake bias adjuster. It comes with a bi-directional knob, mounting plate, and a special cable that hooks directly to the bias adjustment rod on the pedal assembly. The knob should be mounted where the driver can reach it while he's buckled in the seat.

Chapter 1

This rotor is off a Camaro Mustang Challenge race car. Obviously, it has seen some severe heat. The back side of the rotor had a cooling duct blowing on it, and it was not cracked.

Behind the front bumper of this Camaro is a plastic brake duct with a custom aluminum hood to help gulp cool air. The 3-inch racing duct hose helps direct air to the center of the rotor. The hose is secured to the upper control arm, and the front tire does not come into contact with it.

Pushing air into the center of the rotor is the most efficient way to cool the brake rotor and the wheel bearings. Ducting air to the face of the rotor will create uneven heat and wear of the rotor and brake pads.

Performance Friction sells special stickers that show what temperature your rotor or caliper climbed to during use. If you look closely, you can see the sticker on the rotor has been up to higher temperatures than the caliper.

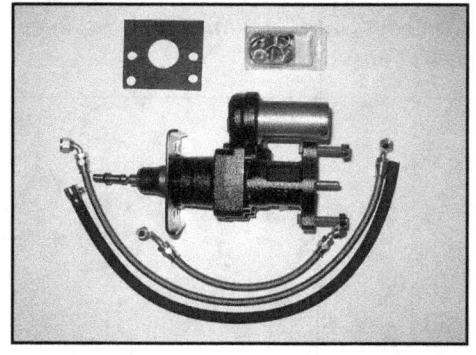

If you want to boost your brakes while keeping clearance for your engine and components, you can get a Hydroboost brake booster. This is a kit offered by Hydratech Braking Systems. (Photo courtesy Hydratech Braking Systems)

Tires

There are a few things to keep in mind when picking your tires. Tire companies measure their tires from sidewall to sidewall, not the width of the tread. Outer tire diameter changes the final gear ratio. A smaller diameter tire will increase gear ratio, and speed up your speedometer. A larger diameter tire will react the exact opposite.

Large diameter, ultra low-profile tires can give your Pro-Touring car a lifted, four-wheel-drive look. For a good look, Kevin Long, tire specialist from Campbell Auto Restoration, says his general rule is to have about 1.5 to 2 times more tire sidewall than space between the top of the tire and the fender opening.

Your driving habits should be taken into consideration when choosing a tire. Are you: driving strictly on the street, auto-crossing, open tracking, or periodically hitting the drag strip? Kevin Long gave some insight in tire choices. For mainly street driving, he suggests ultra-high performance street tires like: Michelin Pilot Sports, Goodyear F-1, BFG G-Force KD, Bridgestone S-02/S-03, or Yokohama AVS Sport. For auto-crossing and open track: Yokohama A-032, Michelin Pilot Club Sport, or Hoosier. For drag racing: BFG Drag Radials, Nitto 555R, or ET Streets. All these options are DOT street legal. He warns that street legal racing tires will not last long on for street use and that drag radials are not designed to go around corners.

Wheels

There are many different wheel companies on the market, and there are different types of materials used to build wheels. The most common wheels used on Pro-Touring cars are the cast-center with spun-aluminum outer, cast aluminum, billet aluminum, and forged aluminum.

Forged wheels are the strongest wheels available. Most forged wheels built today are three-piece designs. The rim is assembled of two pieces, a front half and a back half, and the center piece is bolted in with high-strength bolts. There are also two-piece forged wheels available. Forged wheels are much stronger and lighter than cast wheels. The strength of the forged wheel offers high durability for street use. I've seen many less-expensive, large-diameter wheels bent from hitting potholes and road debris. It's especially easy to damage the large-diameter wheels because guys typically run such low-profile tires with them. The tire's sidewall normally takes the road shock, but with a small sidewall, there is nothing to take the shock.

Large diameter wheels and tires can be much heavier than stock wheels and tires. They increase the rotating mass, which means they require more braking force to slow them down. Big wheels

General Suspension, Brakes, and Tires and Wheels

BonSpeed makes a full line of forged wheels with show-quality finish on the front and backside. This one is called Intense. It is available in 16- to 24-inch diameters, with backspace in 1/8-inch increments for an exact fit. (Photo courtesy Bonspeed)

will also accentuate limitations in your stock drivetrain, so beware.

Wheels are measured between the inner wheel lips, not the outside edges of the wheel lips. An actual 8-inch wide wheel might be 9 or more inches wide when measured from outside lip to outside lip.

Fitting Tires and Wheels

When picking tires and wheels, there are a few things to take into consideration. Are the tires going to fit within the wheel housing (wheelwell)? Are the wheels going to be the right backspacing (or offset) to clear the suspension components? Measuring for correct fitment is critical.

Too much backspacing can move the wheel and tire inward and cause interference with the control arms, ball joints, outer tie-rod ends, brake hardware, brake calipers, shocks, brackets, inner wheel housing, frame, and more. Too little backspacing will move the tire and wheel outward causing the tire to interfere with the fender lip and outer wheel housing. Measuring for proper backspacing is important when you want the biggest tire and wheel package on the front or rear of your car.

The first order of business in getting the correct backspacing is to find the narrowest width of the inner wheel housing. Measure the wheel housing in many different locations, because wheel housings are not always equal widths from front to rear. Keep in mind that the tire needs space to travel upwards in the wheel housing during compression of the suspension. If your car is lowered and the outer wheel housing is shallow and curved inward, like the '69 Camaro wheel housing, you could be limited to a narrower tire than if you made some modifications to the wheel housing. After measuring the width of the wheel housing, subtract 1 to 1.5 inches. This will give you necessary 1/2 to 3/4 inch on the inside and outside of your tire for ample suspension movement. Some extra clearance may be necessary for steering the front wheels. This measurement will be the maximum width of the tire you can run in your wheel housing. Tire manufacturers measure their tires from sidewall to sidewall (when mounted on suggested wheel widths), not tread width.

The next step is to measure backspacing for your wheels. With your car safely supported with jack stands, mock the ride height. With your brake rotors installed, put a straight edge across the mounting face of the brake rotor. With a tape measure or a ruler, measure the distance between the straight edge and the inner wheel housing. Taking the tire clearance into consideration, the remaining measurement will be your backspacing. Measure both sides of the car for proper backspacing, because auto manufacturers don't build square cars. I've seen cars with as much as 7/8-inch difference from side to side.

If you don't want to spend the time doing all this work, for a fee, some performance tire shops offer services to test-fit wheels and tires on your car, or measure it for you. This way you get the correct wheel ordered the first time.

Picking the correct wheel offset is important. The wrong wheel can come into contact with suspension pieces. Someone took a grinder to this tie-rod end to make it clear the wheel.

How to Build GM Pro-Touring Street Machines

Chapter 1

Vince's '69 El Camino

Most guys sell a project when it's done so they can build their next project bigger, better, and faster. Not Vince Asaro, a car builder by trade, and fabricator extraordinaire by virtue. He has rebuilt his '69 El Camino numerous times, and every time the bar is raised. This time, Vince raised the bar to the extreme Pro-Touring level. You would be hard pressed to find something that has not been modified in one way or another.

For lack of space, I'll stick to the car's current state (but it will probably be different by the time this book first hits the stores). At first, you think the car is just a low-slung hot rod. You notice the flush-mounted aluminum bed cover, three-piece adjustable wing, and the extremely straight body, covered in PPG Fleet Black single-stage paint. If you know El Caminos, you might notice the reshaped B-pillars, front wheel openings raised three inches, shaved marker lights, shaved trim, molded bed trim, and late-model Chevy truck door handles.

To see what powers the car, you must open the reverse opening hood. Visibly, you notice the well laid out twin Turbonetics T04B turbos and Deltagate wastegates connected to custom built 1-5/8-inch all-stainless headers. A Spearco intercooler core with owner-fabbed tanks cools the air charge. The custom-built aluminum intake manifold started life as a tunnel ram. What you can't see is the 383's Dart Little M block and its internals, which consist of a Crower stroker crank and rods, Wiseco 8:1 pistons, custom hydraulic camshaft, and headwork done to the Edelbrock Performer RPM heads. Fuel is carried in a custom 35-gallon fuel tank that feeds an SX fuel pump. Liberal use of Aeroquip and XRP fittings and hoses get the fuel to the Aeromotive regulator, Keith Black fuel rails, and 55-lb injectors. An Accel Gen7 DFI with wideband O2 option controls the fuel and spark. So far, the power is estimated at 750 hp on pump gas.

In most cars, 750 hp would be useless, but Vince used all his engineering skills to build a custom de-coupled torque arm rear suspension from pictures and text in Herb Adams' book entitled *Chassis Engineering/Chassis Design Building and Tuning for High Performance Handling*. This system puts the power to the pavement in vicious fashion. The 12-bolt rear end is suspended by Koni circle-track coil-overs with 200-lb springs. This system plants the 17x11-

Vince Asaro's '69 El Camino is considered extreme Pro-Touring, but you need to look closer to see why. You don't see the race-bred suspension and frame. You only see the intake tubes for the twin turbos and the license plate.

From this angle, performance is a little more evident. You can clearly see the adjustable wing, large fuel pump, and big 335 rollers in the rear.

Vince's '69 El Camino (Continued)

inch Centerline Billet Star wheels and Pirelli P-Zero 335/35x17 rear tires like I have never felt 17-inch street tires hook up before. On the front are 17x9-1/2-inch wheels wrapped with 285/40x17 P-Zeros, and they hook up in cornering fashion by way of Stock Car Products hubs, Coleman spindles, custom unequal-length tubular control arms, Koni circle-track coil-overs, Hypercoil 600-lb/in springs, Speedway Engineering hollow sway bar, and all-custom steering

For extra power, Vince installed twin turbos on his small-block 383. The craftsmanship is evident in the fabricated headers, intake manifold, and plumbing.

The rear suspension is controlled by a Herb Adams-esque decoupled torque arm. Herb Adams knows what he is doing. The suspension works like magic. All the parts were ceramic coated or powder coated by Accessories Plus.

The exhaust exits unconventionally, from under the rear wing. The El Camino is an engineering marvel. You can see the large custom fuel cell and some of the cage tubing. Not as visible are the rocker-arm actuated Koni coil-overs.

linkage.

The front and rear suspensions are joined by an ultra-rigid 2- by 3-inch tube frame with a large backbone that doubles as a transmission tunnel. A 12-point roll cage built off the main cage of 2x1/8-inch seamless tubing adds even more strength and keeps the occupants safe while they enjoy the climate provided by a Vintage Air system and tunes from a powerful sound system. The hand formed two-piece aluminum dashboard is a work of art, filled with AutoMeter gauges. The driver selects gears from a Richmond 6-speed transmission coupled with a McLeod Street Twin clutch setup. The 3.5-inch driveshaft from Bayshore Truck Equipment of California turns the 2.56:1 gears and beefed-up Eaton Posi. The brakes are 13x1.375-inch Coleman rotors in front and 12x 1.375-inch in the rear. They are halted by Wilwood Superlite IIA 4-piston calipers front and rear, which are activated by a '75 Corvette manual disc master cylinder. The car is strewn with plenty of other modifications, like the custom exhaust built from 3-inch mandrel bends and straight tubing. Every surface is either painted, or has been powder coated or ceramic coated by Accessories Plus in Belmont, California.

Vince built and engineered the El Camino to be streetable and raceworthy. As low as it looks, it doesn't scrape or rub pulling in and out of driveways around town thanks to the fact that nothing hangs below the bottom of the body, and there's 5 inches of ground clearance as measured just behind the front tires. That in itself shows his engineering and fabrication talents, and I'm sure his next version of the El Camino will be just as well thought out.

Chapter 2

Front Suspension and Steering

Since building a Pro-Touring car is focused around the pursuit of better handling, front suspension is extremely important. This chapter will cover some basics and performance aspects of front suspension alignment. I will be covering separate components and complete front suspension packages. Getting your car pointed in the right direction is important too, so performance aspects of the steering system are also covered. Front suspension and steering work together as a package to increase performance and driveability, and the information covered in this chapter was put together to help you get your car tuned for your style of driving.

This photo shows Steve Broscoe's '69 Camaro undergoing some serious front suspension re-engineering at Campbell Auto Restoration. This is an extreme Pro-Touring front suspension.

Alignment

There are three main settings of front suspension that can affect the performance and driveability of your car: camber, caster, and toe. I will explain the three settings in simple terms, but I will not go into too much detail.

If your front suspension bushings and steering components are loose, worn, or broken, you should have them replaced before considering an alignment. An alignment performed on a car with worn out tie-rod ends or deterio-

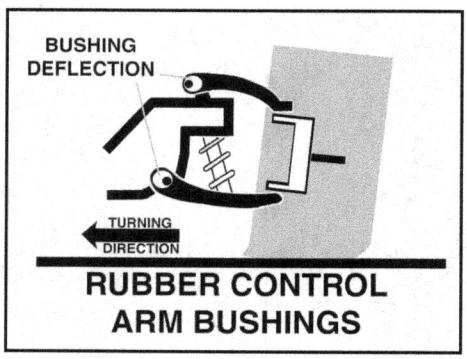

Rubber suspension bushings deflect and distort under hard driving conditions. This distortion helps isolate road shock under normal driving conditions. This movement also allows the suspension geometry to change, hampering handling characteristics. Notice how the spindle is tilted and the tire is barely contacting the ground.

rated control-arm bushings is a waste of time and money because the settings will most likely change before the car gets out of the shop. Worn suspension and steering components are also a safety issue, so take care of these things as a matter of course.

Caster

On a car with upper and lower control arms, the spindle pivots on the axis determined by the upper and lower ball joints. Caster is the forward or rearward tilt of the spindle on this axis as viewed

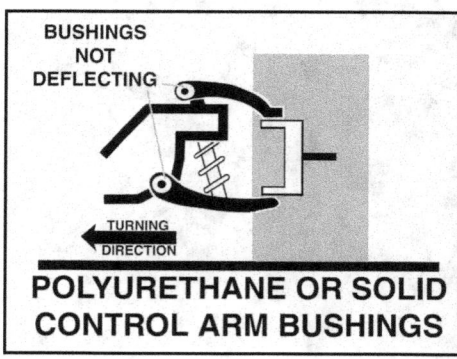

The urethane or solid suspension bushings transfer road feel to the chassis. Solid suspension bushings also help the suspension geometry to stay in its intended position. Notice how the tire is contacting the ground more evenly for better cornering traction.

---

28   *How to Build GM Pro-Touring Street Machines*

Front Suspension and Steering

from the side of the car. On most cars with this type of suspension, caster is adjusted by moving the upper control arm on its pivots using shims. When viewed from the side, if the upper ball joint is behind (towards the back of the car) the lower ball-joint, the car has positive caster. Negative caster is when the upper ball-joint is ahead of the lower. Caster has a tendency to cause the tires to move vertically a small amount as they are steered right or left from the centered position. This vertical movement acts to push the weight of the car off the ground while gravity tries to pull it back down. The force of gravity trying to pull the car down pushes up on the tire. This upward force on the tire causes the spindle to rotate about its axis to the point that the forces on both the right and left spindles find equilibrium. This equilibrium is found when both tires are pointing straight ahead, assuming of course, that the caster is the same on both sides of the car and there is nothing bent or out of alignment on either side. Both negative and positive caster can induce this self-centering action of the wheels and give the car more stability at higher speeds.

The self-centering effect does not come from caster alone. It can also come from steering axis inclination. This is the same basic principle as caster, but in the front view of the suspension. If the axis of the upper and lower ball-joints leans inward at the top, as a lot of cars do, there will again be a force trying to push up on the car. Some cars get this self-centering effect using only steering axis inclination and zero caster. Some late-model Camaros and Firebirds are an example of this. There are probably others as well.

This photo shows the front tire exhibiting positive camber. The top of the tire is pushing outward. If you took a hard corner in this car, it would have understeer. Only the outside edge of the tire is biting the ground.

This front tire is exhibiting negative camber. The top of the tire is tilted slightly inward. This car corners hard. The entire width of the tire tread is able to get traction on the ground.

Camber

Camber is the inward or outward tilt of the top of the tire as viewed from the front of the car. Negative camber is when the top of the tire tilts inward and positive camber is when the top of the tire tilts outward. Positive camber is not desirable for handling, because it makes the outer edge of the tire dig into the pavement. The outside edge of the tire on the ground does not produce as much cornering traction as the entire width of the tire. During negative camber, when the top of the tire is tilting inward, the entire width of the tire has a better chance to evenly plant on the road surface for optimum traction. As with anything in life, negative camber is only good in moderation. Too much negative camber will have the inside edge of the tire trying to keep your car from sliding with unwanted understeer.

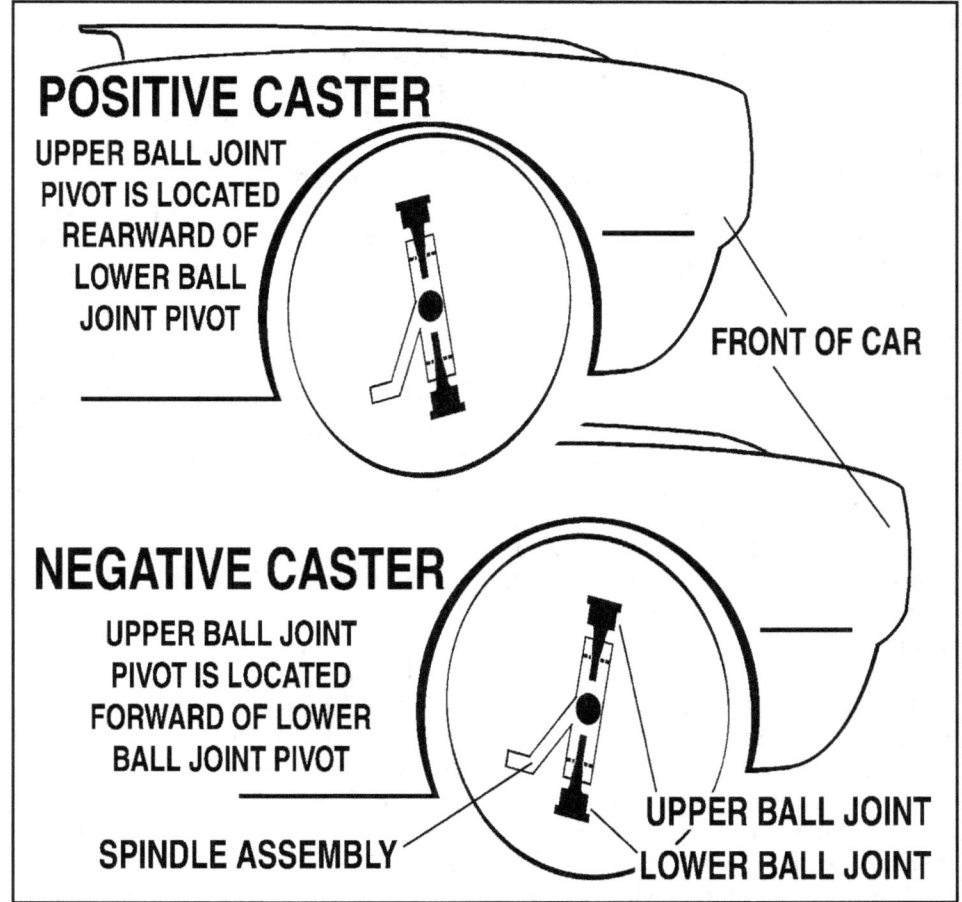

The top of the illustration shows the front spindle in extreme positive caster position. The bottom of the illustration shows the front spindle in extreme negative caster. Positive caster is preferred over negative caster.

Chapter 2

Camber can be set on your car with an alignment. Camber-curve is something completely separate from camber adjustment from an alignment (except in the case of a race-bred suspension with adjustable control-arm pivot points). The camber-curve is affected by the length of the control arms and the control arm pivot points. A positive camber-curve actually increases the outward tilt of the top of the tire during suspension articulation, which is completely undesirable and intensifies understeer. A negative camber-curve tilts the top of the tire inwards during suspension articulation, which is much more desirable for improved handling around corners. I mention articulation because when your car is steered into the corner, the body leans. When the body leans, the outer front tire articulates upward in the fender opening. An extremely aggressive negative camber-curve can be bad too. The key to a good handling car is to keep the largest amount of the tire tread on the road surface as possible.

The top of the photo shows the front tires in zero (neutral) toe. The car will drive straight and have very little rolling resistance. For demonstration purposes, the middle photo shows the front tires in extreme toe-in, and lower photo shows the front tires in extreme toe-out.

Toe

Toe is the relationship between two tires on one end of the car as viewed from above. If, when viewed from above, both tires are parallel, there is zero toe. Toe-in is when the tires are closer at the front than the rear and toe-out is when the rear tires are closer than the front.

Now that you know what zero-toe, toe-in, and toe-out are, you need to know how their settings affect your car. If you aligned the tires with zero-toe, the motion of the car moving forward will actually pull the front tires to a toe-out position from the distortion of the rubber suspension bushings and from road friction on the tires. To compensate for the road friction and movement of rubber suspension bushings, most factory cars are designed with a small amount of toe-in. The goal is to have the tires at zero toe at the intended average speed of the car. Factory alignment specifications are intended to minimize premature tire wear and to lower the rolling resistance of the tires. Since factory specs create less rolling resistance, fuel economy is increased. So, if you are planning on driving your Pro-Touring car across the United States on the *Hot Rod* Power Tour, you may want to have your car aligned to factory specs.

With excessive amounts of toe, whether in or out, your tires will wear out faster and your fuel economy will decrease. Most cars are aligned with around 1/16 to 1/8-inch of toe-in. A setting of 5/16-inch of toe-in is quite a lot. A small amount of extra toe-in increases high-speed stability. Consider 1/32 inch over the factory setting as a practical maximum. Toe-out has a tendency to make the car turn in faster. People looking for the fast way around corners will find benefits from careful experimentation with toe-out settings. Too much toe-out will cause the car to wander back and forth on the straights because the two tires are trying to steer in different directions. Wandering will get worse with increased road speed as a result of toe-out. Keep in mind that altering the factory alignment specs should only be done at the track.

A little toe-out will help your car turn-in around corners and can also help to minimize understeer. What type of driving or racing you plan to do will determine what toe setting is correct for your application.

Just as a warning, beware of the condition of your front suspension components. Worn or damaged bushings, ball joints, bearings, tie-rod ends, and other suspension components will act to alter your alignment settings. Having an alignment performed on your car will not compensate for broken or worn parts.

Street Alignment

If you want your car to handle predictably on the street and want your tires to wear evenly, you should go with the stock alignment settings. However, if you have replaced your rubber control-arm bushings with urethane or solid bushings, you may need less toe-in than the factory calls for. The factory toe-in compensates for the flex and distortion of rubber bushings. Without the flex, you could try changing the toe-in to closer to zero. You may have to look around for a shop that does performance alignments to get the adjustments you want. A street performance alignment will wear the tires a little quicker than normal, but the car will grip better on the street. For cars like the Camaro/Firebird (1967–1981), what you're looking for is the most positive caster you can get while keeping the camber at between zero and about 3/4-degree negative. And for toe-in, keep with the factory specs unless you've replaced the bushings with something firmer than stock. With polyurethane and similar replacement bushings, you may be able to move the toe closer to zero. You may need to experiment a little to get something that works for you, but these specs should get you in the ballpark. These specs will also apply to the early Chevelle, Nova, and full-size Monte Carlo.

The caster recommendation above is done to increase high-speed stability and will increase turning resistance at the steering wheel. The camber is to increase cornering potential, but the further away

Front Suspension and Steering

from zero you get, the twitchier the car will be above about 50 mph or so.

Racing Alignment

If you plan to run your car on an open track or an autocross event, the alignment can be more aggressive. A racing alignment is not good for street use. It will cause the tires to wear very fast, and will be hard to control in a straight line and over rough roads. This makes it very dangerous on the street. If you are going racing, use common sense and trailer your car to the track.

For tighter tracks, you may want to experiment with a little toe-out, but remember, a little goes a long way. On the longer, faster tracks, you may find that zero toe is a better choice. Again, experiment to see what works. Too much toe-out will increase the drag on the front tires and cause the car to wander at higher speeds. Anything over about 1/16 - 1/8-inch of toe-out is probably too much.

On the street, you will probably not be throwing your car into the corners as hard as you do on the track. The increased cornering speed increases your body-roll and suspension articulation, so to increase the camber a little bit for extreme conditions may benefit your handling and your lap times.

Adding a little bit of negative camber is good for increasing traction to your front tires. You can experiment with a little bit at a time. When driving on the street, negative camber increases your rolling resistance and will wear the inside section of tire tread, so the extra negative camber should be left at the track.

Bumpsteer

Bumpsteer describes what happens when the steering linkage affects the intended direction of the tire when the car hits a bump or leans in a turn. This is caused by a lack of engineered geometry of the steering linkage. There are different degrees of bumpsteer; typically, zero bumpsteer (desired) is unattainable with stock suspension components. Most people settle for as close to zero as possible.

Eliminating Bumpsteer

There are several companies that offer bumpsteer checking equipment, as well as other alignment equipment, including Longacre Racing Products and Pole Position Racing Products. You can also build your own low-tech devices. These devices check the amount of fore and aft movement of the tire through the entire range of suspension articulation.

Interchangeable Steering Arms

Replacing the steering arms is not an option on all GM cars. Early General Motors cars had steering arms that are separate from the spindles. Some of the cars have steering arms integrated into the spindles.

Some GMs have steering arms of different lengths that are interchangeable. First-generation F-bodies and second-generation X-bodies are an example of this. They had steering arms of at least three different lengths. The arms came in different lengths for manual and power steering, special options, and by year. The differences in length are approximately 1-1/4 inch from the long arm to the short one. That measurement doesn't seem to be a lot, but when it comes to steering geometry and bumpsteer, a little can mean a whole lot.

Be careful when using longer steering arms, they can limit the wheel offset and size. If the steering arm is too close to the wheel, it can cause the tie rod to dig into the wheel during upward travel of the wheel.

Rod Ends

Bumpsteer can be corrected with the use of spherical rod ends in place of the outer tie-rod ends. Shims of different thickness are used between the rod end and the steering arm to adjust the rod ends up or down as desired. In the past, it was necessary to drill out the taper in the steering arm to use a bolt to attach the rod end to the steering arm. In 2001, Baer Racing Inc. started offering adjustable tie-rod ends called Baer Trackers that utilize spherical rod ends. They offer it for rack-and-pinion and recirculating-ball steering systems. It takes the guesswork out of bumpsteer adjustment, because it comes with special tapered bolts, shims, rod ends, and adjustment sleeves. The Baer Tracker is available for many GM models, but not the first-generation F-body, due to the inconsistency in factory steering components.

Rack-and-Pinion

Bumpsteer can also be corrected on cars equipped with rack-and-pinion steering. The steering rack can be adjusted with shims to space it to the proper position. If shims won't fix the bumpsteer, you may have to modify the steering rack mount, which can be costly and time consuming. In some cases, the engine or other accessories will limit the amount you can move the steering rack.

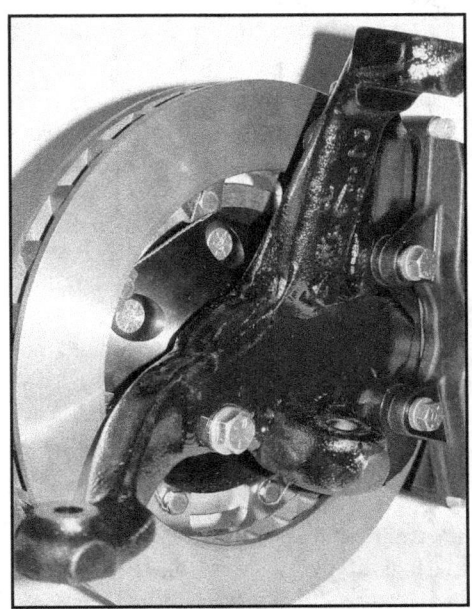

The spindle above is a '71 Chevelle spindle. It has a steering arm that is separate from the spindle. The spindle on the right is from a B-body. The steering arm is integrated into the spindle. Getting a shorter or longer steering arm to fix bump steer is not an option for the B-body spindle.

Control Arms

When it comes to handling, upper front control arms play a large factor. A couple of GM cars are known to benefit from relocating the mount on the frame. Upper control arms are shimmed to adjust camber and caster. Many companies offer tubular upper control arms, but not all aftermarket control arms are created equal.

Stock Control Arms

Stock upper control arms are great for low budget Pro-Touring build-ups. Stock lower control arms are used on any size budget.

Control Arm Relocation

Stock location of the upper control arms can be changed. Guldstrand Motorsports offers a relocation kit for the first-generation F-body and second-generation X-body. The kit includes a template for lowering the location of the upper control-arm shaft on the stock control-arm tower. This modification reduces the unwanted positive camber-gain GM designed into the front suspension. It also lowers the center of gravity, which translates to better handling characteristics.

The Guldstrand modification is a fairly simple upgrade. The bolt holes for the upper control-arm cross-shafts on the control-arm tower are re-drilled in a lower location. To have clearance for the stock control arm after the Guldstrand modification, the tops of the control-arm towers usually have to be trimmed.

Aftermarket Control Arms

Aftermarket suspension companies have been building custom control arms for years. A few of them were made for the application of putting Camaro subframes in sedans from the 1940s and earlier. Unfortunately, they didn't change the suspension geometry. After the Pro-Street craze slowed down, a couple of aftermarket suspension companies saw a market for people wanting to drive fast in a straight line and around corners.

In the mid to late 1990s, a couple of companies started offering tubular upper control arms for General Motors A- and G-bodies. The arms require the use of taller spindles from later GM donor cars. The combination of parts increased handling performance with improved caster for straight-line stability and negative camber curves.

When it came to handling, it wasn't until the mid 1990s first-generation F-bodies and second-generation X-bodies started getting attention. Some of the companies started building control-arm packages and subframes that were too expensive for most budgets. In 2001, a few companies came out with a way to get more performance without breaking the bank. They came out with more affordable upper control arms that increased cornering performance by changing the camber and caster of the front suspension.

As of the date this book was published, there were not any companies building aftermarket control arms for first-generation H- and X-bodies using stock frames. I have listed a few companies offering control arms with modified geometry for Pro-Touring applications.

Detroit Speed & Engineering
3753 Old U.S. 23, Suite 200
Brighton, MI 48114
(810) 227-6343
www.detroitspeed.com

Anyone following Pro-Touring is familiar with Detroit Speed & Engineering (aka DSE). Its founder, Kyle Tucker, has a background in racing and engineering (from working on the Chevrolet Corvette C5 suspension team). From his experience with GM, Kyle got in the habit of building everything with longevity in mind.

Detroit Speed & Engineering builds upper control arms for the first-generation F-body and second-generation X-bodies. With longevity in mind, they computer modeled the control arms and then put them through finite element analysis. Their upper control arms are built with mild steel tubes, CNC milled billet ball joint pockets, custom stainless-steel cross-shafts, stainless-steel hardware, aluminum caster adjusters, and greaseable Delrin bushings. The one-of-a-kind stainless-steel cross-shaft and Caster Tuner Bushings provide ability to align the front end with as much caster as possible without the need for alignment shims. The cross-shaft is available in satin or polished finish.

Detroit Speed & Engineering offers serviceable solid lower control-arm bushings. They have a steel housing that won't distort and can be welded into place. The inserts are made of Delrin, the crush tubes are steel, and the grease fittings are stainless steel. The outer steel housing is available with a zinc electroplate with a yellow chromate corrosion-

Along with improved suspension geometry, Detroit Speed & Engineering's tubular upper control arms feature a CNC'd upper ball-joint cup, CNC'd tube ends, and a stainless-steel cross shaft. It also utilizes Delrin bushings and caster-tuner bushings. (Photo courtesy of DSE)

Detroit Speed & Engineering (DSE) offers an optional service to modify your lower control arms. These have had a plate welded to the underside to eliminate control-arm flex. The plate has countersunk holes for a competition appearance. (Photo courtesy of DSE)

Front Suspension and Steering

resistant finish. The housings are also available bare for those who choose to weld them to the control arm and powder coat the entire unit.

They also modify stock lower control arms for the first-generation F-body and second-generation X-body. They remove the center area of the control arm and weld in a new plate with countersunk lightening holes. This is an old Bonneville trick. It adds rigidity to the arm and allows you to retain the look of the stock control arm.

Global West
655 South Lincoln Ave
San Bernardino, CA 92408
(877) 470-2975
www.globalwest.net

Global West is one of the most diversified aftermarket suspension companies. They make parts for GM A-bodies, B-bodies, F-bodies, G-bodies, and X-bodies. The years span from 1962 to 2002. They also produce aftermarket parts for Ford Motor Company vehicles.

Global West control arms are made from tubular construction. The arms improve suspension geometry with more caster and an improved camber curve, which they call a Negative Roll System. They allow the use of stock upper control-arm shafts, stock replacement offset shafts, or custom billet conrtol-arm shafts, which allow more camber adjustment. Global West also offers custom steel billet cross-shafts for the upper arms, which allow more camber adjustments. Since the Global West arms are designed to utilize the stock control-arm cross-shafts, they also allow the use of stock bushings. Global West offers their control arms with stock rubber or Del-a-lum (Delrin and aluminum) cross-shaft bushings. All bushings for their upper and lower control arms have grease fittings for service.

Global West offers first-generation F-body and second-generation X-body tubular upper and lower control arms, which allow use of the stock spindles. The upper arms have more caster already designed into them, along with a preferred negative camber curve. The lower control arms do not change the geometry. The upper and lower arms are available separately, or as a package with QA-1 adjustable coil-overs. The lower control arms are available with the coil-over mount or coil spring mount for people sticking with the coil spring and conventional shock setup.

For second-generation F-bodies, Global West is also offering tubular upper control arms. They are designed to improve handling with a new camber curve and increased caster.

Upper control arms are available for G- and A-bodies. They provide more caster and have an improved camber curve with Global West's Negative Roll System. The upper control arms for the G- and A-bodies require the use of Global West "tall spindle" brake conversion kits. If you prefer, Global West also provides information on how to piece together your own tall spindle brake kit, or you can see detailed information in the brakes chapter. The tall spindle itself comes from the second-generation F-body, the third-generation X-body, the 1973 through 1977 B- and G-bodies, and a few other models and years. The models and years differ, depending on your quest for 11- or 12-inch disc brakes.

Global West also offers a complete front suspension system for first-generation F-bodies and second-generation X-bodies. It is called a Category-5 system. It converts to a modified taller B-body spindle, along with a slough of other parts so the spindles fit.

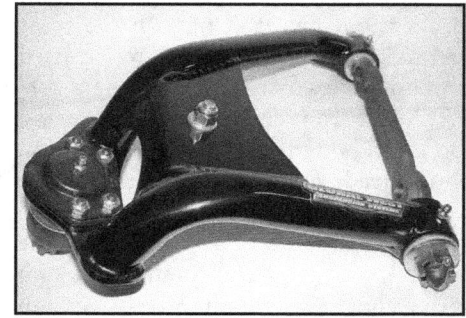

Global West offers upper and lower tubular control arms. The upper arms are available with steel billet cross shafts. They modify the suspension geometry for improved handling.

Hotchkis Performance
12035 Burke Street, Suite 13
Santa Fe Springs, CA 90760
(877) 466-7765
www.hotchkis.net

Hotchkis is best known for their vast line of sway bars. They have many other great products, which include front and rear control arms, leaf springs, and coil springs.

They offer tubular upper control arms for 1964 through 1988 A-bodies and 1978 through 1988 A and G-bodies that allow the buyer to upgrade to a larger set of B- or F-body 11- or 12-inch rotors and spindles. This setup improves the negative camber curve to plant the front tire on the ground during cornering. It also increases caster for increased high-speed stability.

Hotchkis sells the F-body 11-inch brakes and taller spindles as a complete package if you prefer not to spend your time piecing the parts together. If you prefer the B-body 12-inch brakes and taller spindles, Hotchkis doesn't offer them as a kit. If you don't mind going to a wrecking yard and a good auto parts store, you can build your own kit. For information on what cars are donors for 11- and 12-inch brakes and taller spindles, look on page 35 and 36.

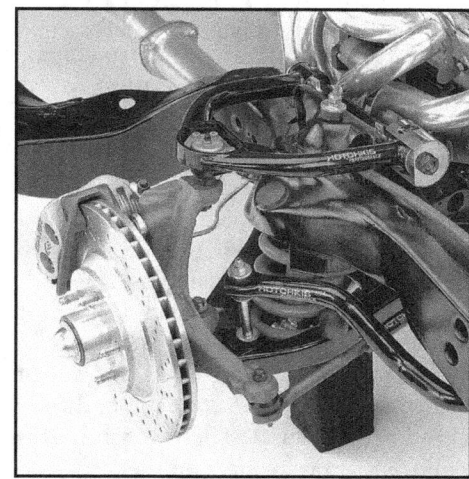

Hotchkis offers tubular control arms for converting your A-body to B-body or second-generation F-body spindles, so you can improve your handling and braking at the same time. (Photo courtesy Hotchkis)

Hotrods To Hell, Inc.
100 East Prospect Ave
Burbank, CA 91502
(818) 842-4360
www.hotrodstohell.net

The owner of Hotrods to Hell applies asphalt and dirt track experience to all his parts. Hotrods' is known more for its truck-arm style rear suspensions, but that is not all they offer. They also offer upper control arms for 1964 through 1972 A-bodies. They are part of a kit to upgrade spindles and brakes at the same time. With the combination of parts, the camber gain and roll centers have been changed so your front tires stay planted on the street when you need them to be. Their kits have springs tailored to big block and small block applications for the best results. The kit also lowers the ride height one and a half inches from stock, as well as offering better handling and stopping.

Pole Position Racing Products
2021 East 74th Avenue, Unit J
Denver, CO 80229
(888) 303-8555
www.polepositionrp.com

The first- and second-generation F-body and the second- and third-generation X-body front subframes have been used in dirt and asphalt modified racing. Since Pole Position Racing Products makes racing alignment tools, it makes sense that they would make a completely adjustable racing style upper control arm.

Pole Position Racing Products offers adjustable upper control arms for first- and second-generation F-bodies as well as second- and third-generation X-bodies. The adjustable control arms allow for caster and/or optimized camber gain adjustment without the use of alignment shims, which can alter the camber during bump and rebound. These control arms can be great performers on the track and street with the right knowledge of front suspension geometry. Without good working knowledge of front suspension geometry, these arms can get you into trouble. If you have your doubts, and don't have the proper alignment equipment, have a reputable race shop install

Pole Position Racing Products offers adjustable tubular control arms. This racer suggests safety wiring the end clips to the cross shafts to ensure that they stay on.

and align them for you. If they are set up wrong, your car can be dangerous.

The options include steel or aluminum cross-shafts and ball joint plates for accepting a Chrysler style screw-in ball joint or stock bolt-in ball joint.

Springs

Obviously, all of the suspension parts, tires, and track conditions play key roles in the handling characteristics of your vehicle. For this section, we will cover front coil springs.

Front coil springs are important to the handling characteristics of your Pro-Touring car. A spring too soft for the weight of the vehicle is great for drag racing. Drag racers need the weight of the vehicle to transfer from the front suspension to the rear suspension for ultimate traction. This is good for straight line driving. Pro-Touring cars don't just drive in a straight line, and rely on the front tires to keep the car going where you need it to go while entering and exiting a corner. A soft front coil spring will give you too much body roll and a loss of traction on the inside tire while cornering.

Pro-Touring cars are meant to be driven on the street, just as much as the track, if not more. If your front coil springs have a spring rate that is too high for the weight and setup of your car, they will give you a harsh ride on the street. The high rate springs may not allow your car to have the body-roll it needs to help plant the outside tire in a corner. Without traction of the outside tire, the car can push, generating uncontrollable understeer.

Choosing the right spring for your application is not easy. If I told everyone to run a 650-lb front coil spring, I would be performing a disservice. I don't know everybody's rear spring rate, front and rear shock dampening, bushing types, tire compounds, etc. Every car is different. Sure, you could throw a set of 650-lb front coil springs in your Firebird. You might get lucky. Truthfully, in most cases, Pro-Touring cars never get pushed to the point where the driver would notice the difference between the performance from a set of 650- or 750-lb front coils. If you believe you might push your car to its limits and want to more education about springs, keep reading. The information may help you with your next coil-spring purchase. In the end, consulting a technical department of your favorite suspension company could help you get the exact spring you need. If a company does not have an educated technical advisor, you may want to get in touch with a reputable spring company.

Stock Springs

Stock front coil springs typically deliver a ride chosen to be comfortable for the mass population. For Pro-Touring people like ourselves, the rate may be too soft, or the ride height is not as desired.

In the past, it was a cool trick to run "air conditioning" or "big block" springs for better handling. A stock coil spring for a car equipped with air conditioning and/or a big block typically has more spring rate than a car without those options. GM engineers knew those option equipped cars were heavier and needed more spring rate to compensate. Since this is not an exact science, aftermarket springs may be a better choice.

Aftermarket Springs — Available Rates

There are so many companies offering different rates of springs, it makes sense to tune your suspension with aftermarket springs. Some companies prefer lower rate springs than others. Each company has its own idea of what is best for each application. One company may believe a car should be set up with more oversteer. Another company may believe a car should be set up with more understeer. Spring rates, sway bars, and tires can affect these suspension characteristics. Coil springs are just another part on your car that can be tuned for maximum performance. Since each company has a different idea of what rate is best for each application, you may want to pick a reputable company and ask them to help. If you talk with too many companies, you may get too much information for your own good. Since you are probably not building a full-on competition racecar, you don't need too much information. Keeping it simple is not a bad thing. With the right help, you may get your optimum coil spring rate within 100 lbs. That would be more than adequate for most Pro-Touring cars.

Coil Spring Basics

There are two different types of coil spring: linear and progressive. They are identified by visual inspection of the windings. The linear coil spring has equally spaced coils throughout the length of the spring, except the very end of the spring. The progressive coil spring has tighter wound coils on one end of the spring than the opposite end.

Coil spring rates are identified by how much weight is required to compress the spring one inch. A 600-lb spring will require 600 lbs of weight to compress it one inch. A 600-lb linear rate coil spring would require 1200 lbs to compress the spring two inches. A 600-lb progressive rate spring could require 1600 lbs to compress the spring two inches.

Linear rate coil springs are used on most production cars. Typically, progressive springs are used in racing applications.

Coil springs are available in 400 to 3200-lb rates. The higher the rate, the harsher the ride will be. Typically, only purpose-built road-race cars need more than 800-lb front coil springs.

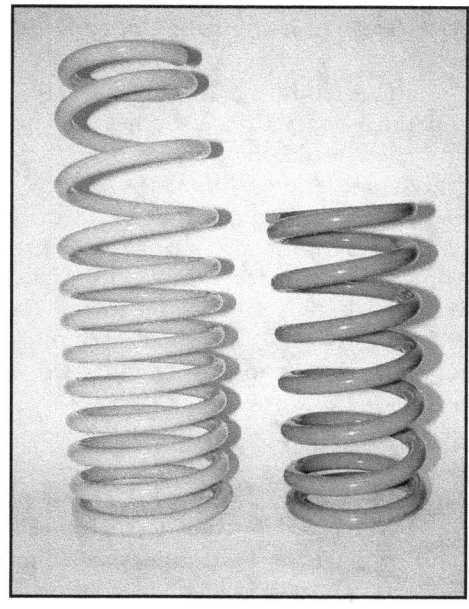

The spring on the right is linear. Its coils are uniform throughout. The spring on the left is progressive. It's identified by its change in winding density.

Spindles and Brakes

First, I want to explain some basics about the interaction between the spindle, rotor, hub, and brake caliper. The following information is on spindles using ball joints, not king pins (old suspension technology). The spindle is the unit located between the upper and lower ball joint. It pivots forward and backwards on the axis between the two ball joints when the steering wheel is turned. The spindle has a "spindle-pin" or a "bearing-pack" for the rotor or a hub to spin on. The spindle-pin is a pin that sticks out of the spindle, for the use of inner and outer wheel bearings. A bearing pack is mostly used on late-model vehicles (such as fourth-generation F-bodies and late-model Corvettes), and looks like a compact hub and bearing assembly. Some rotors mate to a hub, and some have an integrated hub. The caliper mounts over the rotor, so it can pinch the spinning rotor, or keep it from spinning if it wasn't in motion already.

A- and G-Body Spindle Upgrade

1964 through 1972 A-bodies and 1978 through 1988 G-bodies can be upgraded to 11- or 12-inch diameter rotors by using factory donor parts. The taller spindle (in conjunction with aftermarket control arms) not only allows the use of a larger diameter brake rotor, but it also helps correct the factory suspension camber-gain geometry flaws.

The list of donor cars follows this paragraph, and it's broken down by which car offers an 11- or 12-inch rotor/spindle upgrade. You will need a pair of custom upper control arms to adapt your car to these taller spindles. Hotchkis and Global West offer these custom-length control arms. You will need a pair of new Moog outer tie-rod ends (part#ES2033RL) to connect the steering linkage to the steering arm, due to the different taper required. The 1964 through 1972 A-bodies will need a set of custom machined lower ball joints from Hotchkis to fit your lower control arms. If you are installing 12-inch upgrade spindles, you will need pick up a pair of 1988 through 1992 1LE rotors (GM#18016035), since most B-body 12-inch rotors have a wheel bolt-pattern of 5 on 5-inch, instead of the 5 on 4-3/4-inch bolt pattern wheels you already own. The 1LE rotors also have 12-mm wheel studs, so if you want 7/16-inch or 1/2-inch standard threaded wheel studs, you will need to change them. Global West suggests using a 1970-1976 brake caliper, since it is the proper size for the 1LE rotor thickness. They also suggest running a master cylinder with a 1-inch diameter bore and an adjustable brake proportioning valve. For more info on master cylinder choice, call Global West or a brake expert.

Global West warns — they have found two different spindle-pins from 12-inch spindle donor cars. One uses an outer bearing measuring .750 inch, and one uses a larger outer bearing measuring .850 inch. They say to use the spindle with the larger bearing.

If you don't want to put your own kit together, you can purchase complete kits with all the work already done for you. You can purchase the complete brake and B-body spindle packages from Global West, Baer Brakes, and Hotchkis.

After installing any front suspension part, make sure you torque all parts

Chapter 2

to the proper specifications, install all cotter pins, and have your car aligned before driving. (Information courtesy of Global West)

BRAKE DONORS

11-INCH DONORS

F-bodies
Chevrolet Camaro – 1970 through 1981
Pontiac Firebird – 1970 through 1981

X-bodies
Chevrolet Nova – 1975 through 1979
Pontiac Ventura – 1975 through 1977
Pontiac Phoenix – 1977 through 1979
Buick Apollo – 1975
Buick Skylark – 1975 through 1979
Oldsmobile Omega – 1975 through 1979

A- and G-bodies
Chevrolet Chevelle – 1973 through 1977
Chevrolet Monte Carlo – 1973 through 1977
Buick Century – 1973 through 1977
Oldsmobile Cutlass – 1973 through 1977
Pontiac LeMans – 1973 through 1977
Pontiac Grand Prix – 1973 through 1977
GMC Sprint – 1973 through 1977
Buick Riviera – 1977 and 1978

B-bodies
Chevrolet full-size – 1977 through 1981
Buick full-size – 1977 through 1981
Pontiac full-size – 1977 through 1981

12-INCH DONORS

C- and B-bodies
Buick Le Sabre wagon & Electra wagon - 1977 through 1994
Oldsmobile Delta 88, Delta 88 wagon, and Delta 98 - 1977 through 1992
Chevrolet Caprice, Caprice Classic wagon, Impala, Belair, Biscayne - 1977 through 1996
Pontiac Bonneville, Catalina, and Grandville - 1977 through 1986
Cadillac Fleetwood and Deville - 1977 through 1984
Cadillac Brougham and Fleetwood - 1985 through 1994

F-Body 12-Inch Brake Upgrade

The second-generation F-bodies and third-generation X-bodies can be upgraded to 12-inch rotors using B-body spindles, just like the A- and G-bodies. Look at the listing of 12-inch donor cars for the interchange information. The 1LE rotor, wheel bolt-circle, and wheel stud information in the A- and G-body swap information applies to the F-bodies too. You will need a pair of new Moog outer tie-rod ends (part# ES2033RL) to connect the steering linkage to the steering arm, due to the different taper required.

This conversion allows you to keep your original calipers and master cylinder. After installing any front suspension part, make sure you torque all parts to the proper specifications, install all cotter pins, and have your car aligned before driving. (This information was courtesy Brett Klynn and www.nastyz28.com)

S-10 on H-body

The H-body does not get much attention outside of Pro-Street circles, but it is a GM product and deserves attention. Some H-body owners have

The ball joint on the left is a Moog replacement ball joint for a first-generation F-body. On the right is a Moog screw-in Chrysler-style ball joint. Circle track guys run these with a re-tapered spindle, because they are much beefier and easier to replace than the stock press-in ball joint on the left.

Here is the Chrysler ball joint on the control arm. A weld-in sleeve has been added to the arm. Now the ball joint can be replaced at home without a press.

found a way to upgrade the spindles on their cars. The modification uses 1982 through 1993 two wheel-drive Chevrolet S-10, S-15 truck, or Blazer front spindles. There aren't any known suspension geometry benefits to performing this modification, but the modification does allow the use of larger brakes and 5-lug wheels. The stock 1970s H-body has a non-vented 9-7/8-inch rotor that is inferior to the 10-1/2-inch vented S-10 rotor. Baer Racing offers Pro+ kits for their modified S-10 spindles that increase the rotor diameter to a whopping 13.5 inches.

The kit to install the S-10 rotors requires using a simple ball-joint adapter kit offered by Robert Gumm of www.V8monza.com. The kit also requires the use of 1975 to 1980 lower ball joints.

Ball Joints

Circle track guys have been replacing stock style press-in lower ball joints on first- and second-generation F-bodies with larger Chrysler screw in ball joints. The screw-in ball joints are stronger and easier to replace than press-in ball joints. This modification also applies to second-and third-generation X-bodies. The welding and machining required to perform this modification should be done by a professional.

Compared to the stock GM ball joint, the Chrysler ball joint has a larger body and stud. The only way to accomplish this installation is to purchase screw in ball joints and ball joint adapter

Front Suspension and Steering

rings. The stock ball joint sleeve in the lower control arms will need to be cut off. The screw in ball joint sleeves are welded into the lower control arms. Since the Chrysler ball joint has a different taper on the stud, the spindle will have to be re-tapered. A reputable machine shop should be able to perform this task, but they might have to buy the special drill-bit to perform the modification.

Keep in mind that the Chrysler ball joint has a different pivot point than the stock GM ball joint. This modification will change the suspension geometry. Installing a suspension part designed for the stock ball joint might not benefit from the changed pivot point, so be aware of this before you do this modification.

Aftermarket Subframes (20 Questions)

Since the first- and second-generation F-bodies and first-, second-, and third-generation X-bodies have removable front subframes, a few aftermarket companies offer replacement units with upgraded suspension and geometry. Those companies are Campbell Auto Restoration, Chris Alston's Chassisworks, Martz Chassis, and Wayne Due's Chassis Shop. To make it easier for people to compare what is available on the market, each company was sent the following list of 20 questions. The questions were compiled by a large group of Pro-Touring enthusiasts. The answers vary, so each company has a dedicated paragraph of combined answers. I included the questions, so you would know the actual questions asked. If a company left a question unanswered, I did not make a note about it.

1. Does your subframe offer mounts for small-block Chevy, big-block Chevy, and LS1?
2. Will a stock small-block Chevy or big-block Chevy oil pan fit without interference? Will a typical wet-sump road-race oil pan fit your subframe?
3. Do you offer transmission crossmembers for: T-56, Richmond 6-speed, 700R4, TH400, and TH350?
4. What headers will fit your subframe?
5. Would a customer have a choice of bolting Wilwood and Baer Racing brakes calipers on your subframe?
6. What type and size sway bar does your subframe use?
7. What type of rack-and-pinion is used on your subframe?
8. Does your subframe use Mustang II suspension parts?
9. What spindles are used on your subframe?
10. Does your subframe have anti-dive built into it?
11. What is the range of caster adjustment of your subframe?
12. What is the range of camber adjustment of your subframe?
13. Is your subframe engineered to have minimal bumpsteer?
14. Does your subframe use heim joints?
15. Are replacement suspension parts for your subframe readily available?
16. What is the largest tire and wheel combination that will fit without rubbing on the frame or stock fenders using your subframe without modification?
17. Do all factory bumper brackets and body panels bolt to your subframe?
18. Would you suggest using your subframe for 200-mph open-road racing applications (i.e. Silver State Challenge) and road-course racing?
19. Would you suggest using your frame on a car that would be driven 30,000 miles a year?
20. Has your subframe been structurally tested to have less flex than the factory subframe?

Campbell Auto Restoration

The Campbell Auto Restoration subframe is built to the customer's application. The suspension pickup points are set up so well for their subframe, that they integrate the subframe into any car you can imagine. Since the subframe is made to order, it can accept any conventionally mounted engine (with a rear sump or dry sump oil pan) and transmission combination. The

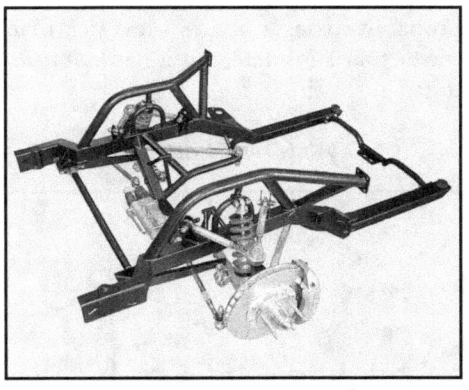

The Campbell Auto Restorations' subframe was conceived in the pursuit of offering the most performance-oriented unit available. From the upper support bars to the Appleton steering rack, you know this subframe means business. (Special thanks to Steve D'Aurora)

headers would be custom built to suit the application. Any brake kit could be mounted to the spindle, so you are not locked into a specific brake manufacturer. The sway bar is a three-piece stock-car style unit, and is available in many sizes. For the best bumpsteer numbers, a racing rack-and-pinion is used. No Mustang II suspension parts are used. The spindles are custom racing units. Anti-dive is adjustable, and the camber and caster is infinitely adjustable for any range desired. The bumpsteer is minimal, at less than .005 inch within 6.5 inches of suspension travel. The frame gets its great geometry from using high-quality nylon-lined chrome-moly heim joints at every pivot point.

In the case of an accident, replacement parts should be purchased from Campbell Auto Restoration, since most of them are custom made for your application. They have been successful mounting 315-width tires within the confines of '69 Camaro fenders, and 275-width tires on the '67 and '68 Camaros. The frame accepts the stock bumper brackets, radiator-core support, and inner fenderwells. Mark Schwartz at Campbell Auto Restoration says he would run a car equipped with this subframe in a high-speed open-road race, open-track events, and even drive it 30,000 miles a year, if it were properly serviced and cleaned on a regular basis. Structurally, the frame is

Chapter 2

probably stronger and has less flex than the factory subframe, but it had not been tested at the time.

Chris Alston's Chassisworks

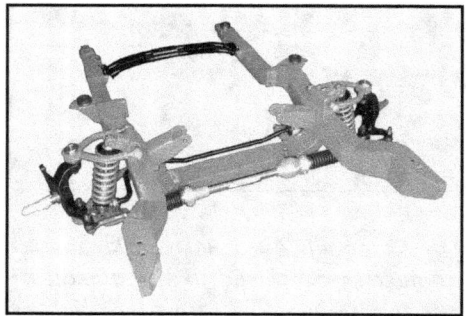

The front subframe produced by Chris Alston's Chassisworks features a custom rack and pinion, rear-mounted sway bar, coil-overs, improved suspension geometry, and a frame that is more structurally sound than the stock subframe. (Photo courtesy Steve Nestlerode Jr — special thanks to Steve D'Aurora)

Chris Alston's Chassisworks has been well known in the drag racing world since 1987. In 2001, he broke into the Pro-Touring world with their front subframe for the first-generation Chevy Camaros and '68 through '72 Chevy Novas. The suspension geometry and components from this subframe are also used on their Chevy II (first-generation X-body) front clip. They offer integral engine mounts for small- and big-block Chevy engines, and are available with mounts for motor and mid-plates, if you have a custom application. They have found oil pans fit if they have less than 4.25 inches of depth in the front. They have transmission mounts for TH-350, TH-400, and 700R4 automatic transmissions, and mounts for 4-speed and Richmond Over Drive manual transmissions. Chassisworks offers their own big- and small-block headers that will fit their frame. The Chassisworks custom spindle has an integral mount that accepts Wilwood calipers exclusively.

The sway bar is a custom Chassisworks 3/4-inch 4130 bar. Due to its mounting position behind the lateral CNC precision-bent tubular frame-rail brace, it is the equivalent of running a 1-inch sway bar on the stock Chevy subframe. The steering rack is built in-house for the correct width of the Camaro and Nova frame. There are no Mustang II suspension parts used. The suspension relies on Chassisworks-sculpted lightweight dropped spindles. The suspension has anti-dive built into it. The bumpsteer is minimal. The system doesn't have heim joints; it utilizes custom adjustable billet rod ends. They have a large inventory of replacement components in stock if the need arises. The subframe has a track width of 60 inches from hub to hub, and allows for the use of tires with a 12-inch rolling radius. All the factory brackets and body components bolt to the subframe. They said they would drive a car equipped with their subframe on a road course, and they would drive the car 30,000 miles a year. They have structurally tested the frame and it exceeded strength of the stock subframe.

Martz Chassis

The Martz Chassis front subframe does not come with the engine and transmission, but it does come with some impressive numbers. Gary Martz has personally driven a car equipped with his Rally and Road Race subframe at 180 mph at Pocono Speedway. (Photo courtesy Bryan Cope — special thanks to Steve D'Aurora)

Gary Martz of Martz Chassis builds subframes for first- and second-generation Camaros, and first- and second-generation Chevy Novas. Their Rally and Road Race chassis for the Camaro is the center of attention for this section. This frame is available with "hoop pipes" that support the frame and mount to the firewall. They have an optional Wide-Track frame available so you can run Corvette-style offset wheels. The frame has extra-long transmission mounting pads on the frame to allow for mounting just about any transmission available. They have two versions of engine mounts available. The most common are the big- and small-block Chevy mounts. The other version is specifically available for mounting a Gen-III small-block LS1 and LS6 engines. Headers available from Hooker, Hedman, and Street & Performance are known to fit the subframe. The customer can choose stock GM brakes, or aftermarket brakes from Baer Racing or Wilwood. The sway bar is a custom one-inch stock-car style setup. The rack-and-pinion is a Mustang unit, and it's available in manual or power. Martz Chassis doesn't use any Mustang II suspension parts. Martz makes their own spindles using heat-treated 4140 chrome moly.

There is no anti-dive built into the subframe, but some feel anti-dive is overrated anyway. The range of caster and camber is unlimited, but typically the caster range is suggested to be set at +2 degrees to +6 degrees, and the camber range is zero degrees to + or – 4 degrees. Their dial indicators show zero bumpsteer in three inches of travel. The frame can be ordered with heim joints or with urethane bushing ends. They have been in business for 33 years, so replacement parts are readily available at Martz. The largest tire they have fit in a stock fenderwell is 8 inches wide. All the factory brackets and panels bolt to the Martz chassis. Gary Martz has personally run a car equipped with his race setup chassis and proper safety equipment up to 180 mph at the Pocono Speedway. His average was 142 mph. He would also run his frame on a road course and drive it 30,000 miles per year on the street. The frame is probably as strong as the stock subframe, but has not been tested.

Wayne Due's Chassis Shop

Wayne Due's Chassis shop has been popularized by Mark Stielow's '69 Camaro project called *The Mule*. Wayne Due builds subframes utilizing '84

Front Suspension and Steering

One of the most recognizable subframes is known to many as "the Wayne Due front clip." With the selling feature of running lightweight C4 Corvette front suspension and components (that obviously worked well for the Corvette), it's no wonder why it's so popular. A subframe with C5 parts would be just as well received. (Photo courtesy Wayne Due –special thanks to Steve D'Aurora)

through '87 Corvette suspension components. These subframes fit first- and second-generation Chevy Camaros and Pontiac Firebirds, and first- and second-generation X-bodies. His frames offer mounting for big-block Chevy, small-block Chevy, and Pontiac engines. His frame utilizes the stock transmission crossmember, but if the customer wanted a custom application crossmember, he could build one. Most production headers made for the body application will fit his frame, with slight modification in some cases. Stock GM Corvette brakes could be used, as well as Baer Racing, Wilwood, or any other company offering brake kits for '84 through '87 Corvettes. They are available with a custom solid one-inch sway bar built by Wayne.

No Mustang II components are used on Wayne's frame. There is 10 degrees of anti-dive built into the frame. The caster adjustment is 3 to 6 degrees, and the camber is zero degrees to plus or minus two degrees. Bump-steer (along with other areas) has been improved since Wayne took over for the late Art Rasmussen (the original designer of the Wayne Due subframe), but no data is currently available. No heim joints are used on the suspension. It uses durable and readily available GM Corvette tie-rod ends and ball joints, as well as all other service parts. The '84 through '87 Corvette aluminum control arms are no longer available brand new from the factory, so used ones need to be purchased and tested for cracks and defects.

Without modifying the fender, you can get a ten-inch wide wheel with a 275-wide tire to fit. The stock bumper brackets and radiator support bolt onto the frame, but the inner fenderwells need to be modified slightly to fit the Corvette control arms, since the Corvette arms mount slightly rearward of the Camaro control arms. Wayne Due says he would drive a Camaro with the proper safety equipment in an open-road race, on an open track, and 30,000 miles per year. His comment was, "I would fly it to the moon." He is sure it's stronger than the stock frame, but actual testing has not been done.

With the introduction of the C5 Corvette, there is another source for lightweight performance front suspension. Art Morrison Enterprises offers a welded front clip that uses a combination of C5 front suspension pieces with their steering rack, sway bar, and coil-overs. (Photo courtesy Art Morrison Enterprises)

Art Morrison Enterprises

Although this is not a bolt-in subframe, it is worth mentioning. Art Morrison Enterprises offers a front frame section that allows the use of C5 Chevy Corvette front suspension. The front clip uses C5 control arms, hubs, brakes, and spindles. It uses Art Morrison coil-overs, steering rack, and sway bar. The welded frame clip is available in different widths. The minimum hub-to-hub width available is 57.5 inches.

Installing a DSE Coil-Over Kit

1. The Detroit Speed & Engineering (DSE) coil-over conversion kit comes with custom upper control-arm mounts with integrated upper shock mounts, two gussets, two dress-up trim rings for the shocks, and two lower shock mounts. The necessary fixture is available from DSE with a refundable deposit.

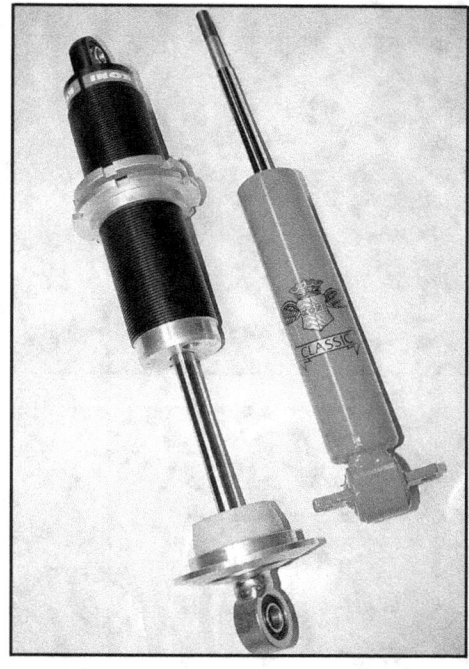

2. Here are two Koni shocks. The bottom one is a performance replacement for the stock shock absorber. The stock configuration uses a stud mount on the top and an eye mount on the bottom. The longer one on the top is the coil-over used for this project. It's custom valved to DSE's specifications. They could be built to your own specs if you chose. Both ends have spherical rod ends for a reduction in the bind found in stock and replacement shock absorbers.

Chapter 2

3. The stock upper control-arm mount is good for average driving. If there has been some trauma to the suspension such as a front-end accident or severe driving with stiff shocks, the mount can develop stress fractures. Once a crack starts, it will get worse as time goes on.

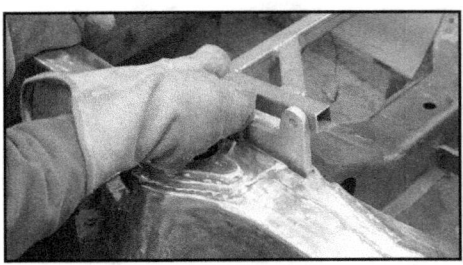

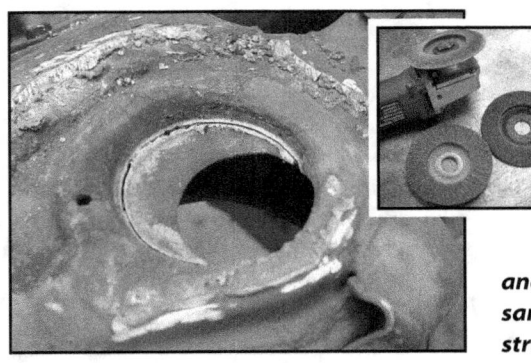

4. There is a hole in the frame for the conventional shock to pass through. Only cut out the crescent-moon-shaped flat plate inside the circular raised radius. Repeat on the opposite side. Using your favorite grinding disc, remove the leftover welds and factory slag. Just remove the necessary metal, so you don't damage the structural integrity of the frame.

5. Remove the engine "stands" (the metal bracket that mounts between the subframe and the motor mount) from the frame. Bolt the control-arm mount fixture to the engine-stand holes. The fixture will locate the upper control-arm mounts in the position for correct fit and suspension geometry.

8. Once you have cut the slots in the frame, bolt the fixture back onto the subframe. Test fit the bracket. Once they fit in the slots and are flush with the fixture, bolt them on. Use 7/16-inch bolts and tighten them up, otherwise the brackets will move around while you weld them.

9. Weld the brackets into place. We started by tacking the brackets in a few places all the way around and checking their position. Then we welded the brackets to the subframe completely around the perimeter of the brackets, as directed by DSE. An experienced welder should do this welding. This bracket needs to have a good quality weld with deep penetration.

6. With the fixture in place, set the new mount flat against it with the bolt holes inline with the fixtures holes. Use your favorite sharp marking pen or tool to mark the frame all the way around the DSE mount. This will be the area you will remove, so check your marks twice before going to the next step. Repeat this process on the opposite side.

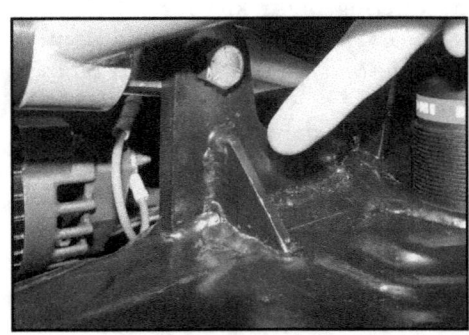

7. Unbolt the fixture so you have access to the area you will cut. Our plasma cutter did the job faster than a cut-off wheel, but was not as precise. Remember, the first rule to cutting is to measure twice and cut once. If you remove too much material, you will have to put it back on, which is not always pretty.

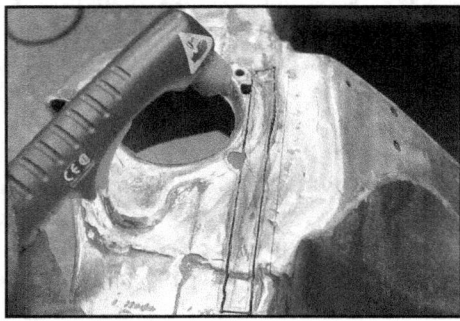

10. Before removing the fixture from the subframe, the triangular gussets need to be welded to the new control-arm brackets. Line them up with the front upper control-arm bolts. Use one gusset per side. This picture was taken after the installation was complete.

Front Suspension and Steering

11. The lower control-arm shock bracket has to be welded to the lower control arm. A four-inch hole saw should be used to remove the original shock and spring pocket. Flip the control arm over, so the arm is bottom-side up. Carefully center the hole saw in the spring pocket. The weight of the front of the car is supported by this mount, so if necessary, have a professional do the job.

12. Trim the trim ring and test fit it. It takes a little finagling to get it to fit down inside the subframe. You may need to file the hole in the subframe a little bit, but don't remove more than is necessary.

13. You can test fit the coil-over shock and the trim ring. They should not interfere when the control arm is fully extended. Mine was really close as you can see. When the suspension is loaded, the coil-over moves more towards the center, so don't freak out when you see how close it is. Remove the coil-over and weld the rings in place.

14. When you are done welding the perimeter of both of your trim rings, clean up all the welds with a high-speed grinding disk. The time spent here will show. If you don't spend the time, people will see it. Countless hours welding, grinding, and finishing were applied to this frame, but they were well worth it. Not everyone has the patience to achieve this show-quality finish. (Photo courtesy of DSE)

Steering

Car builders often overlook the steering system. The stock steering system is great for a family cruiser. If you are going to drive your Pro-Touring car on a road course or just want performance on the street, aftermarket steering systems are available. The steering system consists of a steering gearbox or rack-and-pinion. In the case of a power steering system, there is also a steering pump, fluid reservoir, and hoses.

Power assisted rack-and-pinion and recirculating ball systems have a high and low-pressure circuit. The power steering pump pressurizes the fluid up to 1350 psi and forces it through the feed line into the steering gearbox. The low-pressure circuit is the return line from the steering gear box to the fluid reservoir. From the reservoir, the fluid is sucked back into the pump.

Rear-steer and front-steer refers to the location of the steering linkage and system. The linkage on a rear-steer system is located behind the centerline of the spindles, and the front-steer linkage is located in front of the centerline of the spindles. GM has offered front- and rear-steer in their cars, but they have not offered rear-steer since 1975 when they redesigned the X-body.

Every steering system has a steering ratio. The ratio of the steering box or rack determines how much the wheels turn in conjunction with how much you turn the steering wheel. A wide ratio steering system will require more full revolutions of the steering wheel to turn from lock-to-lock. This could be as much as four and a half complete revolutions. A typical GM 12:1 recirculating ball close-ratio steering box will require three full revolutions of the steering wheel to turn from lock-to-lock. This might not seem like a big difference, but considering how much less the steering wheel needs to be turned when on a road course, a close ratio box makes driving much less work. Road-course driving can be physically draining, so the less energy spent on turning the steering wheel, the better.

A power steering gearbox can be setup with custom-tailored efforts. The effort is the resistance you feel in the steering wheel when you turn it. If the steering box is not built with efforts, the steering will feel as if you could steer the car with one finger when the car is sitting still. This might sound good, but if you would like a little feedback from your steering so you know how your car is reacting to track conditions, you will be out of luck.

This recirculating ball steering box has been rebuilt by DSE. Its ratio has been changed to 12.0:1. All the seals and worn parts were replaced, and the top plate has been safety wired to keep everything together.

Chapter 2

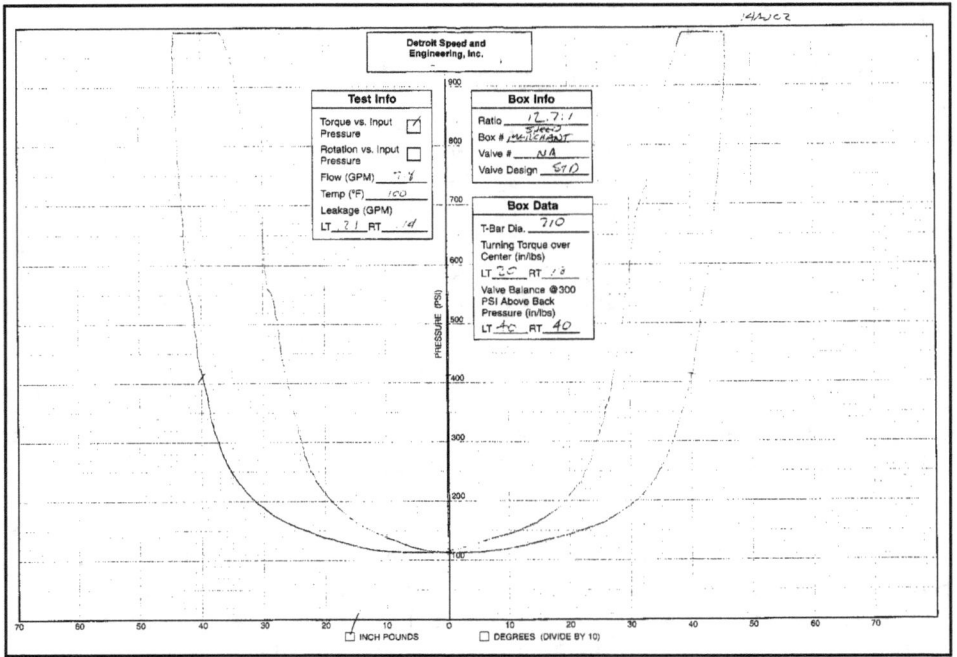

The DSE box has had its efforts modified for better driving feel. The box was tested on a dyno to make sure the efforts match from right to left. A dyno sheet comes with each box.

Recirculating Ball

Recirculating ball is the technical name for the type of steering box commonly found on production cars from the 1950s to the 1980s. It's still used on some trucks and rear-wheel-drive (RWD) cars built today.

Some builders like the simplicity of manual steering, especially drag racers, since they usually have narrow front tires. The narrow front tires are easier to turn with a manual steering box than wide tires when the car is moving less than 5 miles an hour. The narrow tire has less friction since the surface area touching the ground is smaller. Manual steering gearboxes are not commonly used on Pro-Touring cars, because the amount of effort to turn wider tires can be unbearable. Part of Pro-Touring is being able to drive your car anywhere, with the comfort of technological advances.

Most of the 1960s and 1970s GM cars were factory-equipped with recirculating-ball steering systems. Since the most prevalent GM cars turned Pro-Touring are from that era, I will cover the power-assisted recirculating-ball steering system.

Saginaw P-Series Power Steering Pump

Stock Saginaw P-series pumps are well-suited for street use. AGR Performance Power Steering builds performance P-series pumps. They are more than adequate for street and performance street use. AGR modifies these pumps with proprietary components to create significant increase in flow and pressure, over the OEM and remanufactured units you can buy over the counter at your typical auto parts store. These match up well with their performance steering boxes.

This is a Saginaw P-series power steering pump. The reservoir tank is bolted to the pump, and the filler neck is soldered to the tank. The solder can melt when the steering fluid gets too hot during racing conditions, causing the filler to separate from the body.

Saginaw P-Series Reservoir

If you are running a Saginaw P-series pump, you should be aware of the flaws of the reservoir connected to it. The only known design flaw shows up when you are running the pump through high RPM for extended periods of time, such as during road-course racing. If you are not running an inline cooler, the stock system can run at an operating temperature of over 250 degrees. The stock power steering neck has been known to break loose from the reservoir tank when the temperature gets too hot. The neck is only attached with solder. When the neck comes loose from the tank, the fluid quickly empties from the power steering system. It makes a big mess, and is dangerous for the fluid coming into contact with hot surfaces under the hood and soiling your brakes. The fluid on the track is slippery and dangerous. Later in this chapter, you will find information about installing a power steering cooler.

Heat is not the only enemy of the stock reservoir. Extended periods of high RPM on a road course will also cause fluid to splash up on the cap and blow out of the vent hole. The fluid blows all over the engine compartment and hot surfaces. You may think blocking the vent hole would prevent seepage. There is a minimal amount of pressure that builds up inside the reservoir, but it would push fluid through the stock cap seal if the vent hole was plugged. Road-course racers have found a fix for this problem. They put an extended filler neck on the reservoir.

Saginaw TC Power Steering Pump

If you plan to race your car on a road course, you might want to take a serious look at upgrading to a Saginaw TC pump (transverse bearing compact pump). These pumps are well suited for racing and high-performance street applications.

Using a TC pump from a production engine can be a good way to save money, but be careful. Not all TC pumps are the

Front Suspension and Steering

The pump on the lower right is a cast-iron Saginaw TC power steering pump built by AGR. The pump held in the hand is an aluminum KRC Racing pump.

same. Most have low drag bearings on both ends of the shaft. One TC pump in particular has a front bushing instead of a bearing. The bushing creates more friction, causing power-robbing drag, and wears out faster than a bearing. Luckily, it can be easily identified by its 3/4-inch shaft. Using production TC pumps can be challenging since not all of them have the necessary fittings needed to adapt them to your system. TC pumps come in a couple of different versions, with different size shafts and mounting heights. They come with plastic reservoirs mounted directly to the pump or with remote-mounted plastic reservoirs. The factory production TC pumps are built specifically for the pressures needed for the steering boxes or rack-and-pinion units they were mated with from the factory.

If you want less headaches and better performance from your steering system, spend the extra money and get an aftermarket unit. Many aftermarket companies offer new or rebuilt performance TC pumps. They are available in cast iron and aluminum for weight savings. Aftermarket TC pumps usually come with high-temperature seals and O-rings and low-drag bearings (check with the company for specifics). A few companies build their TC pumps with different pressures and flow rates that match their performance steering boxes. Get matching components from one manufacturer for the best results from your steering.

Aftermarket TC pumps are available with all the proper fittings, pulleys, and hardware you will need to hook them up to your steering system. To save you headaches, there are aluminum mounting brackets available for small and big-block Chevy engines. There are even universal brackets if you can't find the bracket that suits your needs. Not all brackets give you room for the locally mounted reservoir in the position you need, so a little research could pay off, or you could run a remote reservoir.

KRC Power Steering Pumps

KRC Power Steering is a racing power steering products manufacturer. They took a good look at the TC pump for racing applications in 1996. They could not improve upon the TC design to make it suitable for the grueling abuse of dirt and asphalt racecars, so they designed their own aluminum and cast-iron power steering pumps to meet their stringent requirements.

The lightweight aluminum pump weighs just 3.2 lbs with pulley. It operates up to 70 degrees cooler than other pumps and can save up to three horsepower. It features adjustable flow rates with optional flow valves. The cast-iron KRC pump meets the same durability requirements and has the same flow features — but it's less expensive. The KRC pumps have the same mounting pattern as the Saginaw TC pump, so they use the same mounting bracket. The KRC pumps are fitted with the necessary AN fittings.

Rack-and-Pinion Steering

There are a few companies offering rack-and-pinion upgrade kits for cars originally equipped with recirculating-ball systems.

Brewers Restoration and Performance offers front-steer rack conversion kits for LS1 converted first-generation F-bodies and second-generation X-bodies. The kit is designed so you can remove the entire stock steering assembly and install the steering rack closer to the front of the car, in front of the spindle centerline. The kit fits when used in conjunction with the LS1 conversion they offer because the engine sits up high enough to clear the rack. The rack is moved to the sway bar location, so they offer a sway bar and relocation kit too.

Racing Rack-and-Pinion

Woodward Machine Corporation makes rack-and-pinion units for dirt, pavement, and road-racing applications. You would find a Woodward rack on an extreme Pro-Touring car. Quite a bit of design and fabrication is involved in correctly mounting one of these units on a front suspension system. There are over 20 different styles of Woodward racks. For help picking the correct rack for your application and installation information, Woodward's contact information is in the source guide. To see a good example of a Woodward rack installed, look at the Campbell Auto Restoration subframe in the subframe section.

A few companies offer racing power steering rack units. They are compact units in widths ranging from 16 to 20 inches, so perfect steering geometry can be achieved. (Photo courtesy Chris Kerr)

Steeroids Rack-and-Pinion Conversion

Pro-Touring guys are always looking for a way to improve upon the stock suspensions. The steering system is no exception. A company named Speed Direct sells a rack-and-pinion conversion kit labeled "Steeroids." The rack is a 12:1 steering ratio, which is the same as the quick-ratio recirculating-ball steering box used in special-optioned muscle cars and IROCs. The Steeroids unit takes up less room so you can run road-racing oil pans that stock steering linkage might not fit. The stock power steering box and components (not including power steering pump) tip the scales at 47 lbs. The Steeroids system weighs in at 32 lbs. That figures out to a 15-lb weight savings.

Chapter 2

Before you spend time getting your car safely up on jack stands and get ready to install your Speed Direct Steeroids kit, lay the parts out and inspect them. Make sure they are all there and in good shape. Manufacturers typically include a parts list in the instructions. This is a good step to perform every time you do a job like this. It's real frustrating to get started on a project, only to find out a part is missing or damaged. All the parts were included and they were in good shape. The next step is to read through the instructions before you start, so you have an idea of the scope of the job. The rack kit installed real easy:

3. The flexible rubber donut that couples the steering box flange and the steering column flange is called a rag joint. Remove the nuts from the rag joint. Sometimes the bolts are tough to get out. Remove them if you can, it will help when removing the steering box.

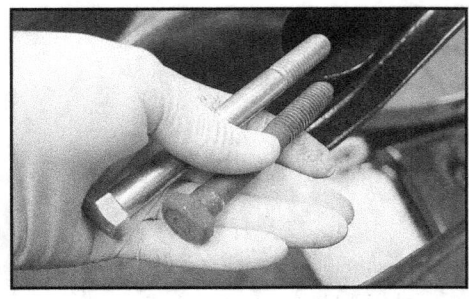

6. The two factory rearward lower control-arm bolts have to be replaced by two longer 1/2x13x5-inch bolts supplied in the kit. I already had my lower control arms off the subframe, so mine were easier to install.

1. All the parts to the Speed Direct Steeroids kit are laid out on the floor. It's good to inspect your parts and make sure they're all there. Before you start, read through your instruction sheet so you don't have any surprises about a special tool or a part you need to supply.

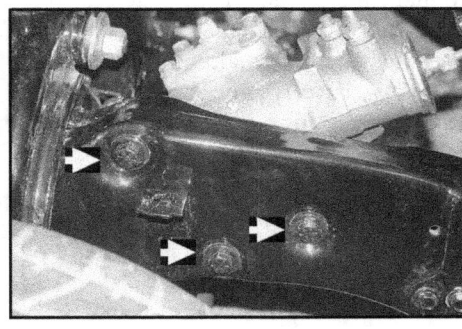

4. Before you remove the three bolts (see arrows) holding the steering box to the frame rail, make sure you have a way to hold the box from falling. It weighs 33 lbs and can be cumbersome and dangerous if it falls on any part of your body. The front brake line is directly beneath the box, and with a little finagling, you can drop the box while the engine is in the car.

7. The rack-and-pinion mounting bracket will not fit if you push the lower control-arm bolts all the way through before installing it. You can see one bolt fits while the other one doesn't. The bracket has to be held in place while you push the bolts through the control arms.

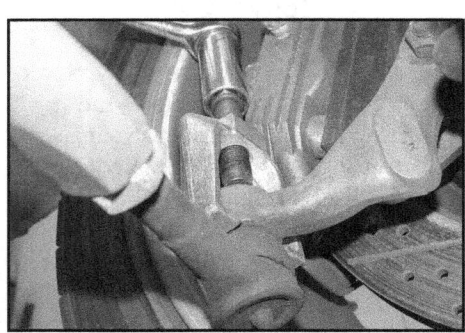

2. Remove the cotter pins from the outer tie-rod ends, idler arm, and pitman arm. Once you have removed the castle nuts, break the joints apart. A ball-joint separator is the best tool for the job. Using a pickle fork to break ball joints and tie rods apart can damage the boots, joints, and suspension parts.

5. Lay the old steering linkage on the ground next to the Steeroids rack with the rod ends on. Match the distance between the outer tie-rod ends from the stock linkage and the rod ends on the rack setup. This will get your front-end alignment close enough to drive the car a couple miles to get it realigned.

8. Install the washers and 1/2x13-inch nuts and torque the lower control arm bolts holding the bracket to 80 ft-lbs. Then bolt the rack to the bracket using the 7/16x14x2.5-inch bolts and washers. Torque those to 59 ft-lbs.

Front Suspension and Steering

9. If you are going to use a power-assisted setup, install the two O-ring adapter fittings supplied in the kit. Speed Direct says: If you are going to use the rack and pinion as a manual steering setup, leave the two plastic plugs in place. They also say that the rack is lubricated from the factory, and does not require additional lubrication. The white arrow shows the high-pressure port. The black arrow is explained later.

10. The headers interfered with the steering shaft. With a couple of bolts holding the header on, I was able to install the shaft on the rack first. At the point of interference, I marked the header with a pencil. Then I removed the header to make clearance.

11. With the header off the car, a ball-peen hammer was used to dimple the primary tube where the pencil mark was. The test fit process had to be done a couple of times before there was enough clearance. If you have solid motor mounts, the clearance can be closer than if you have flexible motor mounts. Movement of the engine can cause damage to the steering joints and shaft, if they come into contact with each other.

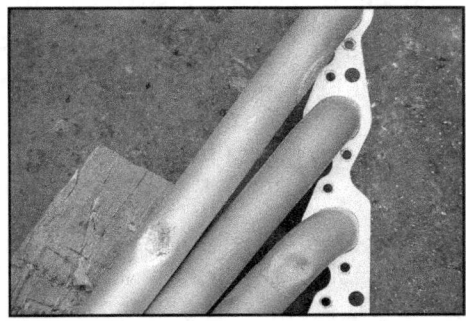

12. Install the shaft once you have enough clearance. Start by installing it on the rack first. The steering joint will install on the rack two ways, but only one way is the right way. There are two setscrews to lock the steering joint to the rack. In the earlier picture, you can see the shaft stub has a flat surface (actually on both sides) and a notch (by the black arrow). Position the lower joint so one of the setscrews is lined up with the notch. Tighten the setscrew, and then install the top bolts and screw (supplied) to the end of the steering-column flange.

13. The kit comes with power steering hoses (two bottom hoses) for use with a factory power steering pump. Since the car is equipped with a Saginaw TC pump, the supplied lines would not fit. The new lines were made from XRP products. The high-pressure side was plumbed with the correct high-pressure hoses and fittings (top), and the low-pressure side was plumbed with standard steel braided hose and aluminum fittings (not shown).

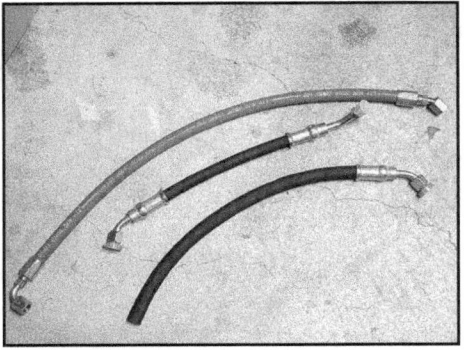

14. In the process of installing the Steeroids kit, I also installed an inline extruded aluminum power steering cooler from Detroit Speed and Engineering. I mounted it low enough on the front of the subframe that it should get plenty of airflow, but not hang down in harm's way. Note that the high-pressure hose connected to the pump on upper left is a different material than the low-pressure hose.

15. After installing all the hardware properly, you can see the rack is an extremely tight fit with this big-block Chevy Milodon road-race oil pan. The rack had to be removed for the engine installation, and fed in through the driver's side. The original stock steering would not fit with this pan without modification or setting the engine back.

Remote Power Steering Reservoir

When running a Saginaw TC pump, it is possible to use a stock plastic late-model-style baffled local or remote reservoir. Remote reservoirs give more options for mounting the TC pumps, since they don't require the pump to be mounted in a specific position. There are good and bad remote reservoirs on the market, so be aware of the differences.

Chapter 2

Power steering reservoir tanks are not created equal. The cheap circle-track tank on the right is not fit for street use. The inlet (up high) is not optimally located. The KSE tank on the left has a superior design.

The inlet on the cheap tank is too high, causing the power steering fluid to aerate. Air in the steering fluid causes loud groaning and erratic operation of the steering box.

This is an AGR power steering reservoir. This type mounts directly to the body of the pump. It is manufactured of glass filled nylon for strength and resistance to high temperatures.

The return line and the feed need to be placed in proper locations. If the return line is too close to top of the reservoir, the fluid will act as a vacuum and pull air in. This is called aerating. The aerated fluid can cause damage to the steering components. The symptoms will be groaning noises and jerky steering when turning the wheel at low speeds. The return line should be located at the bottom or at least one and a half inches below the surface of the fluid.

Power Steering Hose

There are high- and low-pressure circuits on the power steering system. It is important to use the right power steering hoses on your system. If you are running stock power steering accessories and brackets, you can use stock replacement hoses. The stock high- and low-pressure hoses will be made to the right lengths and the correct pressure-rated hose.

If you are using aftermarket hose on your stock steering system or a custom installation, you will probably be required to use custom hoses. Whether you are building your hoses, or someone else is doing it for you, make sure they are using the proper hose and fittings for the job. The pressure spikes on the high-pressure side are too much for standard stainless-steel hose and standard anodized aluminum fittings. Using them for custom power steering hoses is a common mistake, especially on the high-pressure side.

The proper power steering fittings are high-pressure steel, and the hose should be specifically made for a maximum operating pressure 1750 psi. A performance power steering system can operate upwards of 1350 psi, but there are spikes in pressure during operation. There are many high-performance hose and fitting companies. One of them is a company named XRP Inc. They offer specific power steering hose made of elastomer tube, polyester inner braid, single wire braid reinforcement, and a polyester braid cover. They offer a full line of steel fittings and hose ends to make just about any power steering hose for your Pro-Touring machine.

Power Steering Coolers

Power steering systems can generate plenty of heat when driving on the street. While on the track, the temperatures can soar to over 250 degrees. The heat sources are abundant under the hood. In most cases, the power steering box is close to the headers, which can reach over 1000 degrees.

A common mistake in building custom power steering hoses is using standard steel braided rubber hose and aluminum fittings on the high-pressure side of the system. Pressures there can reach 1350 lbs. This hose is only good for a fraction of that pressure.

Front Suspension and Steering

 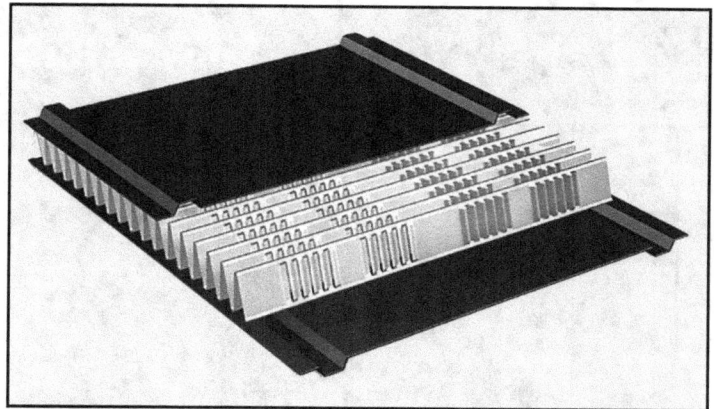

Top race cars run Setrab coolers. If they can endure competition racing conditions, they can work well on a Pro-Touring car. Setrab offers stacked-plate coolers like this one in different sizes and a few other configurations. The close-up shows the cooling fins. (Photos courtesy Setrab)

There are ways to cool down the fluid. People have noted a 30-degree drop in steering system fluid with the addition of a remote reservoir. The addition of an inline power steering cooler is another way to cool the system. There are right and wrong ways to install an inline cooler. Don't install a cooler in the high-pressure side; it puts too much stress on the cooler. Plus, if the cooler were to get nicked by a rock, there would be 1300 pounds of pressure pushing fluid out of the system really fast. Just about any lubricating fluid in contact with hot exhaust is a bad idea.

Put the cooler on the low-pressure return side of the system, between the power steering box or rack and the reservoir. Coolers can be stacked-plate, extruded-cylinder, or round-tube designs. Each design has proven effective in street and track conditions. Be sure the cooler is designed for at least 60 psi and high-heat conditions. A cooler with a 3/8-inch or –6 AN inlet and outlet is best suited for power steering applications. If it is a tube-style cooler, make sure the fittings are not soldered to the tube. The solder will melt and you will have a mess on your hands.

Size matters too. A small 8x4x2-inch stacked plate or 6-inch round-tube cooler will be more than adequate for most Pro-Touring applications destined for the a road course. Anything larger, and the cooling efficiency of the system will be hampered. Some production cars and trucks have been equipped with little in-line coolers. Installing one of these little coolers can reduce the fluid temperature by 30 degrees. The cooler fluid temperature will increase the life of the fluid and the life the pump and steering assembly.

As with any cooler, if it's not placed where moving air can come into contact with the fins, it will be less effective. Place the cooler in a safe place where a rock off the tire, or debris from an unplanned off-track excursion won't cause damage to any part of the system. The factory usually places their power steering coolers on the frame rail in the engine compartment. Unlike with radiators, some moving air for the power steering cooler is better than nothing. Placing the cooler in front of the radiator where cool air is flowing is not always convenient.

Tie-Rod Adjustment Sleeves

Tie-rod adjustment sleeves are a weak link, but they are often overlooked as an upgrade. The stock adjusters are sheetmetal formed into tubes. They flex under hard driving conditions, which causes variances in suspension geometry. The stock adjusters can also bend, causing the front suspension to be out of alignment. The stock adjustment clamps also make aligning a tough job at the track.

A couple of aftermarket companies offer beefy tie-rod adjusters. They are stronger than stock sleeves because they completely wrap around the tie rods and have full thread engagement. Their strength keeps more accurate alignment and suspension geometry under hard driving conditions. Hard driving conditions are not just on the track. The street is full of potholes, train tracks, and debris that can knock the suspension out of alignment. All performance-driven cars should upgrade to these adjusters. Adjusting the aftermarket sleeves is much easier for last-minute track adjustments and alignments at your local shop, because the adjustment sleeves and nuts can be turned with common wrenches.

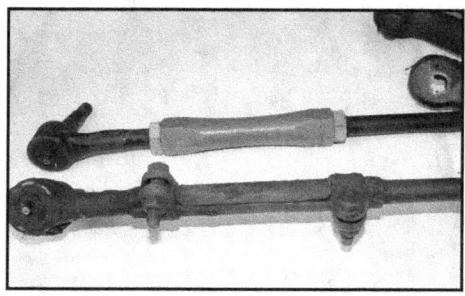

This tie-rod adjuster is offered by Detroit Speed & Engineering. It is much stronger than the stock unit. It is made of 4140 one-inch hex stock. The hex allows for easy adjustment over stock adjustment sleeves. The stock sleeve adjusters are flexible sheetmetal. When they flex or bend, your suspension geometry and alignment changes. Why spend good money on aligning your car and not fully utilize the settings?

Chapter 2

Tony LaRuffa's '81 Malibu

It's not very often you see a Malibu on a road course. No, he's not on the return road from running the quarter mile — at least not in this photo. The car is built to go around corners and periodically sees open-track days. (Photo courtesy of David Nagler)

Tony Laruffa's '81 Malibu has been on the Hot Rod Power Tour a couple of times. The car is equipped with a T-56 6-speed transmission, which is the proper equipment for long journeys and short blasts. (Photo courtesy of David Nagler)

A growing trend is to convert your drag car over to Pro-Touring. Tony LaRuffa found a '81 Chevy Malibu and started turning it into a drag car. He swapped a 327 in for the original V-6, and before long, he was pulling high 12s in the quarter. After a while, Tony wanted more of a driver he could use to tear up the corners and enjoy the open road.

Tony picked PPG Stage Two Black and Strato Blue for his color scheme, which he carried out through the entire car. The body is black, with early Trans Am-esque bold racing stripes running down the center of the car. The seats and interior panels were upholstered in black and blue. Tony installed a full array of 11 AutoMeter gauges to keep tabs on all functions. Tony, Randy Jewell, and Lou Ansuini installed a 10-point cage to add strength and safety. Blue cage padding and safety harnesses were also added.

Tony swapped out the 327 for an internally balanced 462-ci big-block Chevy. Since he was going to run the car around corners, he knew protecting the internals was important, so he purchased a Canton 10-quart road-race oil pan. Those internals are: a steel LS6 crank, Manley rods, and Ross forged 9:1 pistons; all of which get put to the test by a ATI D2 centrifugal supercharger. It blows through a Force fuel-injection intake and Pat Budd Performance reworked Dart Pro-1 325 aluminum heads. The spent gasses exit through Hooker Super Comp headers with 2-inch primaries and 3.5-inch collectors. The air/fuel is distributed by Force EFI, FP Performance management system, and 83-lb/hr injectors. A Comp Cams cam with 0.632/0.666-inches of lift and 260/272-degrees duration opens and closes the valves that move the gasses in and out of the engine. The black and blue theme was carried out in the engine compartment on all the plumbing that carries the pressurized air from the D2 to the intercooler (mounted behind the front bumper) and then to the 1000-cfm throttle body. Power is harnessed by a Centerforce Dual Friction Clutch and a T-56 6-speed transmission, and then transferred to the Currie built 9-inch rear end.

The suspension is equipped with Hotchkis springs front and rear, Hotchkis sway bars front and rear, Hotchkis front upper control arms, Metco rear control arms, and Herb Adams shocks. The brakes are cross-drilled Baer Racing PBR kits with 13-inchers up front and 12-inchers in the rear. The wheels are Vintage Wheel Works 16x8-inch front and rear, wrapped with Yokohama A032R 245/45-16 and 255/50-16 tires.

The body was pretty much left stock, with the exception of monochromatic accents, vent holes in the front bumper for the intercooler, and a VFN fiberglass cowl hood modified to fit the monstrous supercharger and its closed intake air box.

Tony still enjoys blasting down the quarter mile, but the car spends most of its time on the open road. He also enjoys autocrossing, open track events, and driving around the country on *Hot Rod* Power Tour with his fellow Over-Drive Gang members.

The big block is bored to 462 cubic inches, and it has an internally balanced LS6 crankshaft and other hard parts. An ATI D2 centrifugal supercharger and Force fuel injection feed the Dart aluminum heads for a potent package.
(Photo courtesy of David Nagler)

Front Suspension and Steering

Myron Cottrell's '53 Chevrolet Sedan Delivery

Myron Cottrell's '53 sedan delivery isn't your typical Pro-Touring ride. It has C4 Corvette suspension mounted in the front and rear of its custom-built chassis. (Photo courtesy Myron Cottrell)

Myron Cottrell runs Tuned Port Injection Specialties Inc (TPIS) in Minnesota. In good weather, he drives his '53 Chevrolet sedan delivery. He has done some upgrades to make it perform better than the GM engineers intended back in 1953. Myron wanted the delivery to handle the corners and ride better than a tugboat. He started by completely tearing it apart. Myron enlisted Opies Hot Rods Inc. to perform most of the chassis and body fabrication. They modified the frame to accept the C4 suspension. The front suspension is out of an '88 Corvette. It was narrowed two inches to fit within the front fenders. The rear suspension is a Dana 44 unit offered in '84 through '87 Corvettes. For stopping power, the brakes were upgraded to 13-inch discs in the front and 12-inch discs in the rear. The stopping power comes from TPIS calipers in the front and stock Corvette units in the rear. The wheels are 17x9.5-inch Grand Sports in the front and 17x11-inch ZR-1s in the rear.

Since Myron runs TPIS, the delivery features many of their products. The engine started life as a run-of-the-mill 350-ci LT4. It was bored and stroked to a whopping 409 cubic inches by TPIS. The TPIS parts added are: TPIS ported heads, ZZ-X camshaft, LT1/4 mini-ram, 58-mm billet throttle body, billet mass air sensor, oil pan, and headers. The engine produces 548 horsepower and 530 ft-lbs of torque. The power is transferred to the rear axle through a Borg-Warner T-56 transmission.

Opies Hot Rods Inc. modified the wheel openings to look much like a '55 Chevy Nomad. Other than that, the rest of the body is basically stock, except the hood was

The completed '53 looks great with its low stance. The 17-inch ZR1-style wheels are the only hint that this is not a typical street rod. Myron says the delivery drives like it's on rails. (Photo courtesy Myron Cottrell)

nosed and the seam was filled for a clean look. The finish work and Ermine White paint was applied by Chuck and Lance Moy.

The finished car tips the scales at a mere 2,800 pounds. It's well balanced, with just 51 percent of its weight on the front wheels. Even with 548 horsepower, Myron's sedan delivery is efficient enough to click-off more than 20 miles per gallon. This is a different and well-rounded Pro-Touring street machine.

Myron Cottrell works at Tuned Port Injection Specialties (TPIS), so when he started building his '53 sedan delivery, it only made sense to use as many of their injection parts as possible. The engine pounds out 548 horsepower and 530 ft-lbs of torque. (Photo courtesy Myron Cottrell)

How to Build GM Pro-Touring Street Machines

CHAPTER 3

REAR SUSPENSION

As with the front suspensions, the rear suspension is very important to the performance of a Pro-Touring car. This chapter will go over different factory and custom rear suspension systems for GM Pro-Touring cars. Pro-Touring cars are supposed to be driven, and driven hard. This chapter will also cover how to get the best all around performance out of your rear suspension.

Pinion Angle

The pinion angle is simply the angle between the rear end's pinion shaft and a true horizontal line. The transmission angle is the angle between the transmission's tail shaft and a true horizontal line. Together, these angles form the driveline's phase angle. Pinion angles can make the difference between a smooth ride, or a noisy and shaking ride down the freeway. Correct pinion angles are also very important to the life of your U-joints. Over time, the angles can change and become incorrect due to loose factory tolerances, body and frame alignment, and changes in spring rates due to wear. You should check and correct pinion angles any time you change the ride height or modify the rear suspension. Even changing leaf springs can change the pinion angle.

Hot rod shops and seasoned backyard mechanics commonly overlook pinion angles. When I was doing research on this subject, I found out why it seems like there is very little information about it, and the little bit of information available seems to be contradictory. After much research, I decided to enlist the help of Kyle Tucker (an ex-GM suspension engineer).

It turns out that pinion angles are not black magic, though they differ for each application. Family trucksters, production sports cars, and Pro-Touring cars are not built for the same types of driving. I am going to cover Pro-Touring pinion angle settings, since this book is about cars that could be driven daily and hit the road course periodically.

Here are two types of angle gauges. The analog gauge on the left can be purchased from most hardware stores. The digital SmartTool is more expensive. Both show that the rack is very close to zero degrees, which means the suspension is "loaded" correctly.

Rear Suspension

This is another way to lift the car up for measuring the pinion angle. Make sure to do this on a flat, safe surface. Place jack stands safely under the rear axle to compress it as if it were on the ground.

The transmission angle can be measured off the yoke or off the tail-shaft seal. Here, a straight bar was pressed up against the seal with the magnetic-base angle gauge attached to read the transmission tail-shaft angle.

Maybe you're building a full-tilt tube chassis to slide under a Camaro shell. The best chassis designers determine the ride height first, by positioning the rear axle and tires under the body. Once they do that, they set the transmission height and angle, and then build the rest of the car around that. If your car is finished or you are in the middle of a build-up, don't worry. These angles can be adjusted later, but it would be better if the car were designed around the correct angles to begin with.

Checking Pinion Angle

Checking pinion angle correctly is important. Start by getting an angle gauge. A few types are available. The most common is an analog magnetic-base protractor gauge (pictured in photos checking angles). These are about the cost of a meal at your local restaurant. Other types, such as digital angle gauges, are much more expensive. They basically do the same job, but they're much more precise.

Next, find a place to check your angles. Using a 4-post rack or a pit is the most accurate way. The car should be on a level surface and be at ride height. To get the ride height correct, you should fill the fuel tank. Fuel can add up to a lot of weight and change the ride height of the car. If the car is not level on the rack and resting on all four tires, your readings will not be accurate.

If you do not have access to a 4-post rack or pit, then you can use jack stands and/or ramps to simulate fully loaded ride height. Do this on a hard, flat surface and make sure the car is level. You should place jack stands safely under the rear axle tubes. Do not use a floor-jack to support the front of the car. This is very unsafe. The front of the car needs to be lifted exactly as much as the rear of the car. If you are using jack stands under the front of the car, placement is very important. If you place the stands under the frame in front of the centerline of the spindle, you will be placing more of a weight of the vehicle on the rear suspension. If you place the jack stands under the frame behind the spindle centerline, you will be moving some of the load off the rear suspension. This will cause incorrect measurements.

The most precise way to set your car up for measuring pinion angle, without a 4-post rack, is to use two sturdy car ramps and sturdy two jack stands. Start by driving the car up on the ramps, so the front tires are supported by the ramps. Safely place jack stands under the left and right rear axle housing tubes. At this point, the front and rear of the car has to be raised evenly. If the ramps raise the front tires up 9.75 inches off the ground, the rear jack stands should support the rear axle so the rear tires are 9.75 inches off the ground. This will ensure you have lifted the front and the back of the car evenly, for accurately measuring pinion angles. Don't forget: safety first.

The angle on the transmission is typically measured off the back of the transmission, on the driveshaft yoke seal surface. It can also be measured off the engine block, since the oil pan gasket-sealing surface (on GM engines) is parallel to the crankshaft (just take into account that this surface is 90 degrees from the transmission angle). The pinion angle on the rear end is taken from the face of the pinion yoke. Finding the flat surface on the transmission and the pinion yoke is easy, but there may not be space to place your gauge. If you have a metal straight edge, you can rest it against the flat surface, then attach your magnetic gauge to the straight edge.

For a car set up for handling around corners, the optimum pinion angle is different than if you were setting your car up for serious drag racing. Incorrect pinion angles can cause chassis vibration and premature U-joint wear and failure. Without the correct angles, the needle bearings in the U-joint caps do not rotate (as shown in the U-joint section). Those needle bearings need to rotate in order for the U-joint to operate reliably and smoothly.

Chapter 3

Optimum Pinion Angle

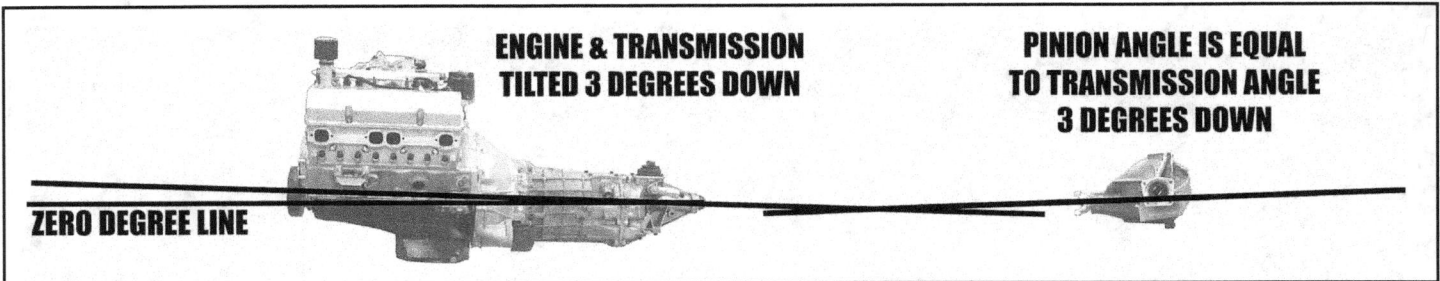

This picture shows phasing angles that should be used for most leaf-spring Pro-Touring cars. Notice the pinion and transmission angles are both down.

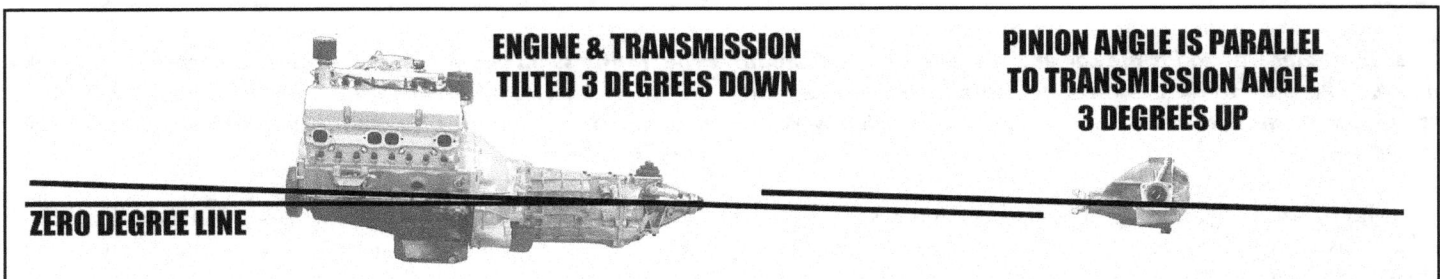

This picture shows how phasing angles are setup on most production passenger cars. Notice the differential pinion angle is as many degrees up as the transmission angle is down. The angles are parallel. Without load on the suspension, the angles total 6 degrees. These angles should add up to a maximum of 7 degrees.

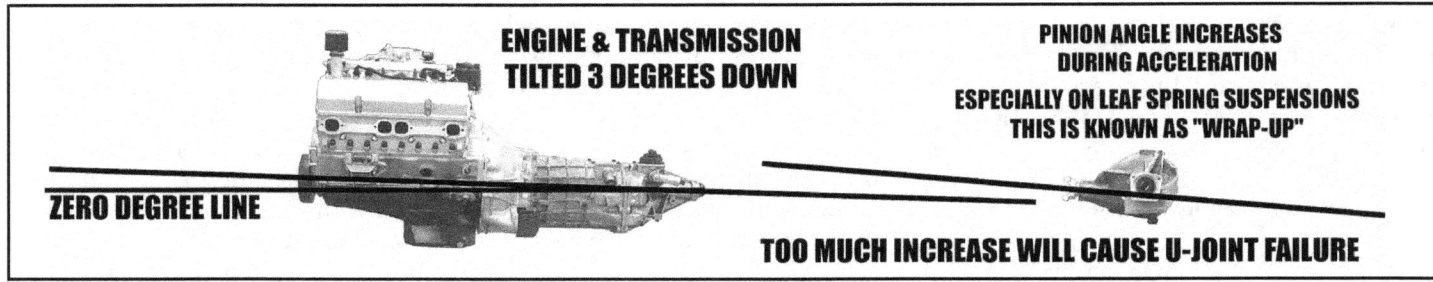

This picture illustrates the problems with running parallel phasing angles. The differential is shown with a torsional load from acceleration. The pinion tries to push upwards, causing the springs to "wrap up." At this point, the maximum tolerable angle of 7 degrees has been exceeded. This is bad for U-joints.

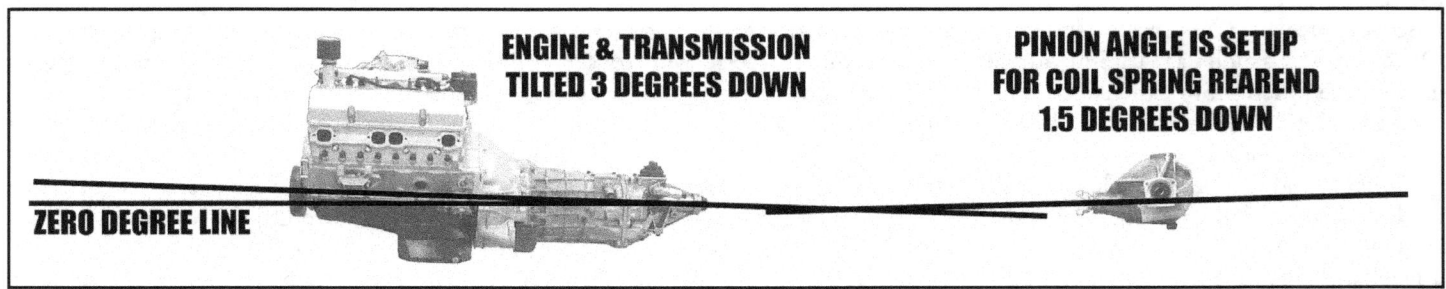

In this picture, you can see the pinion angle is set at fewer degrees down than the leaf-spring setup. This is how short-track coil-spring suspensions should be set up. Unlike leaf-spring suspensions, the trailing arms used in a coil-spring suspension typically minimize upward movement of the pinion.

Rear Suspension

Now that you know how to measure pinion angle, it's time to find the optimum pinion angle. There are many different schools of thought in this area of suspension tuning. I am going to go over pinion and transmission angles. Both angles are equally important when it comes to optimum suspension tuning. When referring to both angles combined and their relation to each other, they are referred to as "phasing angles."

Pinion angle depends on your application. Production passenger cars and basic street cars operate fine with parallel pinion and transmission shaft angles. Many shops still use this old-school design for building cars, and it's fine for street use. However, if you are going to build a car that will be pushed to its limits on a road course, then forget that school of thought. During acceleration, torque causes the pinion to tilt upwards. If you set your pinion angle a few degrees upward, the pinion will want to travel even further upward during acceleration. This is explained in more detail in the leaf spring section. The most common transmission shaft angle is 2 to 3 degrees down. Leaf spring suspensions allow the pinion angle to rotate upward when the springs wrap up under acceleration. Angling the pinion downward compensates for this upward travel. Serious short course race cars run as much as 4.5 degrees down for a pinion angle. Suspension engineers suggest running a downward pinion angle of 2.5 to 3 degrees for Pro-Touring (high-performance street and road course) applications.

The combined pinion and transmission angle should not exceed more than 7 degrees. A combined pinion angle of 3 degrees and transmission angle at 2.5 degrees add up to 5.5 degrees, which does not exceed the maximum. If you run parallel phasing angles like some old-school street rodders have been using, you can easily run into problems. For example, think of the transmission angle set at 3 degrees down and the pinion angle set up 3 degrees to run parallel with the transmission. When the leaf spring wraps up, the pinion angle can rotate upwards 2 or more degrees. If you add the transmission angle at 3 degrees to the pinion angle of 3 degrees, combined, it would add up to 6 degrees combined. During wrap up, the 6 degrees can become 8 or more degrees, which exceeds the maximum allowable range totaling 7 degrees.

Pro-Touring cars equipped with coil spring rear suspensions can run less downward pinion angle. The trailing arms on a coil spring suspension typically limit the amount of pinion lift (where the front of the differential tilts upward), so pinion angle can be set at 1.5 degrees down.

Pinion Angle Adjustment For Leaf Spring Suspensions

On leaf spring suspensions, there are a couple of ways to adjust the pinion angle. The more common way is to install shim-style wedges, which are available in different degrees from several manufacturers. The other method is to install a pair of adjustable leaf spring pads. These are great for project cars that will not be sitting at fully loaded ride height for quite some time. They can be installed early in the process of a project and adjusted and welded later when you are close to finishing the car. They are a nice alternative to welding a stationary spring perch to the differential housing early on in a project and having to use shims to adjust the pinion angle later.

There is an alternative to welding the adjustable perch too. Once they're installed and the pinion angle is adjusted, carefully drill a hole through each perch and axle tube. Then thread the hole in the axle tube to accept a bolt. Disassemble the rear end to clean all metal debris from inside the axle housing, and then reassemble the rear end. This is not the easy or preferred method, but it is an alternative for people without welders.

Pinion Angle Adjustment For Coil Spring Suspensions

Adjusting pinion angle on coil spring suspension systems is completely different than on leaf spring suspension. There are three ways to adjust coil spring suspension pinion angle. The third is the easiest and most common.

Cut the spring perches off the rear differential housing and weld them back on at a different angle.

Modify the length of the stock trailing arms.

Purchase fully adjustable aftermarket trailing arms. These are readily available and are the most convenient way to get full adjustability from your coil spring rear suspension at any ride height.

Many different aftermarket companies offer adjustable upper control arms. These are easy to install, stronger than stock arms, and give you adjustability. More information on these arms is given later in this chapter.

Universal Joints

There are three types of universal joints available:

1. Standard-Duty U-Joint — This U-joint is great for everyday driving. It is completely serviceable, with a zerk fitting located on the body between two of the legs. However, the hole for the zerk fitting can be a weak area when a lot of torque is applied.

2. Off-Road U-Joint — This U-joint is for off-road/road-race applications. It is completely serviceable, but the zerk fitting is located at the tip of one of the U-joint caps. The body is much stronger since the fitting hole is not located near the center. This U-joint is also made of higher-strength steel than the standard-duty U-joint.

3. Race-Only U-Joint — This U-joint is for racing uses only. It is not serviceable and has no zerk fittings. The only way to service this U-joint is to completely remove it, lube it by hand, and then reinstall it. It's stronger because the U-joint body is solid steel, with no internal passages for grease.

Driveshaft angles are very important to the life of the U-joint. Inside of the U-joint caps are needle bearings, which have to rotate inside of the cap when the U-joint is spinning. The needle bearings

Chapter 3

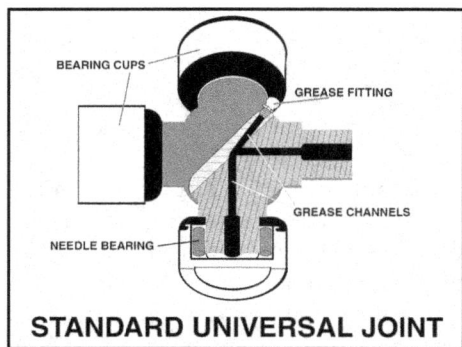

This is the standard U-joint. It is strong enough for everyday driving. If you are going to apply excessive torque and/or sticky tires, stepping up to an off-road-style U-joint is a good idea.

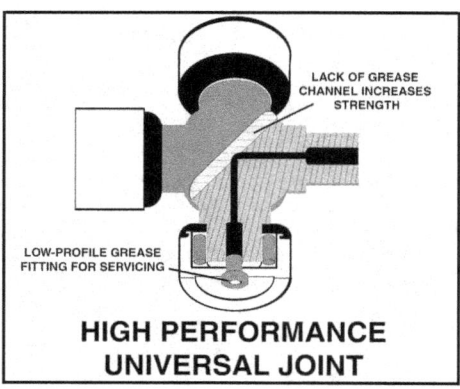

This is an off-road U-joint. They have the grease canal and are made of stronger material than standard U-joints. It is a good compromise between standard and racing U-joints, because it is stronger than a standard unit, but still serviceable.

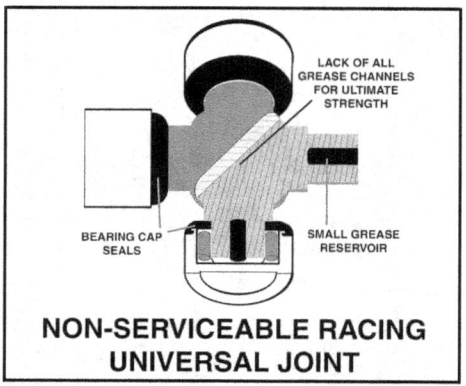

This is the racing U-joint. It has no provisions for servicing. It does not have grease canals, which increase its strength. The only lubrication comes from small grease reservoirs in the end of the U-joint legs.

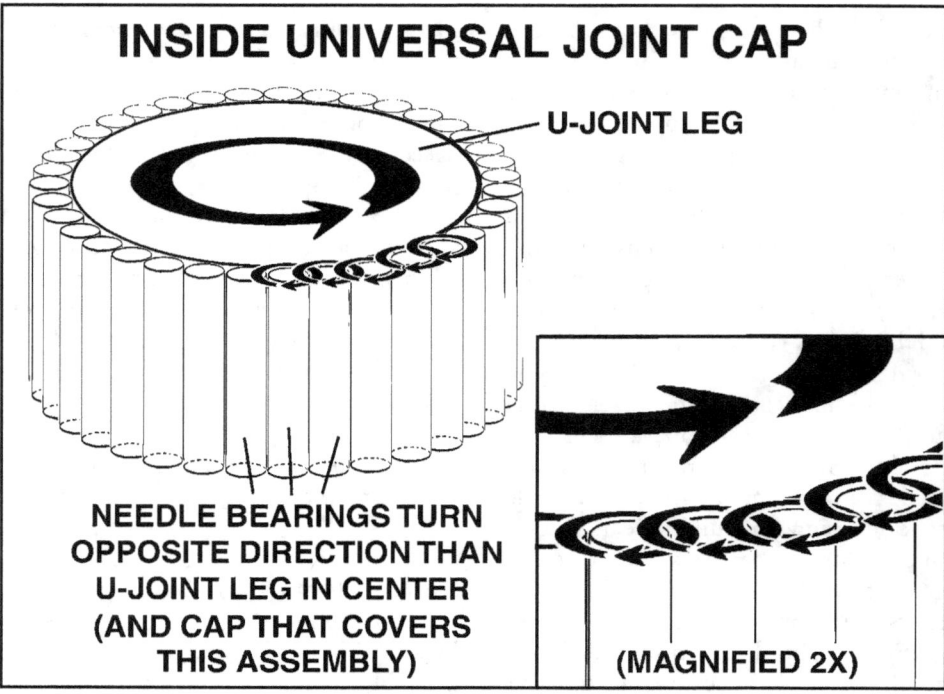

You can see the needle bearings in the cap. When the joint turns, the needle bearings spin, keeping the U-joint from causing vibrations in the drivetrain and having a shortened life.

will not spin if the U-joint is installed incorrectly or the driveshaft angles are incorrect. If the needle bearings do not spin, they wear out. This will eventually cause strange drivetrain vibrations that are hard to pinpoint.

Excessive U-joint wear is usually detectable by hearing a clunking noise from the drivetrain when shifting from reverse to a drive gear. A worn U-joint can cause excessive vibrations in the drivetrain. The most sure-fire way to check the U-joints for wear is to safely put your car up on jack stands. With the engine turned off, but in gear, physically attempt to rotate the driveshaft clockwise and counterclockwise. If you physically feel play or visibly see the pinion or transmission yoke not move in conjunction with the driveshaft, it is probably time to replace the U-joints. There should not be any visible play between the U-joint and its end caps.

Leaf Springs

People overlook leaf springs as an important part of a car's performance. Leaf springs are not only an easy way to locate the differential housing, but they can also mean the difference between a comfortable or an uncontrollable, harsh ride. They also set the ride height for your car. Leaf springs are a single unit, but should be thought of as two separate units that do distinct jobs. The front half of the leaf spring locates the rear-end housing in the chassis. The rear half of the leaf spring is responsible for the ride quality. The spring effectiveness is affected by bias. Front leaf spring bias means the front half of the spring has higher strength and spring rate than the rear.

A two-degree wedge has been placed between the spring perch and the leaf spring. Shims typically come in two- and four-degree increments.

Rear Suspension

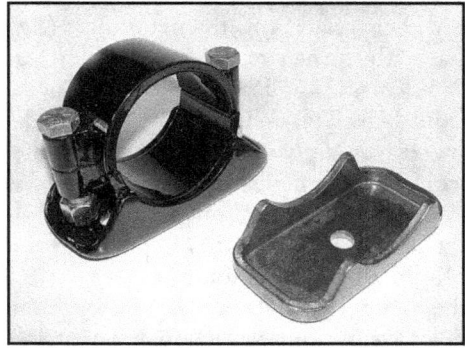

On the right, you can see a stationary spring perch. On the left, you see an adjustable perch. They are both offered by Detroit Speed & Engineering. There are many benefits to using adjustable spring perches.

This is a Chevelle 4-bar suspension with stock trailing arms. These are not adjustable in any way except to cut them to the length you desire, which is more hassle than it is worth.

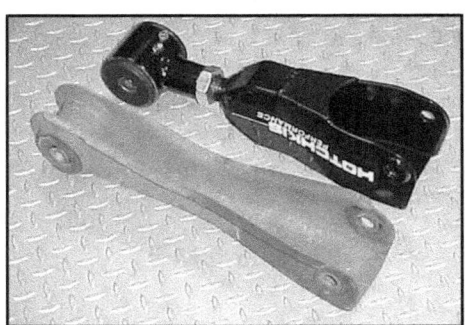

These are A-body upper control arms. The one at the bottom is a stock stamped steel arm with stock rubber bushings. The upper arm is from Hotchkis; it's stronger, has stiffer bushings, and is adjustable for correct pinion angle at any ride height. (photo courtesy Hotchkis)

Aftermarket companies offer many different spring configurations. Each company has a different idea about what design is best for each application. One company may believe that a first-generation F-body would work better with a higher rate (stiffer) spring, which produces more oversteer. Another company may offer less front bias (less front spring strength), causing the leafs to wrap up easier under hard acceleration. Some companies offer just leaf springs. Other companies offer leaf springs with rates that are balanced as a system with their other suspension components to complete a better overall package. The spring rates for leaf springs typically range from 150 lbs to 250 lbs.

If you throw a set of 175-lb springs on your Camaro and install mismatched front and rear shocks and sway bars, you may get lucky and get a great handling car. In most cases, mismatched components can leave much to be desired. This is a good reason to consult a knowledgeable suspension engineer or use a complete suspension package from a reputable company. At the very least, do some homework to increase your own knowledge before spending your hard-earned money on parts that might not work well together.

Wrap-Up

Leaf springs have a major enemy: Wrap-up. Having massive amounts of horsepower and torque under your hood will put a smile on your face. If you cannot get your power to motivate your car in a forward motion, that power is less fun and sometimes downright frustrating.

As you hit the throttle, the torque of the engine is transferred to the rear end via the driveshaft. With the forces of the ring and pinion rotating against each other, the pinion is pushed upward. Since the rear end is mounted to the leaf springs, the springs try to change from their typical arc shape to the shape of an "S" as the rear-end housing rotates upward. This phenomenon is referred to as "wrap-up." This can be more or less extreme depending on the leaf springs your car is equipped with. With any hint of traction, the wrap-up can turn ugly and produce wheel-hop. The way to combat wrap-up is to install a set of leaf springs designed with more front bias.

Leaf Spring Rates

Spring rates are determined by placing the spring on a test-table under a spring press. Mono-leaf springs are laid

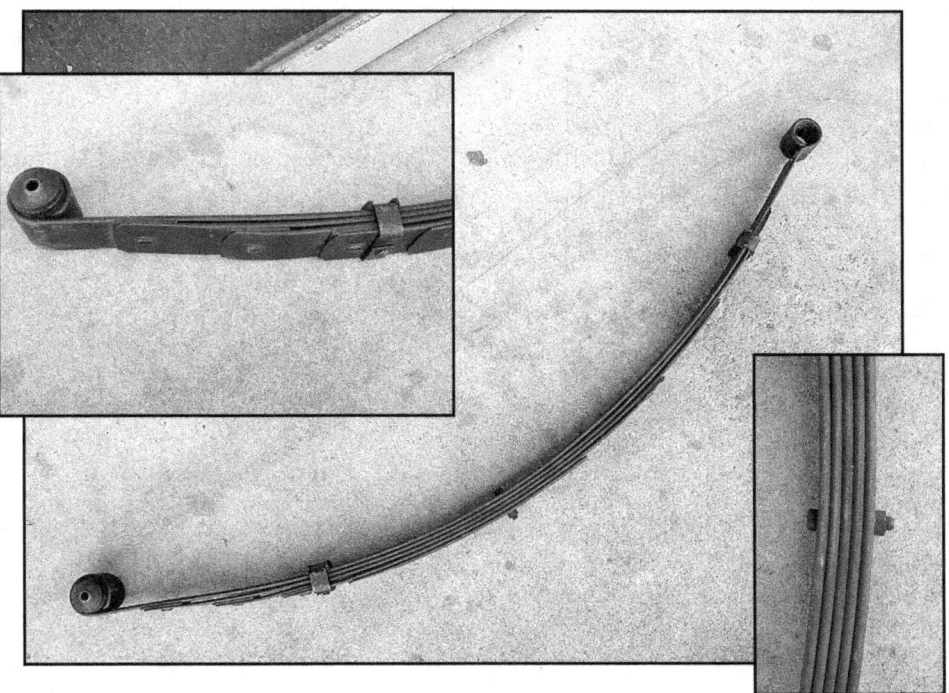

Here you can see the basic parts of a multi-leaf spring.

How to Build GM Pro-Touring Street Machines 55

Chapter 3

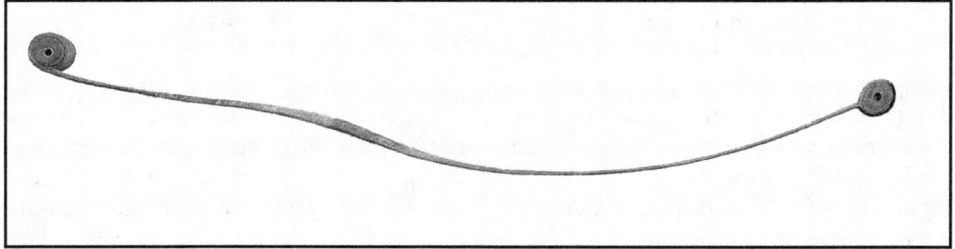

When power is applied through sticky tires and a leaf-spring suspension, the leaf spring can be overpowered if the suspension is not set up correctly. The torque can turn the leaf spring into an "S" shape.

on the table with the arc facing down. This is the exact opposite of the direction in which they are mounted on a car. If it takes 150 lbs of force to compress the spring one-inch, it's a 150-lb spring. The higher the rate, the stiffer the spring. Mono-leafs are pretty basic in this aspect.

Multi-leafs are also rated on a test-table, but they have a progressive rating. The progressive rate comes from the secondary leaves that are stacked in succession with the main leaf. The extra leaves change the spring rate significantly. Before the main leaf can be compressed one inch, the secondary leaves begin to resist compression, and typically increase the amount of weight it takes to compress the spring.

Types of Leaf Springs

There are two common types of leaf springs, mono-leaf and multi-leaf. Mono-leaf springs are available in steel and fiberglass. These types are explained in more detail in the following pages.

Steel Mono-Leafs

The mono-leaf is a single leaf with spring-eyes to hold bushings on both ends. The metal leaf typically gets thicker towards the center of the spring, where the differential mounts, in an attempt to strengthen that area to resist wrap-up. The face of the mono-leaf is wider at the ends to help resist the torsional stresses of suspension articulation while driving. Neither of these features allow the mono-leaf to be effective on a Pro-Touring car.

General Motors (of America) stopped selling cars equipped with steel mono-leafs in the late 1960s. There was a reason for that change. First-generation F-Bodies running factory mono-leafs have been plagued with wheel-hop and poor handling in corners. The single factory leaf is just not strong enough to resist wrap-up. Once the springs wrap up and wheel-hop starts, the car can easily become uncontrollable. Countless people have driven their cars up on a curb or worse, due to wheel-hop of a mono-leaf rear suspension. There are a few companies offering aftermarket mono-leaf springs. These are better than their ancestors are, but they are typically designed for drag racing applications.

Steel Multi-Leaf

General Motors (of America) has changed all of its steel leaf sprung rear suspensions to multi-leaf units. It seems as if every aftermarket spring manufacturer has a different idea of what is best for each application. With that said, not all aftermarket multi-leafs are created equal. I will point out the different features so you can make you decision on what will be the best spring for your application.

Leaf Spring Features

Bias

Think of the leaf spring as a front section and a rear section that are separated at the axle-locating pin (keeps the rear-end housing located). A spring with more front bias will require more leverage to bow the front half of the leaf spring. The secondary leaves change the bias of the leaf spring as a complete package. More front bias can be generated by placement of the secondary leaves and their relation to the main plate (the leaf with spring eyes). A good spring for Pro-Touring applications will have more front bias. This means that the secondary leaves are more prominent in the front half of the leaf spring unit. However, do not forget about the rear half of the leaf spring unit. It is important too. Minimizing the amount of leaves or their lengths in the rear half of the spring saves weight but can hamper your handling characteristics. Without the proper amount of leaves in the rear half, the leaf spring may be more suited for drag racing.

Anti-Friction Pads

Multi-leaf springs are constructed of multiple steel leafs; friction between the leafs makes the spring stiffer. To reduce the friction, some manufacturers include anti-friction pads between the leafs to improve ride quality for street use. This is something to keep in mind, since Pro-Touring cars are meant to be driven as much as possible.

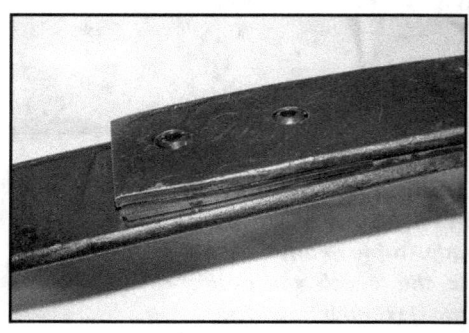

To eliminate bind and friction, pads are placed between leafs. Here you can see the anti-friction pad between the end of a secondary leaf and the main plate (primary leaf). Not all anti-friction pads are created equal.

Lowered Springs

There are quite a few aftermarket companies producing lowered rear leaf springs. Lower springs typically lower the ride height of the car by changing the rate, arc, and overall length of the leaf spring. The benefits are not only the lower stance; you also get lower roll steer (steering changes induced by body-roll), decreased torsional spring twist, decreased sideways movement, and lower roll center (an imaginary line that the body and frame pivot on during body-roll). But beware: Installing lowered springs can change the pinion angle of your rear end. Checking and setting the pinion angle is explained earlier in this chapter.

Lowering Blocks

The most common way to lower the rear of a leaf spring car is to install lowering blocks — basically a spacer that goes between the spring and the rear end housing. Most General Motors leaf spring cars have the rear-end housing located on top of the leaf springs. This makes lowering a car with blocks very easy. GM trucks typically have the rear-end housing located under the leaf spring. Some early GM cars are also designed this way. In this case, you can move the housing and relocate the rear axle mount pads to locate it on top of the leaf spring. After you do this, you can use the lowering block to further lower your vehicle.

Running more than a 2-inch block moves the axle housing too far from the leaf spring. This gives the axle housing more leverage when torque is applied, and will promote leaf spring wrap-up and wheel-hop. If you have to run more than a two-inch block, you should check into getting some lowered leaf springs.

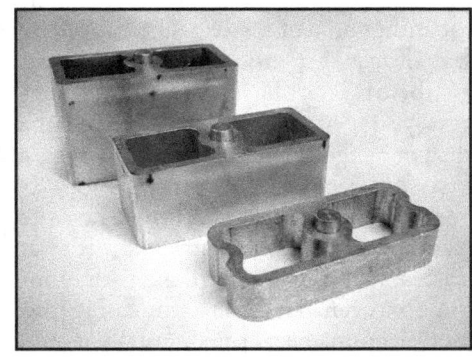

The most common way to lower the rear of a car with leaf spring rear suspension is to install lowering blocks. Here you see the different sizes of lowering blocks. BellTech offers lowering-block kits, which include longer U-bolts, nuts, and blocks.

Re-Drilling Spring Hangers

On some leaf spring suspensions, the pinion angle can be changed by repositioning the leaf spring perches; this modification lowers the car a little too. Suspension engineer Herb Adams is a proponent of this modification for second-generation F-Bodies ('70 through '81 Chevrolet Camaros and Pontiac Firebirds). This modification was intended to be performed with stock suspension components. If your second-generation F-body rear suspension has already been modified, this might not give the desired benefits.

The front perches of the rear leaf springs are modified to reposition the mounting location of the spring. The spring bolt hole is drilled 3/4 of an inch upwards, and a relief hole for the spring eye is made on the top side of the spring

Manuel Scettri's 1973 Pro-Touring Firebird is powered by a 455 backed by a 700R4 automatic transmission. Second generation F-bodies can benefit from modifying the rear suspension's front spring perch. (photo courtesy Manuel Scettri)

These cage nuts can lead to hours of frustration when they break. Restoration companies such as OER sell these. If you own a first- or second-generation Camaro, it is a good idea to have six of these in your toolbox, even if you are not doing this modification.

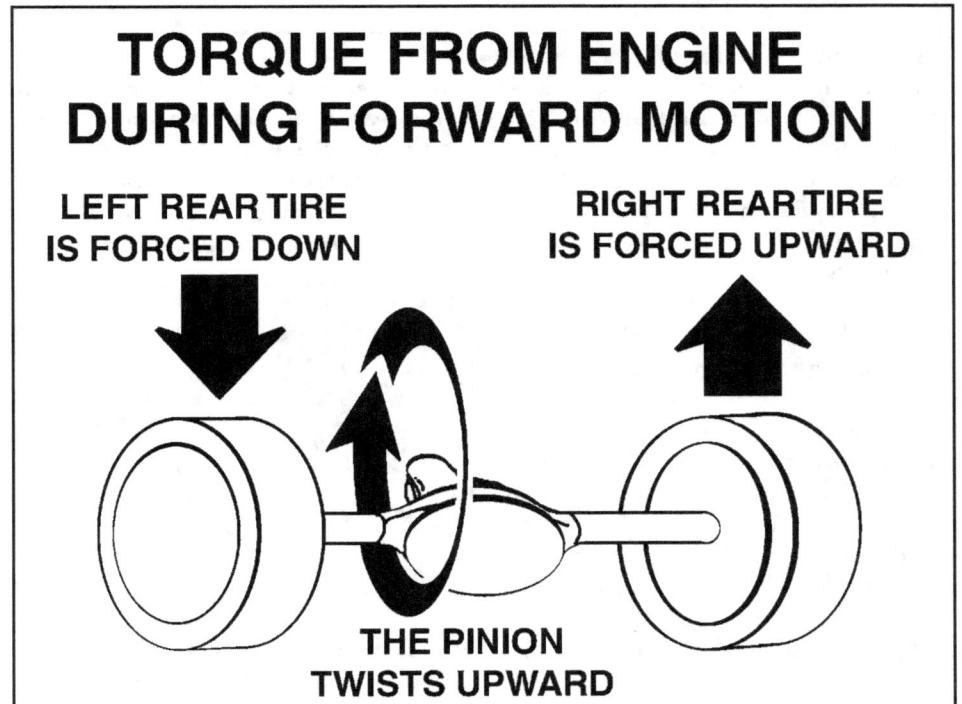

When power is transferred to the rear differential, the forces twist the pinion upward. At the same time, the left rear tire is forced downwards and the right rear tire tries to lift upwards.

Chapter 3

If a bolt has a broken cage nut, you will need to pry the hanger down a little bit to put pressure against the bolt. If this does not work, the bolt head will need to be cut off.

The new through-bolt hole has been drawn out on the hanger. It is 3/4 inch higher than the original hole.

A window is cut in the top of the hanger to accommodate the leaf spring eye. The second-generation F-bodies' floorpan has enough clerance around the window for the spring eye.

perch. The second-generation F-Body floorpan has enough clearance above the perch to leave room for the spring eye. First-generation F-Bodies ('67 through '69 Chevy Camaros and Pontiac Firebirds) do not have this clearance, so you would have to modify the floorpan to eliminate interference between the spring eye and the sheetmetal above it.

This modification will lower the car about a half inch, but lowering isn't the intent. The real goal is to improve the car's handling. It is designed to increase traction and allows more use of acceleration out of a corner by reducing roll oversteer and increasing anti-squat. Anti-squat is a term used for counteracting the squatting force of the rear suspension, by way of rear suspension link placement.

Before starting this project, I suggest you get six bracket nuts for the spring hangers. In fact, if you own a first- or second-generation F- or X-body, I suggest you call your favorite restoration parts company and order at least six of these. Keep them in your toolbox even if you are not doing this modification, because eventually you'll need them.

Start by removing the hangers from the front of the leaf spring. Be careful — be sure the car is supported by stout jack stands, and that the rear end is supported as well. Beware when removing the mounting bolts, the nuts holding the bolts are made of stamped steel, and they break easily. There are three of these nuts in the floorpan for each hanger. These can be a real pain in the neck — 9 times out of 10, at least one of these nuts will break. If you happen to break a nut when removing the perch bolts, there are a few things you can do to extract the bolt. If you have air tools, you can try to use your impact gun to remove the bolt. If the bolt just spins in its hole, then start by removing all the bolts holding the hanger in place. Then you can try to pry the spring hanger down a little to put pressure on the bolt head. Now try to use your impact gun to remove the bolt. If you don't have an impact gun, or air tools for that matter, pry the hanger down a little and use your ratchet to loosen the bolt. If you still cannot get the bolt out, you are going to have to break the bolt head off. Either way, this is not fun. When you get the three mounting bolts out, you can remove the through-bolt that attaches the leaf spring to the hanger.

Once the spring hangers are out of the car, drill new through-bolt holes 3/4 of an inch higher than the originals. Next, you will have to open the top side of the hanger to accommodate the front leaf spring eye. With the "window" cut in the top of the hanger, you should test fit it on the spring. Check to see if the hanger can freely move with the through-bolt installed in the new holes. With the hanger moving freely, it is ready to install. After all the parts have been re-installed, check your pinion angles to ensure they are correct.

Leaf Spring Pads

When putting your car together, you will need to make decisions on how you want your car to perform. There are

The rubber pads on the left are best for a soft ride, and are available from restoration companies like Year One. The urethane pads (on right) from Prothane will transfer road shock to the leaf springs faster to increase handling abilities.

Removing the pads will cause the rear suspension to react faster and make a more predictable ride. The shims shown take up the slack of the removed bushings. In this case, a thinner set of shims might have been better — notice the U-bolts are slightly angled.

different levels of performance available with just about every part. Leaf spring pads are not the exception.

General Motors commonly installed upper and lower rubber pads between the rear-end housing and the leaf springs. If you are restoring your rear suspension, you can replace your old worn out rubber leaf spring pads with replacement units from restoration companies. You can go one step better and replace the rubber pads with urethane pads. The urethane units will increase the shock to the spring from the road, but will also increase the overall performance of the car.

The leaf spring pads could be removed entirely for even better performance. With the housing directly mounted to the leaf spring, lateral movement will decrease and wrap-up rate will increase, causing the suspension to react faster, and the overall spring rate will increase. Even under braking, the suspension will react faster, making the car more predictable for performance driving. Be careful though. If your rear end has spring perches designed for the rubber pads, you may have to install aluminum spacers to take up the space previously occupied by rubber. Spacers are not necessary if you can solidly clamp the housing to the leaf with the rubber pads removed.

Leaf Spring Bushings

Leaf spring bushings come in three types: rubber, urethane, and solid.

Kyle Tucker of Detroit Speed and Engineering has found using the combination of rubber in the front spring eye and urethane in the rear spring eye keeps the road shock to a minimum for the most comfortable ride. Since the front eye of the leaf spring takes most of the road shock, using rubber makes sense. The urethane bushing in the rear eye minimizes lateral (side to side) movement of the leaf spring. Kyle went with this setup on his famous '69 Chevy Camaro named *Twister*. He mentions that he would have netted better handling with all solid bushings, but he planned to drive it everywhere, so he opted for a comfortable ride.

Kyle Tucker built Twister *to drive on the track and across the country. For all-around driving, he compromised and used rubber bushings in the front eyes and urethane in the rear eyes of his leaf springs. (Photo courtesy Anders Odeholm)*

Rubber

Rubber leaf spring bushings are great for stock cars. They minimize the transfer of road feel to the chassis of the car, and they do not bind. In fact, they allow the rear suspension to travel in ways you may not want it to, due to the deflection in the rubber bushings. This deflection can make the car unpredictable in high-performance driving.

Urethane

The next step up in performance is to replace the rubber spring eye bushings with urethane bushings. The urethane bushings don't distort like rubber bushings, so they allow the springs to stay in proper position. They help reduce body roll and torsional movement of the leaf spring. Urethane leaf spring bushings should be installed with the manufacturer's suggested lubricant. In harsh conditions, they should be serviced on a regular basis to reduce squeaks. Since urethane is denser than rubber, some people feel the ride becomes too harsh, especially when using them in rear leaf springs. Using a urethane or solid bushing in the front and rear spring eyes increases the transfer of road shock to the car. When pulling in and out of driveways at an angle, you will get some binding in the front spring eye. This binding can periodically cause noises under the rear seat.

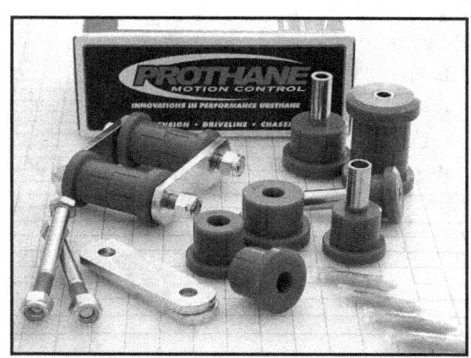
These are leaf-spring bushings. They come in different forms: rubber, urethane, and solid. Each has different characteristics, so do your research, and choose which is best for you.

This Global West solid bushing does not bind in radial motion. The center and sides are not attached. This allows the center to turn while the sides are bound.

Chapter 3

It sounds like someone dropped a water balloon on a car from a second story window (not that I would know). Even the twisting motion of the leaf springs under hard braking can produce this sound. Most of the road shock and binding come from the front spring eye.

Solid

If you do not care about an extremely comfortable ride, you can completely do away with flexible bushings and install solid bushings made of aluminum and Delrin. Unlike urethane and rubber bushings, solid bushings have a solid center with solid sides that are separate. This allows the center to turn in a radial motion without binding on the sides. Solid bushings do not bind, they resist chassis roll, and promote more predictable handling. It is frustrating to drive a car on a road course and have it turn into a corner differently even though you entered it exactly as you had every other time. These are for the Pro-Touring cars built for frequent road racing. However, solid bushings create a harsh ride because they do not absorb as much energy from uneven road surfaces.

Coil Springs

In the U.S., General Motors has not used parallel leaf springs in any car line since 1981. They are still using them on their truck lines.

Typical GM coil systems have two coils and four locating arms. The coil springs simply locate between two spring pockets. The length of the springs, the control arm articulation, and the weight of the vehicle all work to keep the springs in place.

Aftermarket coil springs are available from many different manufacturers. They come in stock and lowered heights. Different spring rates are also available. As with leaf springs, coil springs with higher rates are stiffer than lower rate springs. The rate is measured by how much weight it takes to compress the spring one inch. If it takes 650 lbs to compress the spring one inch, then it has a rating of 650 lbs.

Not all coil springs are created the same. Coil springs are available in stan-

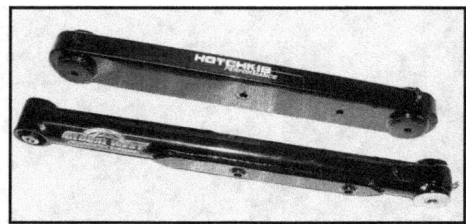

These are aftermarket control arms. They are stronger than stamped stock control arms. The top one is a Hotchkis arm with polyurethane bushings, and the bottom one is a Global West arm with Del-A-Lum on one end and a spherical bearing on the other.

The spherical aircraft bearing offered in many Global West products offers a full range of motion without bind.

dard and progressive rate. A standard rated 650-lb spring takes 650 lbs to compress the spring one inch, and 1300 lbs to compress it two inches. A progressive rate coil can take 650 lbs to compress it one inch, and 1600 lbs to compress it two inches. Progressive coil springs can be identified by their windings. Usually one end of the coil has more windings per inch than the other; sometimes the thickness of the coil wire changes as well.

As with leaf spring manufacturers, each coil maker has its own ideas about which rate will work best with your car. Some manufacturers design their systems to produce more or less oversteer than the others. They can accomplish these differences by changing spring rates or sway bar diameters front and rear. Because of this, it is a good idea to talk with each manufacturer about your car and how you plan to drive it. A good aftermarket suspension manufacturer carrying full front and rear packages can offer technical advice to help you with your application.

The rear of the stock torque arm is solidly mounted to the differential, while the front of the torque arm is mounted to the transmission with a rubber mount from the factory. The factory torque arms on third- and fourth-generation F-bodies are stamped steel. C4 Corvette torque arms are stamped aluminum.

Live Axle Rear Suspension

There are two typical types of rear axles: live axle, and independent rear suspension (IRS).

The live axle consists of a rigid housing that contains the axle shafts and differential, with wheels mounted solidly on both ends, it's the rear end that most of us are used to seeing under cars. Any travel or motion from the left tire directly affects the right tire, since they are both attached to the axle. A live axle is attached to the car's frame using links, bars, or leaf springs. There are many different configurations of links. When it comes to locating the live axle, the concept is basic. The axle needs to have limited fore and aft movement. It also needs to have limited travel from side to side. All this is done while still allowing the axle to move up and down. From those basic principals, live axle rear suspension gets complex.

Trailing Arms For Coil Spring Rear Suspension

Coil-spring and coil-over rear suspensions locate the rear-end housing with links commonly known as trailing arms. Factory trailing arm setups have two upper and two lower arms, or a combination of two lower trailing arms and a torque arm. Both setups will be covered in this section.

Rear Suspension

Many different aftermarket companies offer upper and lower trailing arms with different bushing ends for different types of driving. Not all trailing arms are created equal. Some are better for drag racing than they are for running on a road course. Some trailing arms are great for both types of driving. Pro-Touring cars are meant to be driven as much as possible, and would benefit getting power to the ground in a straight line or around a corner.

Most aftermarket trailing arms have urethane bushings in the ends. These are better than stock, but are not the only designs available. At least one aftermarket suspension company offers trailing arms with spherical aircraft bearings. The urethane bushings have "stiction" (or static friction) and will also wear out over time (as will any moving part). When the bushing wears out it distorts and allows fore and aft movement of the arms, which will change suspension geometry. The most effective trailing arms available have spherical bearings on one or both ends. Some applications will not benefit from having these spherical bearings at both ends. Some applications require a more lateral "fixed" position of one end of the trailing arm. Some rear trailing arms are designed to keep the rear axle housing in a certain position for proper geometry and articulation with a certain degree of bind. In these cases, one end may require a solid bushing and a spherical bearing in the other end. The spherical bearings offer full range of motion without bind or the possibility of distortion.

The 1981 F-body was the last car-line General Motors offered with leaf spring rear suspension in the U.S. In 1982, General Motors F-body cars started using a three-link rear suspension, commonly known as torque-arm rear suspensions. This setup had been introduced in the 1970s H-bodies with much success. With the introduction of the torque arm, the upper control arms were not necessary. The torque arm absorbs axle torque from braking and accelerating forces. When added with the lower control arms, this system resists wheel hop during braking and acceleration.

As with any part on a car, aftermarket companies have studied the torque arm and improved its design. Some companies offer non-adjustable replacement units that are simply beefed up. A few companies offer units that change the pivot point closer to the differential. With the right geometry, these units offer improved traction with adjustable pinion angle. Be careful — most of these units are designed for drag racing, but a couple of companies have designed their units with turning corners in mind.

There is one company offering a trailing-arm system that uses only two

This is the Hot Rods to Hell Inc. Cassette Truck Arm Suspension. It uses longer suspension arms like those used on Winston Cup and other big-buck racing series cars. This system has proven itself on the track, and now on the street. It is available for many Chevrolet models, including early X-bodies, F-bodies, A-bodies, and 1937 through 1957 sedans.

The half-shaft transfers power from the differential to the hub assembly. For high-powered applications, heavy-duty half-shafts might be necessary. Dynotech in Troy, Michigan, built this custom half-shaft.

long lower trailing arms without uppers. This system is similar to those used by Winston Cup, Busch Grand National, Craftsman Super Truck, and IROC racers. Longer trailing arms have proved to be more stable in high-speed open-road racing too. A company named Hot Rods to Hell Inc. (HTH Inc.) offers this long-arm suspension. They call it Cassette Truck Arm Suspension. To help locate the rear differential in its proper location, they use an adjustable panhard bar. It also comes with fully adjustable ride height.

HTH Inc. offers these kits for most 1937 through 1957 Chevrolet models. They also offer it for first- and second-generation X-bodies, first-generation F-bodies, '64 through '72 A-bodies, and some truck models. Their complete kits can be installed at home or they can install them for you. They have designed these kits to install with optimum suspension geometry. HTH Inc. has a '38 Chevy Coupe equipped with their Truck Arm Suspension that can duke it out with newer European sedans in the corners.

Independent Rear Suspension

The design of an independent rear suspension (IRS) is completely different from a live axle design. With IRS, the left and right tires are not solidly attached to the differential housing. The differential

For added simplicity, the transverse mono-leaf can be removed and coil-over shocks can be used in place of the shock absorbers. Due to diameter of coil spring, the upper locating point must be moved forward for clearance with the half-shaft.

Chapter 3

is solidly mounted to the frame between two half-shafts (also known as drive axles). Half-shafts rotate hub assemblies mounted to the wheels. This design allows the travel and movement of one tire to not directly affect the other tire. Compared to live axles, vehicles equipped with IRS have less weight directly attached to each rear wheel.

Factory IRS

The most popular IRS for street rods is the early Jaguar rear end. The Jaguar IRS lacks forward trailing arms and upper locating links. It allows torque steer when high horsepower is supplied to sticky tires. Toe and camber problems are also common. The early Corvette IRS has similar problems, even with trailing arms. The most popular IRS for Pro-Touring applications is the later Chevrolet Corvette rear end. The Corvette IRS has been more desirable since its redesigned introduction in 1984. It is almost a completely self-contained unit. This makes it a great upgrade for many applications.

In most cases, production-car suspension engineers have to cut corners on their overall design. A good design may not give the most comfortable ride. Another large barrier for factory engineers is cost. A superior design may be overlooked because it is deemed cost-prohibitive by the bean counters in the corporate office. Compromises are made in just about every part of a production car. Some compromises are larger than others.

Some years of C4 ('84 through '96 Corvette) IRS rear ends are more desirable than others. With the improved geometry introduced in 1988, builders with intentions of blistering around corners started drooling. Some chassis could accept these rear ends with limited modifications. Other cars are not as easy to adapt. The '84 through 1987 IRS was 62.5 inches wide, hub to hub. The 1988 through 1996 were a little wider at 63.5 inches hub to hub. The emergency brake system on the 1984 through 1987 used small brake shoes inside the rotor. This system is not the preferred way to go. The 1988 through 1996 emergency brake system was part of the caliper. This later system has fewer parts and is easier to work with. All C4 rear ends can be upgraded with aftermarket alignment products. The transverse leaf spring is a little bulky behind the rear differential cover. To give more space when installed in tight spaces, the leaf spring and shocks can be removed and replaced with coil-over shocks. When putting coil-overs in place of standard shocks, the upper shock mount location must be moved forward. If not, the half shafts will most likely rub on the coils.

The C5 IRS rear ends are not as self-contained as the C4 IRS. They have upper and lower control arms. The upper control arms are attached to the frame. The lower control arms are attached to an aluminum cradle under the differential. The C5 IRS is wider than the C4. It measures 66 inches hub to hub. Unlike the C4 transmission connected to the IRS with a torque arm, C5 has a transaxle mounted on the end of a torque tube. The torque tube is rigidly mounted between the IRS transaxle in the rear, to the bellhousing on the back of the engine. The torque tube can be shortened with some major modifications. This design is definitely not as easy to adapt to other chassis.

Aftermarket IRS

Unlike production-car manufacturing, aftermarket companies are less governed by cost. Racing aftermarket companies worry about cost even less. Their target market cares more about function than they do about cost. A few aftermarket companies are producing redesigned Jaguar-style IRS units. One aftermarket company in particular is producing a completely new IRS. Daryl Armstrong from Precision Brakes Company designed a racing IRS system for the Factory Five Cobra chassis. With extensive frame modifications, this kit could be installed in just about any GM chassis.

This system was designed with performance driving in mind. It has no bumpsteer. It is fully adjustable and tunable. The system is built in a self-contained cradle. It is designed to use a Ford 8.8-inch differential, which mounts directly to the cradle. The upper (rocker arm) and lower control arms have three different positioning holes to tailor the track width to your application. The adjustable hub-to-hub width ranges from a minimum of 54 inches to an unlimited maximum width. For extra-wide requests, they will build a wider cradle without changing geometry.

This system has upper and lower control-arm mounting points that are far apart so they limit fore and aft movement. This helps eliminate toe and camber changes under hard-driving conditions, which is common for most other IRS systems. Greaseable urethane bushings are used on inboard pivot points to cut down on road noise. Inboard rocker-arm points are bushed with Delrin to promote accuracy under load. All hub-carrier pivot points are handled by self-lubricating Teflon/Kevlar bushed spherical bearings. This system is designed to be used with 12- and 13-inch Wilwood brake systems. Custom heavy-duty drive axles are made for each application. These features all allow the system to be very durable under hard-driving conditions.

The rear control arms look very similar to front control arms. Unlike the C4 IRS, the upper control arms on this C5 are attached to the frame and the lowers are attached to an aluminum cradle below the differential. This C5 has upgraded Baer rotors.

Rear Suspension

Britt Guerlain's '76 Vega

Britt Guerlain's '76 Vega is a prime example of the possibilities of Pro Touring H-bodies. Huge Baer brakes hide behind the 17x 8-inch wheels that help this Vega stick to the asphalt. (Photo courtesy Britt Guerlain)

The stance is right. It has www.vegamods.com front and rear spoilers for looks, and for business it has an 8-point roll cage, racing seats, and harnesses. The suspension is a combination of bolt-ons from other GM car models and custom parts. (Photo courtesy Britt Guerlain)

When you mention the term H-body to most car guys, they don't know what you are referring to. Try talking about building a serious Pro-Touring machine, and the conversation goes well, until you mention your H-body idea is a Vega or Monza. All of the sudden the conversation loses steam. Why? The H-body is a light car with a straight-line performance reputation. Imagine having a light car with a powerful little small-block Chevy stuffed under the hood. Imagine being able to modify the suspension and brakes to actually perform equally well on a road course.

Britt Guerlain had these ideas. With a lot of research with fellow H-body owners, his thoughts became reality. His starting platform was a fairly clean '76 Chevy Vega. The previous owner had already installed the 1992 L-98 LT1 350-ci Chevy with a Borg-Warner T-5 and LT1 performance clutch. Britt added a TPIS cam and ported the intake and runners. The headers necessary for this swap are a set of Sanderson CC13HO headers. These are shorty-style headers, which allow the use of the original steering system, and don't hang down under the car and limit ground clearance. Fenderwell-exit headers would have required cutting the fenderwell and limited the front tire width, due to clearance issues. They also would have heated the brake fluid in the nearby front lines.

Britt took the car a few steps further by installing www.v8monza.com S10 Chevy truck spindle adapters. With these ball-joint adapters, he was able to upgrade to Baer Brakes 13-inch S10 front spindles and brakes. The rear braking was handled when he installed a rear axle from a 1990 1LE Camaro that had been narrowed to stock Vega width. It mounted using a combination of Camaro and Vega brackets. With the Camaro rear end, Britt easily upgraded to rear discs using a Baer Track system. Britt made some adjustable tubular control arms and a panhard bar to help keep the rear end in position. The 2.77:1 rear gears and the 2650-lb curb weight propel the Vega to speeds in excess of 155 mph. The chassis was

With this late-model TPI 350 stuffed in the engine compartment of this svelte H-body, this car is a real rocket. (Photo courtesy Britt Guerlain)

stiffened up adding an Alston 8-point cage. The steering was handled by installing a Cosworth steering box and center link. Springs are 420 lbs in the front and 185 lbs in the rear. Britt found the available sway bars to be inadequate, so he built his own from hollow 1.25-inch 4130 chrome-moly in the front and 1-inch in the rear. The bars are available to the public through www.vegamods.com. The wheels are 17x8-inch, with 3-inches of backspacing. The tires are 235/40x17 Yokohama A032R race tires all the way around. Bilstein shocks keep the car planted.

The interior was upgraded with Recaro seats, 5-point harnesses, a carbon fiber dashboard from www.vegamods.com, and a full array of AutoMeter Phantom instruments. For some hard-driving tunes, Britt installed a full Rockford Fosgate system. The body was upgraded with a www.vegamods.com front bumper/air dam and wrap-around rear spoiler. The hood was upgraded with a cowl scoop.

Now you know what an H-body is, and Britt's Vega is the prime example of a Pro-Touring H-body. Those two terms aren't typically used together in the same sentence, but in Britt's case they belong together, because this car performs well on the street and has proven itself on the track several times.

How to Build GM Pro-Touring Street Machines

Chapter 4

Frames

Frame Types

General Motors has designed a few different frames over the years. Two basic frame construction types are full-frame and unit-body (or unibody).

Full-Frame

The oldest frame design is full-frame. Typically, the frame rails are constructed of .120-inch wall stamped steel that runs the length of the vehicle. GM used full-frame construction in their car lines until 1996. They still use full-frame construction in truck lines.

X-Frame

The X-frame was used in B-bodies from 1958 to 1964. As its name suggests, it was shaped like an X. The X met in the center of the chassis. It relied on the less-than-rigid floorboards to add strength. It was susceptible to twisting forces and lacked occupant protection during side impacts.

Ladder

The ladder frame is the oldest full-frame design. It typically consists of two long frame rails that run parallel for the length of the vehicle. The frame rails are separated by lateral supports. This design lacked strength in the early years. Early GM's only had one lateral support in the rear and one in the front. This design relied on the floorpan and body to add strength. It was extremely susceptible to twisting force.

Perimeter

When GM decided to get rid of the short-lived X-frame in 1964, they switched to the perimeter frame. The perimeter frame is a version of the ladder frame. The front and rear frame portions were approximately 12 inches inward of the external body panels. Notice, I refer

The B-bodies from 1958 to 1964 had an X-frame. The frame came together in the center of the car. This frame flexes easily and would need to be extensively modified for handling purposes.

The ladder-style frame consists of two frame rails that run parallel to each other, with one or two bars separating them. All the lateral supports shown were added to accept a truck-arm suspension. (Photo courtesy Hot Rods To Hell, Inc.)

Frames

The perimeter frame went around the outside edges of the body. Since it only has a couple of lateral supports, it is susceptible to flex. The frame is much stronger when the body is bolted on to help tie things together. (Photo courtesy of Hotchkis)

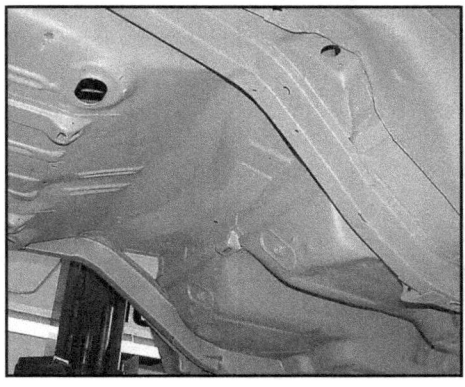

Unibody cars don't have full-length frames. The first- and second-generation F-body had a stamped sheetmetal rear frame and a front subframe. Here you can see the two rear frame rails of a '67 Camaro.

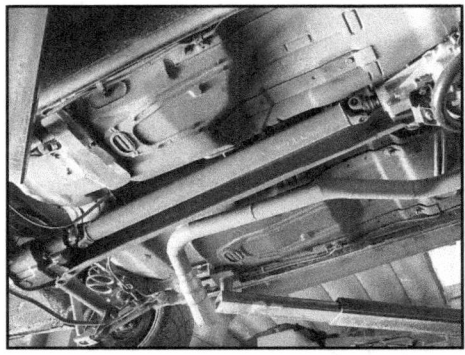

Some unibody cars don't have any resemblance to a conventional frame. The entire frame on this H-body is made of stamped sheetmetal, much like the frame construction used on all of today's GM production cars.

to the frame in portions, not sections. This is a full frame, made as one unit. The front and rear portions were not much different than the front and rear portions of the older ladder frame or the X-frame. The center portion of the frame was the difference in design. The center portion of the frame ran around the outside of the passenger compartment. It was usually only an inch or two inward from the external body panels. This design is more resistant to flex and much stronger in a side impact.

Unibody

The term unit-body is short for unitized body. The most common name for unit-body is unibody. This construction design was used by other automotive manufacturers well before GM did. Unibody construction is best described as body construction that incorporates body structure and chassis floorpan as one unit, to form a single, strong structure. Unibody construction was adopted by General Motors as a technological advance. It was introduced on the 1960 Chevrolet Corvair, along with other new designs that would be used well after the Corvair line was dropped. In 1961, the Pontiac Tempest hit the market with another version of unibody construction. In 1964 the Pontiac Tempest was redesigned. It shared the perimeter style full-frame with the Chevrolet Chevelle. Since then, the unibody has been refined. All GM car lines are now using unibody construction.

Subframe

With the introduction of the unibody in 1960, it was only a matter of years until GM engineers capitalized on its design. In 1962, GM came out with the Chevy II (first-generation X-body), which incorporated a modular type of frame. This new design incorporated a front frame section that could be completely removed from the body and the floorpan. The subframe on the first-generation X-body was unitized sheetmetal construction. The front subframe was bolted rigidly to the body firewall and floorpan. The second subframe design came out on the '67 F-body. It was a sub section of a full-frame. The factory attached the subframes on these cars with large rubber isolator bushings. The entire front suspension was attached to the subframe, making it a self-contained unit. It was a simple design that could be incorporated into more than one GM car-line at the same time. Pontiac, Oldsmobile, Buick, and Chevrolet took full advantage of this formula for many years. GM redesigned the F-body in 1982. The new design incorporated front suspension struts. The subframe was replaced with a large bolt-in K-member.

Here you can see that the front frame has been completely unbolted from the main body shell of this '63 Chevy II. Since the 1960s, companies have been building replacement front subframes for drag racing. Now, a few companies are offering bolt-on subframes with Pro-Touring in mind.

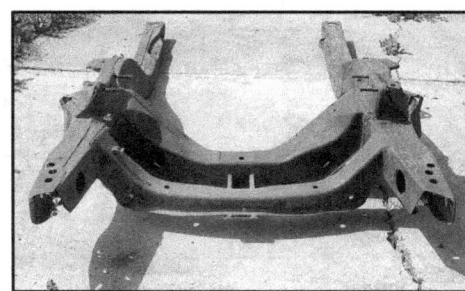

The stock front subframe is bolted to the body with six large bolts that attach it to the sheetmetal floor and the radiator support. From the factory, the six bolts have rubber bushings to isolate chassis vibration from the body.

How to Build GM Pro-Touring Street Machines

Chapter 4

This stock rubber body bushing is distorted and cracking, which is a common sight. The typical hot rodder does not know how much better his car would ride if he replaced these worn-out bushings.

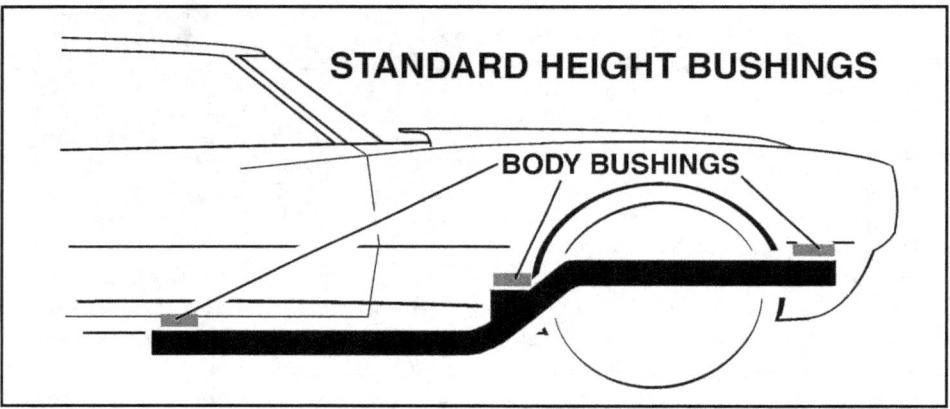

This drawing shows stock bushings (gray) installed. The bushings locate the frame to the floorpan of the body.

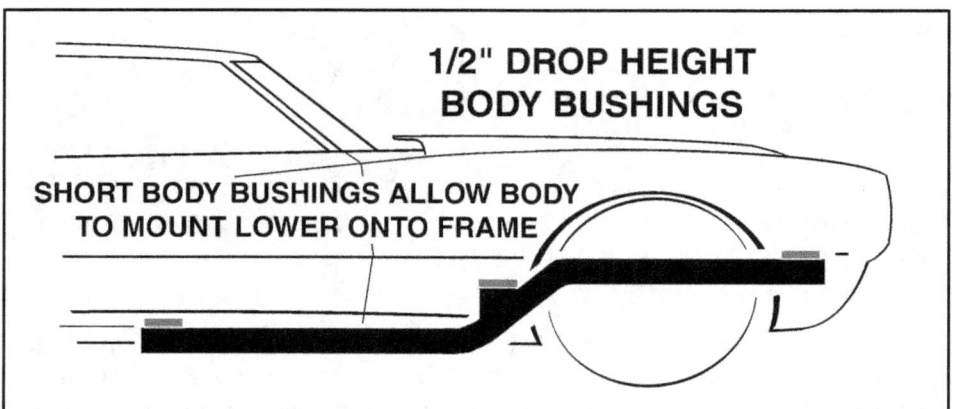

This drawing shows lowered bushings (gray) installed. The bushings allow the body to be lowered over the frame without sacrificing the extra ground clearance.

Frame and Subframe Bushings

Stock Rubber

Full-frame and subframe constructed cars typically have bushings between the frame and the floorpan that they attach to. The factory bushings are usually made of rubber. These bushings help isolate the road noise and road "feel" to the chassis. For instance, when the tires of your car hit the little reflectors that separate lanes on a highway, or they hit uneven pavement, the rubber factory bushings keep the jolt from being transferred to the body structure. That same design allows the frame or subframe to flex and twist under hard cornering.

Here are two aftermarket solid body-bushing kits. Detroit Speed & Engineering's version of GM's interlocking body bushing (shown with optional stainless hardware) is on the left, and comes hard anodized for added corrosion resistance. Global West's less-expensive version is on the right with standard anodizing.

Poly Compounds

The poly compounds are commonly known as urethane, polyurethane, and polygraphite. Body bushings made of these compounds are a compromise between flexible rubber mounts and the solid aluminum types. Poly bushings allow a little flexibility without distorting. Usually these don't come with the isolator sleeves. After many years of deterioration, the rubber mounts will almost fall off of the isolator sleeve. Unfortunately, the sleeves might be damaged from rust and abuse. If the sleeves are not reusable, you will have to go to a wrecking yard in search of good used ones, or go to a store and buy new ones. If you have to buy new ones, you will need to remove the rubber and just use the sleeves.

Solid

The solid body bushings are made of aluminum. Solid body bushings must be used when installing weld-in subframe connectors, due to the rigidity they offer. There are a few different types of solid body bushing kits. Some types are a single-sided bushing kit, which only supply the bushing that goes between the frame and the body. It uses the original (and usually rusty) body bolts and portions of the original rubber body-bushing sleeve. The other types are double sided, and are usually interlocking, like the stock design.

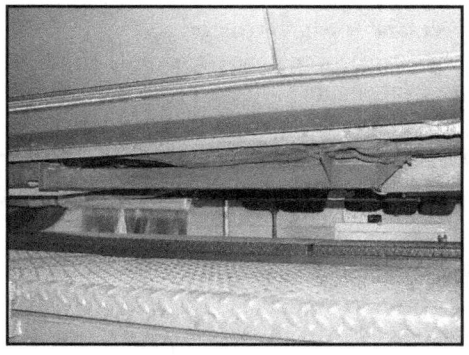

This bolt-in subframe connector is great for drag racers and guys not worried about ground clearance. They are not very strong, but they do add some torsional resistance to the body.

The double-sided bushing kits supply a bushing that installs between the body and frame and also one between the bolt washer and the frame. This type sandwiches the frame and is much cleaner-looking compared to the single sided kits that require the use of the original isolator sleeve, which is usually in bad shape after years of abuse. Compared to poly and rubber, these bushings give a little more road noise and feel.

Subframe Connectors

When building a car with a high-powered engine with a lot of torque, keep in mind that unibody cars tend to twist and flex. The flexing caused by driving a unibody car on a road course also leaves much to be desired. Forces from engine torque and flex from severe driving can cause fatigue in the body and frame structure and also make the car more unpredictable on a road course. To strengthen the car, sub-frame connectors can be installed. Subframe connectors attach the front subframe to the rear frame. This reduces the torsional flex that the sheetmetal of the body structure usually absorbs and makes the car more predictable on a road course.

Before installing subframe connectors in your car, be sure to inspect your frame and all of its components. If you install subframe connectors on a cracked frame or have worn out rubber sub-frame bushings, you will not be able to fully utilize the connectors. Subframe bushings are important parts to look at before installing subframe connectors. Read the section on bushings to learn more about them. It is also a good idea to align your frame before installing any type of weld-in subframe connector.

Subframe connectors come in many shapes, sizes, and designs.

Non-Integral, Bolt-In Subframe Connectors

The easiest subframe connectors to install are the bolt-in type. These reduce body flex. Along with being easy to install, they are also the least effective of subframe connectors. Bolt-in subframe connectors are only as strong as the bolts that connect them to the chassis. If you are going to attempt to strengthen the chassis with bolt-in connectors, the rubber body bushings should be replaced. You can get more effectiveness from connectors with polyurethane or solid body bushings. Polyurethane bushings are not as rigid as solids, but they are more than rigid enough for use with bolt-in connectors.

Bolt-in connectors could be welded in, but they were not intended for that purpose. If you were going to weld them in, you may as well step up to stronger connectors if you are going to make them a permanent part of your car. In most cases, they also reduce the ground clearance.

Detroit Speed & Engineering subframe connectors for a first-generation F-body are the best integral connectors on the market. Here they have been installed on the convertible pan. The picture shows an extra connector being held up for presentation.

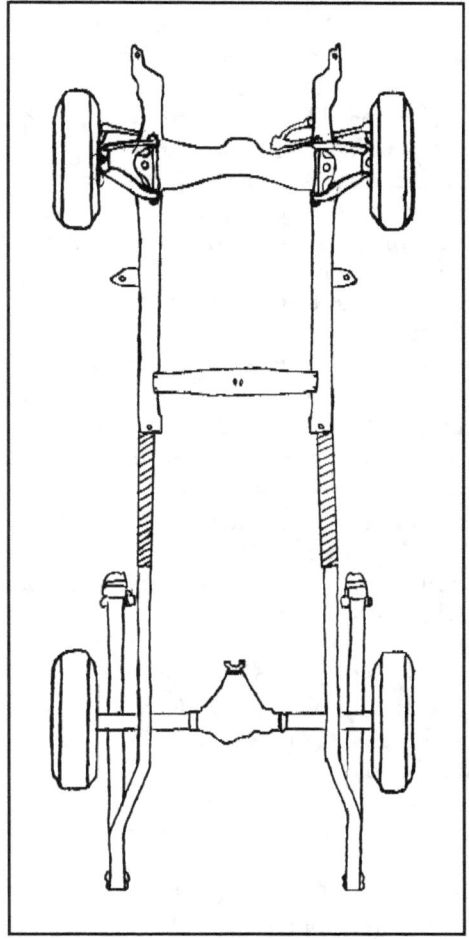

This drawing shows the front subframe and rear unibody frame connected in the center by a two striped black lines that represent subframe connectors.

Non-Integral Weld-In Subframe Connectors

Before going as far as putting a set of weld-in subframe connectors in your car, you will need to take a serious look at your subframe and all of its components. Any time you weld the subframe to the car, you should replace the rubber body bushings with polyurethane or solid bushings. Earlier in this chapter is information on body bushings. Check the alignment of the frame before welding it in with subframe connectors.

This type of subframe connector is a weld-in type, but doesn't require serious modification to the floorpan, if any at all. They perform better than the bolt-in type. Depending on the car, these can reduce ground clearance. If your Pro-Touring car is limited on ground clearance, you may want to take a serious look at installing some integral weld-in connectors. Depending on the application, these types of connectors can be much less effective than the integral type. For instance, a non-integral weld-in connector that hangs down under a first-generation Camaro is tying the front and rear frame together. But, it can still twist, unless a gusset is welded somewhere in the center of the connector to the frame. A non-integral weld-in connector on a fourth-generation F-body tucks up close to the floorpan and does not hang down, which minimizes chassis flex, due to minimized leverage points. To get a mental picture of this, which do you think is going to resist twisting (not bending), a straight or a U-shaped piece of tubing? Obviously the straight piece is stronger, unless you add a gusset or two near the center of the bend.

Keep in mind, the only complaint ever heard about subframe connectors in general is about reduced ground clearance. I've never heard anyone complain about a chassis being too stiff. Weld-in connectors are typically noticeable the first time you pull your car into (or out of) an inclined driveway, at an angle. Chassis flex should be non-existent.

This is a '68 Firebird hardtop. The floorpan itself is just stamped sheetmetal. There are no extra braces under the floorpan, so there is a lot of body flex.

In most cases, convertible cars have a floorpan that is more rigid than the coupe floorpan. This '69 Camaro convertible has more bracing than a coupe.

Integral Weld-In Subframe Connectors

This weld-in subframe connector is the mother of all connectors. These require the most work to install, but are also the most rigid type of connector. For all practical purposes, the strength added when doing this type of connector installation is just short of installing a full frame in your vehicle. They connect the front and rear frame sections. The connectors are typically stronger than the actual frames they connect. This type, if done correctly, will also not reduce your ground clearance under the car. Integral weld-in connectors protrude into the driver's compartment, and with a little insulation movement, they can be hardly noticeable.

As with all subframe connectors, to get full effectiveness out of them, you must replace the rubber subframe body mount bushings. Integral weld-in connectors require some serious flex-free bushings. Some builders think using polyurethane body bushings will work okay. Other builders will not install integral connectors without the use of solid body bushings. If you are going to go through the trouble of installing integral connectors to increase the rigidity of your car, why not use the most rigid body bushings to compliment the package? Polyurethane does not flex as much as rubber, but they do flex a little bit. Don't do the job half way. Any flex in the front subframe after installing integral subframe connectors, and you will find fatigue cracks in the frame where the connectors attach. And don't forget to align the frame before making it a permanent part of the car.

Some companies offer these connectors pre-made for specific applications. Just to name a few of those companies: Competition Engineering, Chassis Engineering, Global West, and Detroit Speed & Engineering all offer integral and non-integral weld-in connectors.

Homemade Weld-In Subframe Connectors

This job can be done at home with simple hand tools with the exception of the need for a welder to install them. You can purchase the metal tubing down at your local metal scrap yard. Most homemade connectors are made from 2x2-inch square or 2x3-inch rectangle tubing with .120-inch wall thickness. Using any smaller tubing or thinner wall thickness will minimize the effectiveness of all your hard work.

Front Support Systems

You may not think the factory engine compartment braces are much help. Think again. Without those braces that triangulate the front sheetmetal structure, the front fenders and radiator support are flimsy. When metal twists constantly, it gets fatigued. That fatigue shows up as cracks in the radiator support and other sheetmetal attachment points.

Factory steel front inner fenderwells add strength to the fenders, radiator support, and subframe. You may recall some GM cars having plastic front inner fenderwells. Those cars were all full-frame cars. The steel inner fenderwells are there for a reason. The steel inner fenderwells act as factory bracing for rigidity. Removing them reduces weight, but it also reduces the rigidity of the front sheetmetal and subframe. If you have to remove them, make sure you have some added support for the front subframe. The addition of front braces and subframe connectors is always a good idea.

Spreader Bars

Some frames have a tendency to flex and compress under hard cornering. This movement causes changes in suspension geometry and unpredictable handling. The movement also weakens the entire structure causing permanent damage, such as bent or cracked frame rails. Spreader bars reduce flex and minimize compression of the frame rails. Spreader bars come in different configurations.

Guldstrand, Vette Brakes & Products, and other companies offer spreader bars for '63 through '82 Corvettes. This spreader bar mounts between the two upper control arm towers. It minimizes flex, which can lead to eventual cracking of the towers, especially when larger and stickier tires are used on the front. The bar also minimizes unwanted camber changes. Most of the spreader bars for this application have heim-jointed ends to allow for pre-loading the towers.

Global West offers a spreader bar for third-generation F-bodies. It's called a "steering box brace." The steering box introduces extreme loads into the unibody. The steering box brace keeps the frame rails from twisting and bending under hard driving conditions, especially with wide sticky tires. For this application, the ends are rigid and non-adjustable. I have seen these on Camaro Mustang Challenge cars, and they're pretty simple to install. The steering box brace mounts between the sway bar and the unibody.

Another type of spreader bar looks similar to the strut tower brace, but does the same job as the others. Some front braces (described in the next section) benefit from use of spreader bars to keep the braces apart. Some racers use non-adjustable solid ends and some use adjustable heim joints. This is usually based on personal preference.

Front Braces

Front braces are also known as forward struts or hoop bars. A few companies have sold these front support bars with their aftermarket subframes as a package. Herb Adams' VSE sold them for use with the stock subframe. VSE called them Structure Braces. These braces help minimize flex at the front of the frame and the bodywork attached to it.

The non-adjustable tower brace is located in front of the engine. It helps keep the front bars and uprights from flexing under cornering conditions.

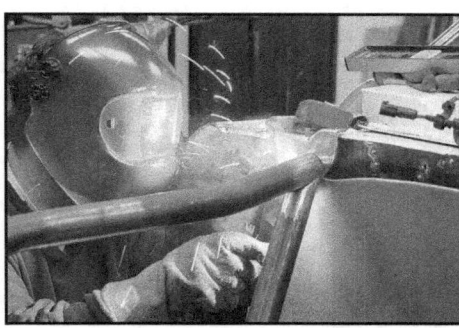

In this picture, Mark Deshetler tack welds some structure braces on a '68 Camaro. You can see the bolt-on plate on top of the firewall. It will fit between the body and the front fender. The rest of the brace will be welded to the frame.

The structure braces are fully welded and painted. Combined with weld-in subframe connectors, they will add a lot of strength to the front subframe. In an accident, the extra downward braces will help keep the top brace from going through the firewall.

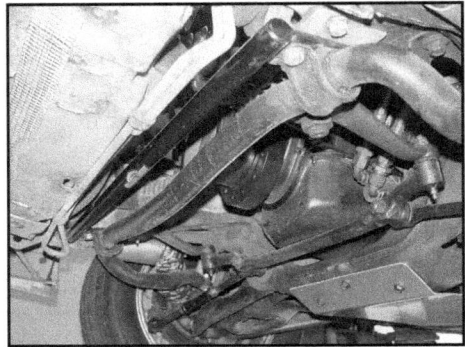

The black brace located between the sway bar and the bottom of the radiator is a Global West steering-box brace. The third-generation F-body suffers from flex in the front frame by cornering loads twisting the steering box and the frame around it.

This front brace is tied to the roll cage inside of the car. It protrudes through the firewall and drops down to the frame in front of the control arm. This adds rigidity to the front frame, which is nice, since this car has no inner fenderwells.

GM full-frame and early unibody cars have removable fenderwells. Structural integrity of the front sheetmetal and frame is reduced when the inner fenderwells are removed. Unfortunately, front wheelwells don't offer the clearance for tires of larger sizes. This is especially true when the ride height is reduced. Without the inner wheelwells, the front frame is able to flex more than desired. The inner fenderwells also protect the paint, engine, etc., from rocks that fly off of the tires. For these reasons, it's a good idea to either modify them or make some new ones that will fit. Whether or not you have fenderwells, it's a good idea to use some type of bracing to reduce flex.

On early Chevelles and Novas, as well as cars with McPherson struts, the front braces are attached at the firewall on one end and to the top of the shock tower on the other. The most strength, however, comes from attaching these bars to the main roll cage inside the car in the dash area.

In the absence of a full roll cage with front braces, these bars are typically attached to the firewall with a reinforcing plate. The preferred method is to weld steel plate approximately 4x4-inches to the area of the firewall or strut-tower where you intend to mount your braces. It's best to weld continuously around the perimeter of these plates and plug weld these plates to the host sheetmetal in a few places to further increase their resistance to fatigue. Material thickness should match the wall thickness of the tubing used for the braces. Picking a strong anchor point is critical for strength and safety, so try to attach the bars near bends or corners in the attachment area as these areas are inherently stronger. As with any design, the structure is only as strong as its weakest link. If you anchor the braces to a weak area of the firewall, the brace will break the sheetmetal. Also be aware that during a frontal collision, a poorly placed brace could easily come into contact with the driver, injuring or killing him. Anchoring the brace to the frame in more than one location would be the strongest and safest design.

Frame Boxing

Some full-frame cars came with c-section frames, also known as open-channel frames. These types of frames can be strengthened by a method called boxing. The object is to plate the open section of frame to box it. One trick is to use cardboard as a template for the boxing plates and then transfer the template onto the steel sheet. It's best to use material of the same thickness as the frame. The plates are cut out and deburred once they are welded in. This process significantly increases strength. This is a method used by hot rodders for decades.

Tubbing

Getting the widest tire possible under the rear fenderwell has been a goal since hot rodders figured out that wider is better for traction. It's not easy getting 13-inch wide tires under the stock quarter panels of an early Camaro, or any other car for that matter. Tubbing involves removing the fenderwells and the floor from behind the front seat to the taillight panel. After all the original sheetmetal has been removed, the frame rails are cut off about 18 inches forward of the rear axle centerline and moved inboard enough to get the necessary clearance for the new tires. New wheelwells can be purchased from any number of companies or can be fabricated out of either sheet aluminum or steel. Steel tubs are stronger, more durable, and generally provide for a quieter interior. This is why the majority of Pro-Touring cars are built with steel instead of aluminum tubs.

Mini-Tubbing

Mini-tubbing is the process of cutting the wheelwell front to back at the largest diameter and widening the well by adding in a strip of sheetmetal between the inner and outer halves of

This is a modified wheel tub. It measures 13.5 inches from the quarter-panel skin. Also note the outer wheel tub has been modified to give more room for the outside of the tire, a necessary modification for some '69 Camaros wanting that extra bit of clearance.

This '69 Camaro stock rear wheel tub measures 10.75 inches from the quarter panel skin (on left). These wheel tubs have an inner and outer shell. To make room for larger rear tires, the inner tub must be widened.

This is a complete Deep Tub kit from Detroit Speed & Engineering. The kit comes with everything you will need to mini-tub your first-generation F-Body. They even include a video to show you the installation process. (Photo courtesy Detroit Speed & Engineering)

the well. Sometimes it is also necessary to notch the frame rail slightly to clear the tire. This process is less time consuming and less expensive than a full tub job. This is the process used when the wheelwell can be enlarged enough to clear the desired tire without having to move the frame rails. For early Camaros, Detroit Speed & Engineering offer a set of deeper than stock inner wheel tubs that replace your factory tubs. Ask around or search the net for similar parts for other body types. Not all mini-tubs are constructed of steel, and not all of them look "factory."

The stock wheel tub is dwarfed by the new, larger wheel tub. The new tubs will allow John Parsons to fit 335s, whereas 235s were a tight fit on his '67 Chevy II with the original tubs. (Photo courtesy of John Parsons)

Rear Frame Rail Tricks

When working with frames or suspension systems, excellent welding and fabrication skills are required to do this work safely. So if you aren't 100% confident in your welding or fabrication skills, it's best to have this work done by a professional welder/fabricator.

If you have to notch the frame to get clearance, it's a good idea to reinforce the area that gets cut out with sheet steel that is the same thickness as the original metal. It's also a good idea to use cold rolled steel rather than hot rolled, due to the higher strength of cold rolled steel.

One company named Metal Works Fabrication builds new frame rails that resemble the original first-generation F-body frame rails. One feature that sets them apart from other rails is the welded top plate, which makes them easier to attach to the floorpanel. There are also several companies that make universal rails out of 2x3-inch box tubing. Chris Alston's Chassis Works and Art Morrison Engineering are some of the best, but there are others.

In order to narrow the frame rails on a full frame car, the rails are cut off about 18 inches forward of the rear axle centerline and moved inboard. When figuring out how far to move the rails inboard, make sure you end up with enough clearance on both sides of the tire. Try for at least one inch of clearance on each side of the tire and more if possible. If you are going to reuse the original rails, the end of the forward rails need to be capped with a plate that covers the entire open end and continues inboard the distance you want to move the rail. Use 3/8-inch or thicker steel for these plates. Next, reattach the rear rails to the plated end of the forward rail, then box in the areas ahead of and behind the plates with sheet steel that is the same thickness as the rails.

These custom rear frame rails mock the factory frame rails in shape, but mount parallel to each other in the floorpan, rather than angling out towards the rear like the stock ones. (Photo courtesy of Kip Valdez)

Moving the frame rails inboard, the rails to try to twist under suspension loads, so you need to add a fairly large X-member above the axle housing to prevent twisting. Use 2x3-inch box tube or something equivalent. When installing this X-member, make sure the axle won't hit it at full bump. You may end up moving the X-member to just above and behind the axle for clearance.

Nearby is a picture of a '66 Chevelle frame that shows a partially finished, sectioned stock rear frame. To get an even lower stance, the frame rails were not only moved inboard, they were also moved upward. The reinforcing plates mentioned above have not been finished yet.

If you've decided to narrow your frame, this would be the best time to consider changing to coil-over shocks

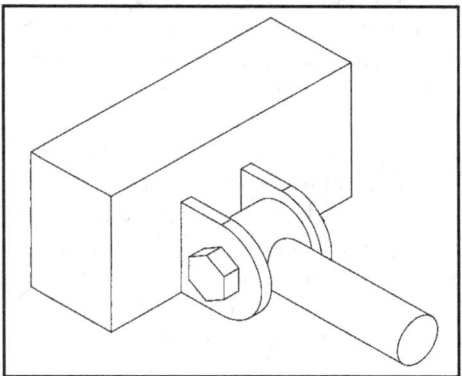

This illustration shows the proper way to mount a suspension or load-bearing link. The suspension link is located by two mounting tabs. This mounting method is referred to as double shear. A single mounting tab would be insufficient and unsafe. (Illustration courtesy of Vince Asaro)

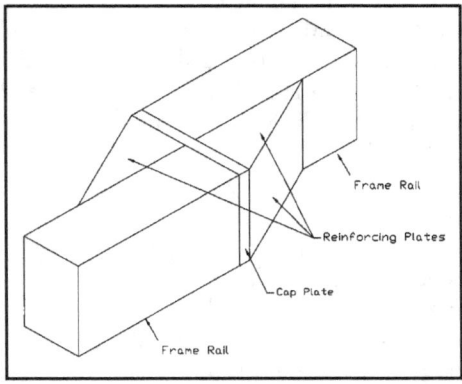

This illustration shows the method for narrowing rear frame rails. The frame is cut, a cap plate is welded into place, the frame is welded the desired distance inwards, and then reinforcing plates are added for strength. (Illustration courtesy of Vince Asaro)

Chapter 4

John Parsons purchased some mandrel bent frame rails and built a new frame for his entire car. This in-progress shot shows custom exhaust routing through the frame and the integral driveshaft loop. (Photo courtesy of John Parsons)

and a link type axle locating system. Of the different link systems, the most common is the 4-link. This is popular in drag racing, but unless it's modified slightly, it won't make for a very good candidate in a Pro-Tourer. Either the top or bottom links need to be angled front to rear so as to converge as closely as possible. This allows for more axle articulation than is possible with parallel links, which helps keep the tires planted in the turns. Angling two of the links approximately 20 to 30 degrees to the centerline of the car also eliminates the need for a panhard bar, which, by the way, locates the axle side to side in the car.

Something worth mentioning is that for strength, all suspension mounting points should be double shear, and the mounting tabs preferably should be made of cold rolled steel. Double shear means that there is a mount plate on either side of the suspension link. On page 71 is a drawing of a link mounted in double shear.

Another common type of link system gaining popularity in the Pro-Touring crowd is the 3-link. The 3-link uses two lower and one upper link and eliminates the inherent binding of the 4-link design, allowing for complete axle articulation. Using only one upper link means that the link and its attaching mount have to be extremely strong. Consider using at least 1 1/2-inch diameter thick-wall tubing for this link, and no less than 3/4-inch diameter bolts for attachment. On the lower links, use at least 1 3/8-inch tube and 5/8-inch bolts.

On the subject of attachment bolts, consider using airframe (also called AN bolts) bolts, as they are of very high quality. The 3-link design, as well as the 4-link, needs some type of side-to-side axle locating mechanism, such as a panhard bar or a Watt's link. The panhard bar attaches to the axle on one side and the frame rail on the other. For more complete info on the different axle locating options, check out *Chassis Engineering* by Herb Adams.

Aftermarket frame rails can be purchased from many different companies. Similar construction techniques to narrow stock frame rails are used to install aftermarket frame rails. The majority of the time, when narrowing rear frame rails on leaf-spring rear suspensions, they are converted to coil-over suspension systems. If you use narrowed rear frame rails, a narrower fuel tank will most likely be required.

Roll Bars and Roll Cages

Production bodies and frames were not originally designed to withstand the rigors Pro-Touring guys put them through. Along with increased safety, the strength of the body and frame are increased with the addition of a roll bar or roll cage.

The following is an explanation of the terms used when dealing with roll bars and cages. Windshield posts are referred to as the A-pillars, and in succession, the next body posts toward the rear of the car are known as the B-pillars and then C-pillars etc. Roll bars can be identified by the number of points that attach to the chassis or floorpan. A four-point cage consists of the main hoop and two rear braces that attach from the top of the main hoop to the rear frame rails or reinforced floorpan above the frame rails. A six-point adds another set of bars from a point between your shoulder and elbow on the main hoop to a reinforced area on the floor near your feet. Another version of the six-point uses bars that run forward from the top of the main hoop, follow the A-pillars down past the dash, and finally terminate at reinforcing plates on the floor near your feet. It's also common to combine the two versions of the six-point in one cage for more strength. An eight point adds bars running through the firewall to the front frame horns (or shock towers on a unibody car). These two bars typically attach to the bars of the six-point where it passes the dashboard. Ten-point cages are basically eight-point cages with extra bracing for strength and safety.

This wagon seems to be a good car to explain pillar designations. The first pillar at the windshield is the A-pillar. The next one behind the front door is the B-pillar. The next pillar is the C-pillar, and so on.

Frames

The main hoop in this car is tied to the upper door bars with a smaller diameter tube. This distributes load better than any small gusset. The bars are tight fitting to the roof too.

When planning a roll bar or cage, it's a good idea to keep in mind that, if you eventually want to race your car, your car will most likely have to pass a safety inspection and will need to be designed according to a rulebook. With Pro-Touring cars you will most likely need to abide by rules established by the SCCA and/or NHRA. Each have their own requirements as far as tubing material, diameter, thickness, placement, etc., so if you plan on racing in more than one venue, it's a good idea to be sure you're legal for all the rules that apply. If your design doesn't follow exactly what is described in the rulebook, don't hesitate to call the technical inspector and ask questions before beginning work.

In the process of designing your bar/cage, keep in mind that the joints need to be welded all the way around, and this isn't easy to do with the cage tucked up against the sides of the body and headliner. First you should form and install all of your floor reinforcing plates. Lightly tack these in to keep them in position, but they will have to come out for the next step, so keep the tack welds small. The trick is to mock the cage together with light tack welds first and then mark the floor around where each bar will attach with a Sharpie pen. Next, remove the cage pieces and floor plates. Now use a hole saw about 1/8 inch larger than the bar tubing and drill holes where you marked the floor. Deburr your holes and re-tack your floor plates in using two small tack welds as they are coming out again shortly. Next, reinstall your cage bars and tack the cage together lightly. With the cage all tacked in, go around all the bars and put four or five tacks on each bar. Now remove the floor plates and let the cage slide through the holes in the floor a few inches and voila! Now you can weld all the way around the tubes without having the sides of the body or headliner get in your way. When fitted tight to the inside of the body, a roll bar or cage will add considerable strength to your car and give it that wicked race-car look.

Roll Cage Safety

Roll bars and cages are there for your safety as well as the safety of those around you, so if you're not extremely confident in your welding or fabrication skills, have this part done by an expert. An incorrectly designed or installed roll bar or cage could seriously injure you. If a bar breaks off in an accident, it could impale you. Make sure any companies or shops you deal with have a good reputation and employ highly skilled workers. Again, if you have the slightest doubt about your design or welding abilities, have a professional fabricator do the job. Roll bar padding is another safety issue. An unpadded bar within arms-length or close to your head could cause a broken bone or worse. Also know that in an accident, seat belts can stretch as far as 12 inches.

Here you can see the drawback to having an awesome cage on the street. If you don't want to look like one of the Duke boys every time you get in and out, you can strategically place bars for easier entry.

Pinch weld guard comes in different colors, sizes, and types. The two on the left have metal inside them to help create a positive grip. The other type is just rubber, which can be seen between my radiator and core support. It helps cover sharp edges in interiors and engine compartments.

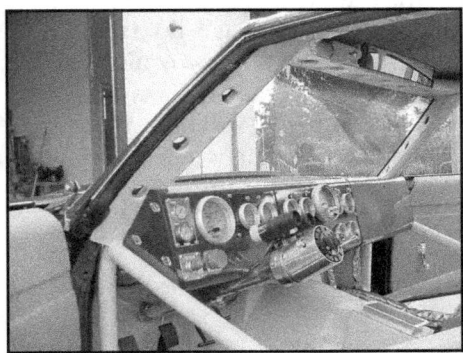

Mike Face tied his roof hoop and A-pillars to the shell of his '70 Chevelle. He cut holes in the panels and countersunk them for an extra clean and competitive look. (Photo courtesy Mike Face)

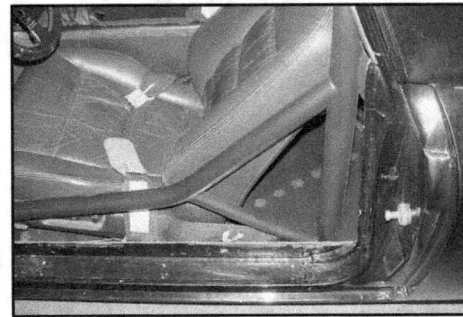

Vince Asaro put a lot of thought into installing these door bars. They match his seat angles and the downward bend is backed up with another bar for triangulation.

Chapter 4

If you are going to have a back seat for passengers, keep the passengers in mind when installing a roll bar or roll cage. On the street, passengers could easily come into contact with the bars too. If it's possible they could be in danger, don't take the risk. Give them a ride some other day.

Roll cages and roll bars benefit from the addition of gussets. The gussets add strength by triangulating the mounting point and distributing the loads over a larger surface area of the tubing. Be careful of sharp edges of gussets or any other object within reach of your limbs or head. Sharp exposed edges are extremely unsafe and have no place anywhere in your car, especially in the passenger compartment. Take a little extra time and smooth any exposed edges or burrs.

Exposed sharp edges that can't be reached with a file, sandpaper, etc., should be covered with some type of edge trim. Edge trim is available in a variety of different colors. Make your car as safe as possible. If your car gets damaged beyond repair in an accident, you can build another one, if you are still alive.

Bolt-In Roll Bars/Cages

Bolt-in roll bars and cages are for people who have commitment issues. Some people want to use their car for dual purpose. The car can be daily driven without the roll bar or cage, and it can be installed for race days. Some people have plans to put their car back to "stock" condition someday. Yeah, right. Whatever your reason is, it's your car and bolt-in roll bars and cages are perfectly fine when welded and installed correctly.

If you ever plan to race, make sure to check rules and find out if they accept bolt-in roll bars and cages. Some bolt-in cages are not legal at some drag strips. Some racing associations accept bolt-in roll bars and cages only for specific classes. Other sanctioning bodies require the use of large hardened washers or metal plates that sandwich the floorpan sheetmetal. The hardware helps ensure the bar or cage is anchored securely to the floorpan and will be harder to pull through the sheetmetal. Some associations also require the use of fine thread grade-8 bolts with two nuts locked together. The doubled nuts ensure the first nut won't come loose, causing the roll bar or cage to fail in an accident.

Weld-In Roll Bars/Cages

As with bolt-in roll bars and roll cages, make sure that you check the racing association rulebook you plan to race with. It seams every sanctioning body has a little different idea of what design and tubing size is required to keep you safe. Some sanctioning bodies also allow the cage to be tied to the body for added strength.

Roll cages have been around for a long time, and there are some issues that keep surfacing. Two of the most common issues are headroom and door bars. Whether you plan to drive your car on the street on a regular basis or not, take entering and exiting the car into consideration. Some people choose cage integrity over ease of access. There needs to be a happy medium. On the one hand, you want the cage to be strong to absorb a hard impact, and on the other hand, you need to be able to get out fast in case of a fire.

An expertly designed and installed cage is not intrusive into the passenger compartment. The roll bar or cage would also be as close to the inside of the body as possible.

Buildings and roll cages have a few things in common, but the most important feature they share is the foundation. If the foundation isn't strong, the integrity of the roll cage will only be good for visual effect — and also as a weapon. The floorpan and the frame must be in good shape. A rusted floorpan is not a good place to anchor the cage. Fabricators prefer to anchor a cage to frame structures rather than sheetmetal, but this isn't always possible. In the case of a unibody where the cage

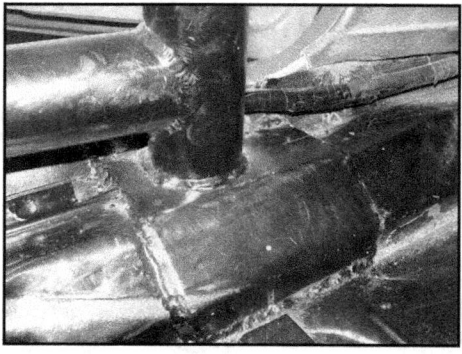

Attaching a roll bar or a cage requires a good foundation. Welding a bar straight to the sheetmetal is worthless. You must have an anchor plate to build strength. As with a building, a good foundation is important.

The main hoop comes from the floor behind the passenger seat, goes up and over to the driver's side, and then flows down to the floor behind the drivers seat. Some classes require the main hoop to be larger than the rest of the cage, so check any rules if you plan to race.

In this main hoop is a diagonal bar that ties the passenger side lower section to a point just over the driver's head. This bar is very important for strength if you plan on road-course racing. A horizontal bar without a diagonal bar does not limit torsional stress as well as a single diagonal bar, which matters much less for drag racing.

must attach to a sheetmetal structure, use large load spreading plates between the tubing and body metal. Again, use a rulebook as a guide to accepted practices. The rocker panels are typically made up of multiple sheets of formed steel sheet welded to create a strong structure, making this area a good attaching point for the cage.

Roll bars and roll cage main hoops need to be anchored to the floor behind the front seats. In unibody cars, the rocker panels are the only place to anchor the main hoop. Most fabricators use 0.090- to .125-inch thick mild steel for fabricating anchor plates. The anchor plate is typically formed to take the shape of the floor area it will be welded to. Anchor plates need to be welded around the entire perimeter for maximum strength.

The main ingredient of a roll cage is the main hoop. The main hoop is the bar located just behind the front seats. A good example of a main hoop can be seen in the photo on page 74. All driver protection bars attach to the main hoop. Some racing rulebooks require the main hoop be made out of larger diameter tubing than the rest of the cage. In some rulebooks, the diameter of the main hoop tubing is determined by the weight of the car. The use of larger diameter tubing, such as 2-inch, can cause headaches when attempting to bend it, as most fabrication shops don't have the proper dies. If the fabrication shop you have in mind doesn't have the size dies needed to bend your tubing, ask if they are willing to purchase them in order to do the job. Or maybe a nearby shop can be commissioned to bend the tubing.

Either way, there are only two ways to do things: the right way, or over and over again. Build the cage strong and safe, it might save your life someday.

Roll cages are not all created equal. Cages designed for drag racing are generally not as torsionally rigid as road race cages. In road racing, it's important that the chassis/cage be as rigid as possible so that the suspension can work under the extreme loads of braking and turning. Most all road-racing roll bars and cages have a diagonal bar from the bottom of the right side of the main hoop running up to a point near the top of the main hoop on the left side. Adding this bar to the main hoop helps reduce twisting forces in the chassis, but more importantly, it helps keep the main hoop from trying to collapse downward in a rollover.

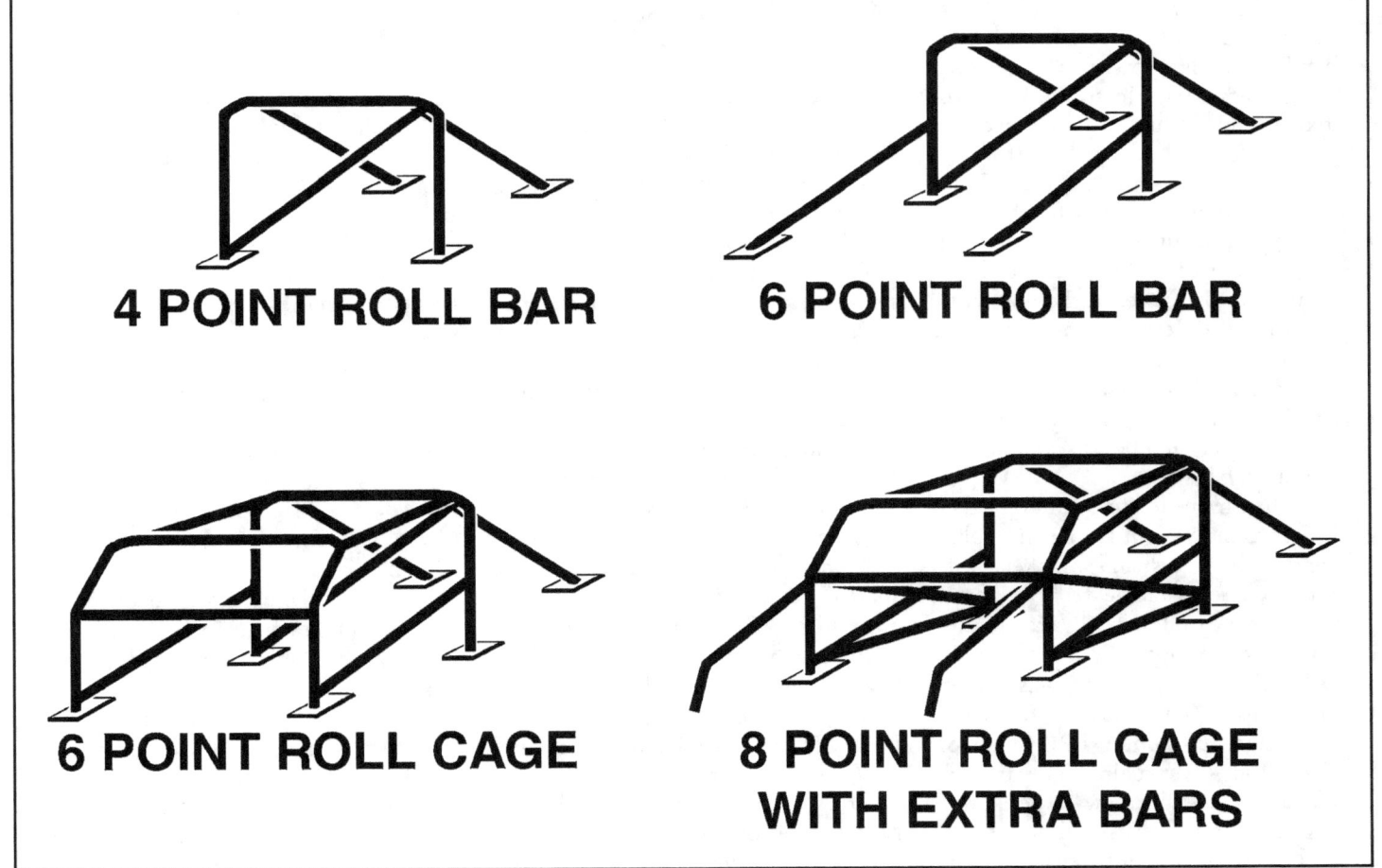

A roll cage is built off of the main hoop of a four-point roll bar. Roll cages come in many shapes and sizes. They are referred to as 6-point cages, 8-point cages, etc. Basically, the points come from how many points the cage intersects the chassis.

Chapter 4

Jeff Schwartz's '82 Fleetwood Brougham D'elegance Coupe

Another atypical Pro-Touring car is this monumental '82 Fleetwood Brougham D'elegance Coupe built by Jeff Schwartz. It's been on 6 Hot Rod Power Tours and gets raced on open track days. (Photo courtesy Jeff Schwartz)

On the bottle, this '73 500 Cubic inch Cadillac engine produces 710 hp and 850 ft-lbs of torque, and propels the 3960-pound car to a quarter-mile time of 11.80 seconds at 118 mph on street tires. (Photo courtesy Jeff Schwartz)

Jeff Schwartz always wanted a car that would be luxurious, but also out-handle and out-power most production sports cars. He started with the luxury end of his idea. In Texas, he found a rough, but rust-free, low production '82 2-door Cadillac Fleetwood Brougham. Only a few hundred D'elegance Coupes were produced. It took 2 years to build the car for luxury and performance. In the nine years that followed, Jeff made modifications to bring the car the state you see in the accompanied pictures. He modified in small steps to keep from getting "project burnout," and he was able to drive the car in between.

The car needed to be put on a diet, so Jeff found weight savings in replacing the bumpers and brackets with some custom fabricated 10-pound units, front and rear. Brake ducting was integrated into the front bumper. Other than that, the body was left virtually stock. The body is covered in two-stage, two-tone PPG Deltron black and silver paint. The interior was upgraded with new carpet, a new dash pad, and a new headliner. A GM leather Trans Am steering wheel with Cadillac Catera center emblem was also added. The instrument panel was modified to house all new AutoMeter gauges. The shifter was upgraded to a B&M unit, and the original seats were swapped out for a set of Recaro seats custom upholstered in two-tone leather. The full power memory GM seat brackets were retained and integrated into the new seats.

All suspension bushings were replaced with serviceable Delrin and steel versions. The rear control arms were boxed to rigidly locate the non C-clip GM 8.5-inch ten-bolt rear end, which is loaded with 2.73:1 gears and a limited slip. The front coil springs were shortened, and Hellwig front (1 5/16-inch) and rear (1-inch) sway bars were added. A 14:1 WS6 Trans Am steering gear box is connected to a custom-made aluminum steering shaft. The wheels are custom forged aluminum Centerlines, measuring 17x9.5 inches in front with 5-inch backspacing, 17x11 inches in the rear with 7-inch backspacing. The tires are Nitto NT555R 275/40ZR17 front, and 315/35ZR17 rears. To make room for the 315s, the rear frame rails were narrowed one-inch on each side. The brakes are original 12-inch front disc brakes with Performance Friction "95" pads, and the rears are 12-inch '94 Corvette brake rotors mounted with custom brackets. To help balance the system, Jeff installed an adjustable proportioning valve.

The original 350-ci Olds Diesel V-8 engine was discarded and a '73 500-ci Cadillac engine was mounted to a TH400 transmission and a 13-inch W-30 converter. The block was deburred and the heads were ported and milled. A MTS / Competition Cams Extreme Energy 230/236-degree duration, .562-inch lift hydraulic cam and kit were installed. The modified 850-cfm Holley was "flowed" to 980 cfm, and sits atop a custom carbon-fiber heat shield, an NOS Big Shot plate system, and an Edelbrock intake. The fuel is ignited by an MSD ignition. The spent gasses flow out through custom headers built from Hedman big-block Chevy headers modified with custom Cadillac flanges. On the engine dyno, the engine pounded out 710 hp and 850 ft-lbs of torque on the bottle.

The Cadillac took first place in *Car Craft Magazine*'s Real Street Eliminator competition, where it left some spectacular cars in the dust. With the assistance from some nitrous oxide, he was able to blast down the quarter mile in 11.80 seconds at 118 mph on street tires, which is impressive considering the car's overall weight of 3960 lbs. It also has the capability to pull 1.0 G on the skidpad, and has been undefeated in attended High-Speed Autocross events. He accomplished everything he set out to accomplish and more. Jeff Schwartz has the ultimate, and most original, Pro-Touring ride.

Chapter 5

Engines

There are a few areas of the drivetrain that should receive extra attention when building a Pro-Touring car. Some of these areas don't get much attention on street rods and Pro-Street cars. Most of those cars don't see the hard driving a Pro-Touring car will see. When you push your car to the limits and beyond, weaknesses in your engine, cooling and oiling systems, transmission, and clutch will become more evident. The following chapter will be dedicated to these areas and more.

Engine Swaps

To start off, this section will have information some purists will deem ludicrous and downright horrible. With that said, read on.

Swapping in a non-original engine is done for many reasons. Here are a few of them: gain more power, increase the "oooh" factor, save money, or just use what you have laying around. The most common engine swap in the world is to swap from a small-block Chevy to a big-block Chevy or vice versa. Any transmission that fits a big-block Chevy will fit a small-block Chevy. Buick, Oldsmobile, and Pontiac (commonly referred to as BOP and BOPC when Cadillac is added) transmissions interchange with each other, but require different flywheels or flexplates in some cases.

The finger in the picture is pointing to the frame stand. It bolts between the frame and the motor mount (which bolts to the engine block). If you had Pontiac Firebird frame stands, you could bolt them to this Chevy Camaro frame. This makes it easy to install a Pontiac engine in a Camaro, or vice versa. GM did this to save money and time. It helps when doing engine swaps too.

Frame stands make swapping easy with some cars. The frame stands I am referring to are the metal brackets that bolt between the subframe and the engine mount. All the first-generation F-body and '68 through '74 second-generation X-body engine stands can be interchanged. All the second-generation F-body and the '75 through '79 X-body engine stands interchange. All A-body engine stands interchange, and so do the B-body frame stands. The frames either have multiple drilled patterns for the different engine stands, or the frame stands use the same holes. GM did this to save money and time when engineering and assembling at the factory. To you and I, this all means that with right frame stands, a '68 Pontiac 400 engine can be bolted in a '69 Camaro or a '74 Oldsmobile Omega. With all the different frame stands available, and all the interchangeability, just about any GM engine will mount in just about any GM body. Of course, there might be some interference with a firewall here and there, depending on what distributor you use.

This '70 Pontiac GTO owned by Andrew Borodin is equipped with a 502-ci big-block Chevy. The swap was easy since the GTO frame was shared with the Chevy Chevelle. Andrew installed Chevelle frame stands, so the 502 bolted right up. The Pontiac transmission would not bolt directly to the Chevy engine, but he installed a T-56 to fix that problem. (Photo credit Andrew Borodin)

How to Build GM Pro-Touring Street Machines

If you have a rear-wheel-drive 1963 through 1992 (in some cases, earlier and later) Chevy that was available with a small-block engine, and want to stick with a Chevy engine, that is easy too. The inline 6, small block, and big block all had different frame stands. Just swap the stands and bolt in a Gen-I and -II small block or a Gen-IV, -V, or -VI big block.

Then there are the guys who use what they have laying around the garage. Using what you have laying around is a good way to save a little money when building your project. Maybe even go as far as swapping an engine from a different manufacturer. Take Ron De Raad for instance. He is building a '68 Camaro. It's mini-tubbed, has a Martz Chassis front clip under it and a full cage, as well as all the full-on Pro-Touring goodies. He just happened to have an 800+ horsepower twin turbocharged 302-ci Ford engine lying in his garage from a project that came and went. It only made sense to use a nice powerplant like that in a nice project car.

H-Body Engine Swapping

The only four-cylinder GM I am covering in this section is the H-body, so they get their own section, due to modifications specific to them. If you own one and want to swap out the 2300 four cylinder engine for something more powerful, you could try to scrounge up a rare 122 cid twin-cam Cosworth and drop it in, or you could choose from many other more powerful and readily available engines. A Saturn DOHC, a Quad4, or Buick V-6 will give you more power than the 2300. An LS1 or LS6 would be nice and light for a V-8. You could go the traditional route by bolting in a Gen-I or -II small-block or big-block Chevy V-8 and buy special engine mounts and other H-body parts from Robert Gumm of www.v8monza.com. He sells custom rubber mounts that allow you to bolt small- and big-block V-8s into the '71 through '80 H-body. They are modeled after the factory mounts (which are no longer available).

Just like any car, when installing a V-8 where a much smaller engine was previously housed, check all front suspension and drivetrain components to make sure they are in tip-top shape. Builders have found weaknesses in the H-body front frame when applying lots of V-8 torque. The front frame rails start to spread. The K-member under the front of the engine is stamped steel and has slotted mounting holes. The stamped steel flexes and the slotted mounting holes allow too much play. Welding extra bracing to the K-member and closing the slots so they are round holes increases the rigidity.

The exhaust gets tight in the Vega-sized engine compartment. Full-length headers usually hang down too low, and the fenderwell exit versions limit the front tire width and tend to bake the master cylinder and brake fluid. Sanderson makes a beautiful set of shorty headers that fit the small block. The steering shaft runs between two of the primary tubes, so the shaft must be removed and reinstalled once the header is in place.

The Vega looks a little sedate with Chevy S-10 15x7-inch wheels, but it really moves with an LT1 and the light body. It has a 700R4 transmission, a Monza rear-axle housing equipped with Moser axles, and some '98 S-10 12-inch rear disc brakes. The front brakes and spindles are adapted from an S-10 using special adapters from v8monza.com. (Photo courtesy Dave English)

Gen-II Engine Swaps

Putting a Gen-II small block (LT1 or LT4) in a car previously equipped with a Gen-I small-block Chevy is basic, since the transmission and engine mounts are the same. The Gen-I and -II engines share the same transmission bellhousing bolt pattern, so the transmissions from either generation fit. Other than that, there are a few differences that make the swap more difficult. The LT1 is externally balanced, so they use a specific counterweighted flywheel or flexplate. Radiator hose routing is tougher due to the placement of the water inlet and outlets on the engine. The stock fuel-injection intake manifold is very low profile, so hood clearance is not an issue unless you swap it for something else that is taller. Using the factory accessory brackets may require notching the frame if you intend to use the low-mounted air-conditioning compressor. The oil pan from the Gen I starting in 1986 fits the Gen II, so there are plenty of oil pan configurations available. One should be able to fit your engine compartment and frame constraints.

When hot rodders first started putting the LT1 put into older cars, the factory engine management system was used. Using the stock wiring harness proved to be a huge job. These days you can save yourself some time by using custom wiring harnesses and accessories by Painless Performance Products. Or you can totally bypass the factory management system by tossing it in the scrap pile, and install a complete aftermarket engine management system, such as an ACCEL/DFI.

This LT1 was swapped into a '69 Camaro. You might think that is a typographical error, but it's not. The engine was converted back to an earlier-style rear distributor. The owner, Bob Spears, decided the stock GM OptiSpark distributor was not reliable enough. The water pump is the only hint that this is an LT1.

Engines

Gen-III Engine Swaps

The Gen-III small block (LS1 and LS6) has been available since 1997. Like all aspects of hot rodding, not even specific to Pro-Touring, it was only a matter of time until people wanted the latest technology in their older vehicle. People like Tyler Beauregard have taken the Gen-III swap to a whole new level. They are swapping in the Gen-III engine along with the C5 Corvette torque tube and rear mounted transaxle. This is highly involved because the torque tube and drive shaft have to be lengthened or shortened to the correct length of the car's wheelbase. In some cases, builders are getting more extreme and lengthening the chassis and bodies of the vehicle to fit the stock length C5 drivetrain.

The less invasive use of the Gen III is to swap in the engine along with a transmission from the '98 through '02 F-body, since it has a different transmission bolt pattern than the Gen I and II. This has been made fairly easy by a few aftermarket companies offering custom motor mounts. One of those companies is BRP Hot Rods. They offer custom Gen-III mounts so you can bolt directly into the frame stands in the car. The stock GM accessory mounted air-conditioning compressor mounts low like the LT1 system, so notching the frame for clearance is necessary on most older GM frames. The coolant hoses come out of the water pump housing at an awkward position, which adds a little difficulty to the swap. If you want to mix a little old technology with new technology (and less wiring hassles), you can bolt a carburetor on top of your LSx engine by using a GM Performance Parts or Edelbrock intake manifold. Since these engines don't have distributor, MSD Ignition and Edelbrock offer an electronic controller to help make the swap easier. Painless Performance also offers a wiring harness to take some of the pain out of connecting the factory engine management system to the Gen III. GM is currently offering three different oil pans for Gen-III engines. They are for trucks, F-bodies, and Corvettes. The Camaro version hangs down 5.5 inches

A modified LS1 puts out 426 hp and 400 ft-lbs of torque at the rear wheels of this '88 SS Monte Carlo. It pushes the Monte through the quarter mile in 12.04 seconds at 115 mph. The LS1 is backed up by a 6-speed transmission, an 8.5-inch positraction rear end, and a set of 4.10:1 gears. It sits low and has 17x8.5-inch Arrow wheels wearing 275/40ZR17 tires. (Photo courtesy of John Bzdel)

Katech Inc. worked with GM on the Cadillac XV16 concept engine for the Cadillac Sixteen concept car. The engine is LS1 based, and might be nice to stick in the right Pro-Touring car. Imagine the power two all aluminum LS6s would produce. (Photo courtesy of General Motors)

The LS1 has an aluminum block and heads, which makes it a lightweight and powerful engine to swap. John Bzdel used a modified F-body oil pan and homemade engine mounts to shoehorn the engine into his '88 SS Monte Carlo. It is a clean installation, and at a glance looks like it was meant to be there. (Photo courtesy of John Bzdel)

This unfinished '68 Camaro is highly modified with the entire running gear coming from a C5 Corvette. The original frame was tossed to make room for one custom-built by Wayne Due. It has the C5 front and rear suspension and a modified torque tube, so the LS1 and rear-mounted 6-speed transmission could be retained. This should give the car good front-to-rear weight distribution. (Photo courtesy Tyler Beauregard/Wayne Due)

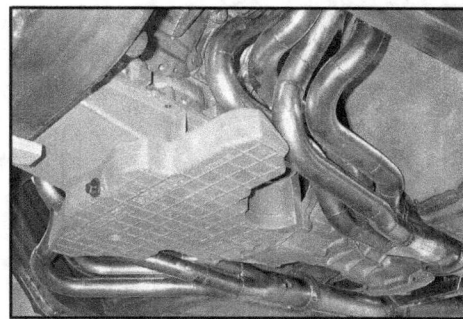

The Corvette LS1 pan has a lower-profile sump than the Camaro, with only 4.75 inches of rear sump. Its big wings make it 21 inches wide, which limits its use in a lot of cars. Those wide wings help control oil and increase the oil capacity to 6.5 quarts. John Parsons decided to use it in his Chevy II, and even built custom full-length headers to fit. The GM part number is 12561828. (Photo courtesy of John Parsons)

How to Build GM Pro-Touring Street Machines

from the pan rail, has an oil capacity of 5.5 quarts, and is the most popular for Pro-Touring applications due to its unobtrusive shape. The truck 5300 Vortech oil pan holds 7 quarts of oil, but has a deep sump that hangs down 8.5 inches from the pan rail, which is too deep for most Pro-Touring applications. The Corvette holds almost 7 quarts of oil and hangs down 4.75 inches from the pan rail. The C5 pan is perfect for open track abuse due to its oil control and shape. The shape of the pan is the problem. It has large "bat wings" on both sides. They are perfect for the tight C5 chassis, but not exactly a great fit for Pro-Touring chassis.

Cadillac 32V Northstar Engine Swaps

If you are going for high-tech engine swaps, swapping in a Cadillac Northstar 32-valve (32V) engine is an option. Compared to the small-block Chevy's 540 lbs, the 32V Northstar tips the scales at approximately 470 lbs complete with all accessories (it only weights about 415 lbs without them). The 4.6-liter (280 ci) came from the factory with 275 – 300 horsepower and 400 ft-lbs of torque. The Northstar was only available as a transverse mounted engine in front-wheel-drive cars. Well, a few companies are offering conversion parts to adapt them to rear-wheel-drive applications. For a low cost solution, Phoenix Transmissions in Texas offers an adapter kit to bolt the Northstar to a late-model V-6 Camaro manual transmission bellhousing or 700R4 transmission. The kit does not require welding or torque converter modification, which is otherwise required and more expensive.

Cadillac Hot Rod Fabricators also offers parts for Northstar conversions. The stock computer system could be adapted if you have too much time on your hands and you want to run the factory fuel injection. If not, Cadillac Hot Rod Fabricators offers a few different intake manifolds, including a single four-barrel version that has bosses so fuel injection can be added.

Engine Parts

Pro-Touring engines are usually loaded with performance parts. I could write a separate book on engine upgrades, but there are plenty of other CarTech books covering the subject. I will keep this section fairly short, and try to include parts that sometimes increase the durability of your engine. Some of these parts also give the engine back its horsepower. You may be asking what I mean by that statement. An engine makes power that is robbed by parts bolted to it. For instance, a cooling fan bolted to the front of the water pump robs power from the engine. The inertia of the rotating mass and wind drag of the fan robs power from the engines overall output. When you remove the manual fan and install an electric fan setup, you give the power back to the engine. Of course, the fans would draw more electrical current from the alternator putting a little more strain on the engine to operate the electric fans, but the power difference between manual and electric fans would be substantial. Some parts rob less than one horsepower, but some losses are over ten horsepower.

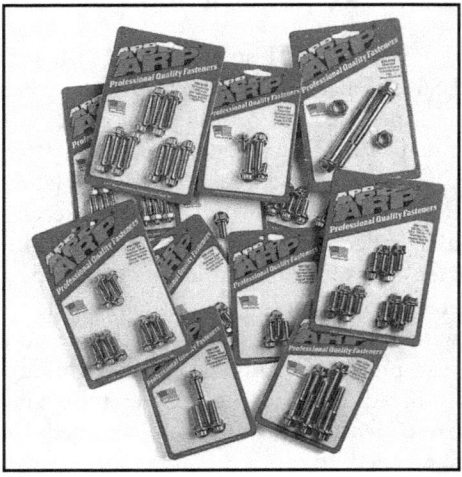

The most popular bolt company in the aftermarket industry is ARP. They offer bolt kits for just about every engine component, including all the accessories on the outside, like water pumps, starters, etc. They offer bolts in bulk if you are interested in getting the best quality bolts for your body or suspension components. Don't be fooled by other bolts that are advertised as aircraft quality. ARP has higher standards than aircraft applications require. (Photo courtesy of ARP)

Bolts

Some people find it hard to justify spending money on engine bolts, since they don't increase your power. They are very important in certain applications. Going to your local hardware store to purchase bolts to use for bolting on your timing cover is fine, but buying hardware-store bolts there for your heads and main caps is a really bad idea. Even if you bought some grade-8 bolts from the hardware store, they are not designed for this application, and you're just asking for trouble. I've been around cars long enough to see people build engines with grade-5 bolts as head and main bolts. Even if you are on a budget, any good engine builder will tell you to spend the extra money to buy good quality fasteners. The professionals I asked said they would use a minimum of quality rod bolts, main bolts or main studs, and head bolts when building an engine. They all use Automotive Racing Products (ARP) fasteners.

Don De Raad had an engine sitting in his garage when he picked up his '68 Camaro. It was a twin-turbo 302-ci Ford engine with an expected output of 800 hp. He decided not to let the engine sit around and collect dust, though some people see this swap as sacrilegious. It always keeps the costs down on a project when you can use parts you have lying around the garage. (Photo courtesy Ron De Raad)

Engines

If you have the extra money, you should consider replacing all your engine fasteners to high-quality nuts and bolts. Some of you may be thinking that using ARP fasteners in such areas like the oil pan and the intake manifold is overkill. Figure that most small engine bolts are commonly over-torqued. Think of what kind of hassle it will be to remove the remains of a broken intake manifold bolt that broke on the third time you reinstalled it because it was of inferior quality. Maybe you think you will never remove your intake manifold or timing cover after you install it the first time. The average engine is disassembled and reassembled at least ten times in its life. Quality fasteners will save the threads in your block, untimely hassles, and save you money in the long run.

Bolts are different than studs. A stud only has to be installed once. For instance, a main bolt must be removed every time you remove a main cap. If you remove a main cap attached with main studs, the nut is the only fastener necessary to remove. This saves the threads in the block. When installing studs in the mains or any other location that is blind (a hole that does not have opening at the bottom), it is best to bottom-tap the hole. This means that the threads need to extend to the bottom of the hole, so the bottom face of the stud will have positive contact with the block. The studs will have more integrity. So, if you are using studs because you want more strength, you should do the job completely.

Using head studs can save the threads in the deck of your block, since you can leave them screwed into the block during head service. Imagine how much deterioration the cooling system can cause to the head-bolt threads in the block. Removing the bolts time and again can eventually pull the threads out of the block, requiring the need for a Helicoil. The only drawback to running head studs is lack of serviceability when the engine is in the car. The head must have room to slide perpendicular to the deck (head mounting surface) of the block, for the length of the studs. This is usually fine on the passenger side, but the driver's side is usually obstructed by the brake booster/master cylinder. Using good quality head bolts instead of head studs will not help you save the threads in the deck of the block, but they allow easier serviceability while the engine is in the car. Usually serious racers with head studs don't have any obstruction for head removal, or they have spare engines to swap for faster repair.

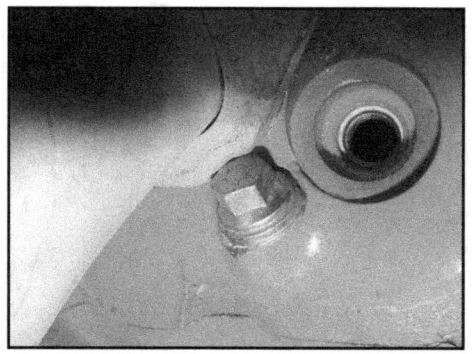

Sometimes aftermarket head bolts and studs will interfere with mounting accessories, since stock head bolts have shorter heads. This picture shows the header flange hitting the head of the head bolt. The flange had to be ground down a little bit so it would seal properly. It's frustrating to replace header gaskets a few times before noticing the interference.

Cooling System

Internal combustion engines create enough heat to destroy themselves if they are not equipped with a good cooling system. The cooling system also circulates hot water to warm the engine in colder climates. Since most Pro-Touring cars won't be driven in icy and extremely cold environments, only cooling systems will be covered in this book. To simplify the cooling system, it consists of a few basic components: a radiator, a pump, water, and a fan to cool the system. The stock cooling system is great for a stock engine in a moderate climate. Stock systems in the sixties, seventies, and the eighties were inadequate in extremely hot environments. With the addition of computer-controlled engine management systems, the cooling systems have become more efficient.

The Buick, Oldsmobile, Pontiac, Gen-I small-block Chevy, and big-block Chevy engines all have similar cooling systems. The coolant is drawn out of the lower portion of the radiator and forced into the front of the block. The water flows around the cylinder walls and then up into the heads through holes in the head gaskets. Then the water flows up even further to the crossover under the thermostat, where it is restricted until the water gets hot enough to open it. After the water flows through the open thermostat, it flows through a hose into the top portion of the radiator. Once it is in the radiator, it transfers heat to the cooling fins and starts the whole process all over again. Other smaller details about steam and water jacket differences, coolant transfer tubes, and other changes throughout the years have helped the performance of the coolant system, but are too numerous to list within the scope of this book.

In 1955, Chevrolet designed the most well-known and prolific V-8 in the U.S. I am referring to the first-generation small-block Chevrolet V-8. Its cooling system didn't change significantly between its introduction in 1955 and 1992 when the LT1 was introduced. Before the LT1, there was the L98. It was introduced with a reverse rotation water pump. Since the earlier small block was first introduced with clockwise rotation of the water pump, it has been labeled as "standard rotation." The reverse-rotation pump was not a redesigned water flow system. When GM switched from the limited configuration V-belts to serpentine belts, they were able to completely redesign their accessory-drive system. Serpentine accessory belt configurations allowed the use of the back side (flat side) of the serpentine belt on the water pump pulley, which turned the pump in a counter-clockwise direction. The standard-rotation pump could no longer be used, so GM designed the reverse-rotation water pump. Standard-rotation pumps will not work on reverse-rotation accessory-drive system, and vice-versa. They will fit, but the blades on the impeller are designed to turn only one direction.

GM introduced the LT1 (Gen II) small block in 1992. The most significant change from the earlier version of the small-block Chevy was the cooling system redesign. It was equipped with a reverse-flow cooling system, which allowed the heads to be cooled first, where the highest heat source is located. This allowed GM to use higher compression, more spark advance, and create lower emissions using lower octane fuels, without the side effects of detonation. The wear on the cylinder walls decreases dramatically when the cooling system operating temperature is 180-degrees Fahrenheit or hotter. The water flowing to cool the cylinders is hotter than it is on standard flow cooling systems, but the cooling of the cylinders is more uniform. On standard-flow systems, the cool water entering the cylinder cooling jackets keeps the number-1 and -2 (front two) cylinders cooler than the other six. This allows the rear cylinders to run much hotter. The thermostat in the LT1 recirculates some of the hot water back into the heads to keep the cooling more uniform and keep cold water from "shocking" any part of the system.

The Gen-I cooling system has water passages in the intake manifold that are susceptible to leaks. The LT1 does not have these. The water pump bearing on the standard-flow system also suffers from side loads from the belt. GM wanted the water pump to last at least 100,000 miles, so the LT1 water pump is driven off of the camshaft, where the bearing and seal are less susceptible to wear. The drawback to having the water-pump seal over the front of the engine is that the Optispark ignition system is right below it. The Optispark is very finicky, and it doesn't like water. If you do so much as mention water around an Optispark distributor, it won't work. You had better hope the LT1 water pump shaft seal doesn't leak.

In 1997, General Motors introduced the LS1 (Gen III) small block. Its cooling system is one that more closely matches that of the Gen-I small block. It utilizes a belt-driven water pump. The water pump feeds cool water directly into the block, where it cools the cylinders first. It then flows up into the heads. The newly designed thermostat system mixes hot water with the incoming cool water. The coolant in the block stays at a more constant temperature, which allows the computer-controlled engine to operate more efficiently.

The LT1 has a transfer tube that connects the back side of the heads together. It allows trapped air and steam to escape from the heads, which can create dangerous hot spots. The transfer tube runs to the upper portion of the radiator. The tube running to the radiator was trimmed off and the hole was threaded so we could run our own fittings and steel braided hose for a better appearance. The tube between the heads was not modified.

Water Pumps

Every cooling system needs a pump to circulate fluid to help minimize hot spots, and automotive cooling systems are no exception. Without a pump to circulate water through the engine, the water surrounding the cylinder walls would boil. That boiling would allow air pockets to form around the cylinder walls. These are called hot spots. Air does not cool as efficiently as water, so these hot spots would allow the cylinders to overheat and cause severe expansion in the block. These extreme conditions could cause the block to crack and other engine parts to seize or fail. The pump moves water around inside the engine and through the radiator, where cooler water resides. The cooler water helps to equalize the system temperature.

An impeller inside the water-pump case circulates the water. The impeller has small blades, which cup the water. The impeller is designed to work in only one direction. Chevrolet small- and big-block water pumps turned the same direction as the crankshaft (clockwise if you are looking at it from the front of the engine) until the mid 1980s. They are referred to as "standard rotation." Reverse-rotation water pumps started showing up on Chevrolet cars and trucks in the mid to late 1980s.

Stock Water Pumps

Most stock water pumps have a stamped-steel impeller. Stock water pumps work great on low-horsepower daily drivers. The impeller fins are designed to move coolant into the engine block at an operating RPM designated for normal driving conditions. The stock water pump impeller loses efficiency because of the straight blade design and it does not have tight tolerances between the case and the blades. GM did not design the stock cooling system with high RPM and excessive heat-producing horsepower in mind. At high RPM, the pump cavitates because the impeller turns too fast. When the pump cavitates, the water is not pumping cool water into the hot engine. Without cool water cycling into the engine, the water gets even hotter. This is not efficient and can cause damage or at least headaches if the system goes through this cycle too often within a short period of time.

Belt-Driven Aftermarket Water Pumps

You should upgrade to an aftermarket water pump when producing more horsepower than your engine had from the factory, considering some track time, or just want to improve the efficiency of your cooling system. Pumps are available in cast iron and aluminum. Meziere, Milodon, Stewart Components, Edelbrock, and FlowKooler are just a few companies offering these pumps. Some pumps are designed to flow better at lower RPM for streetability, and some are designed to operate at high RPM for full-race applications. Make sure to contact the manufacturer for guidance on their products before making a purchase.

Some companies offer OEM housings with upgraded impellers. Others offer completely new designed housings and impellers. Each manufacturer is different. Most aftermarket pumps are

Engines

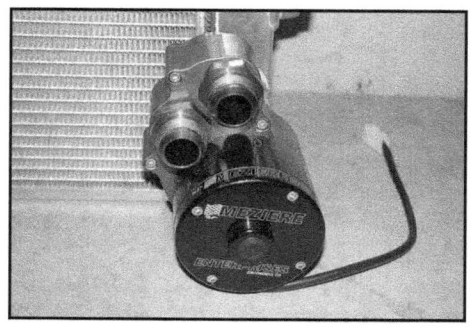

This electric water pump offered by Meziere mounts on the radiator, instead of the front of the engine block. These are rated at 2400 hours of operation before servicing. That is a lot of hours. After you drove your car 2 hours, every single day, for three years, you would need to start thinking about servicing the electric motor.

equipped with low-drag bearings to reduce horsepower needed to drive the unit. If you are worried about weight, aluminum housings are lighter than cast-iron units, and can shave approximately ten pounds off the nose of your engine. Ten pounds does not seem like a lot, but it can add up when coupled with other weight-saving parts. The aluminum also dissipates heat better than cast iron.

The higher-performance water pumps have larger bearings and pump shafts for strength in higher-performance applications. The larger shaft will require a pulley with a larger shaft hole, or you can modify your current pulley. Chevrolet small- and big-block water pumps are available with standard and reverse rotation, so be sure to get the right pump for your application. Chevrolet has offered different pulley bolt patterns, so make sure you are aware of the bolt pattern of your current pulley, if you plan on using it. Some aftermarket pumps come with double or triple bolt-pattern flanges to help with pulley fitment.

Electric Water Pumps

In the past, electric units were made for drag racing only. A drag-racing cooling system has minimal requirements. The pump doesn't need to produce much pressure and the engine is producing extreme heat for twelve seconds or less.

Car owners tried the original belt-driven electric and stand-alone electric water pumps on their street cars with very little success. These bad experiences gave electric water pumps a bad name. There have been some superior advances in electric water pumps in the last 10 years. Not only have the engineering designs changed for the better, but they have also become more reliable. Even with advanced technology, electric water pumps still have a stigma.

A few aftermarket companies offer reliable, high-quality electric water pumps. Meziere Enterprises Inc. is one of those companies. They offer electric units for the Chevrolet small block, TPI, LT1, LT4, LS1, Chevrolet big block, Buick V-6, Buick V-8, Oldsmobile V-8, and Pontiac V-8. In some applications, these pumps can free up as much as 15 horsepower. Depending on the application, these pumps range from 35 to 55 gallons per minute (gpm). Some of these applications require the use of a fitting for use with the lower radiator hose. The fittings are available from Meziere to match your required hose size. These aluminum-bodied pumps are available in red, blue, purple, black, and polished.

Electric water pumps should be running when the engine is on. At any time the pump is not running, the engine could be building up air pockets around the cylinder walls, insulating them from water. This can happen very fast and you would not know it. The gauge won't even register fast enough to show this condition, so do not run the engine without the electric water pump turned on. The beauty of the electric pump is the ability to run the pump even after you shut off the engine.

Electric water pumps operate at the same RPM, no matter fast the engine is running. If you have a 35-gpm water pump, it will be pumping at the same rate at 1000 or 6000 rpm. This helps keep the engine cool at an idle, as well as high RPM. If you get stuck in traffic, the system will be flowing better than a belt driven system.

With the advances of electric water pumps, new remote water pumps have started to become available. The remote pump allows the complete removal of the pump from the front of the engine. This can be useful in custom applications where space between the radiator and a conventional water pump is cramped. Maybe you are installing a turbo or a supercharger, and you need extra space. If you simply want to clean up the front of the engine for an ultra-clean look, a remote pump might be the ticket.

Meziere Enterprises Inc. offers a few different electric remote water pumps. They offer three models that can be mounted in the fenderwell or somewhere near to the lower radiator outlet. They also offer a remote version that mounts directly to the radiator when used with a special bracket that can be tig welded to most aluminum radiators. When using the remote water pump, you will be completely removing the conventional pump from the front of the engine, so you will need special port adapters. These adapters allow you to run hoses directly from the pump to the front of the block.

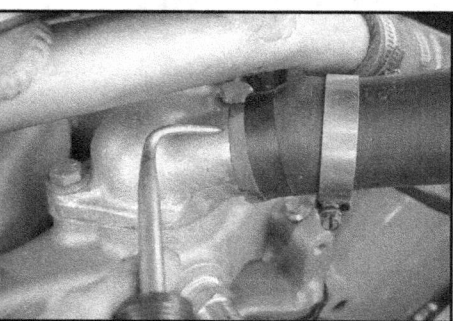 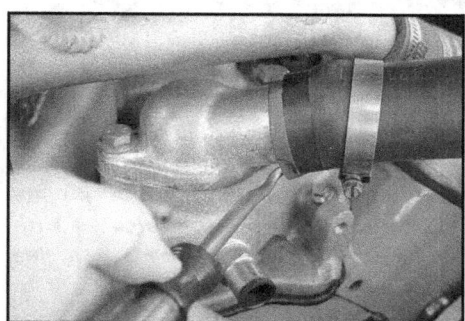

Here is a tip for removing any kind of hose. Stick the curved tip of a cotter pin removal tool between the hose and the water-neck fitting, and move the tip around the circumference. This will break the seal loose so the hose will be much easier to remove. That way you might be able to remove the hose without having to cut it off.

Chapter 5

The port adapter allows the remote pump to hook to the engine block by way of AN fittings and hoses. It has an O-ring that seals against the engine block and eliminates the need for sealant. The paint and sealant were completely removed from the surface that the O-ring will seal against, resulting in a leak-proof seal.

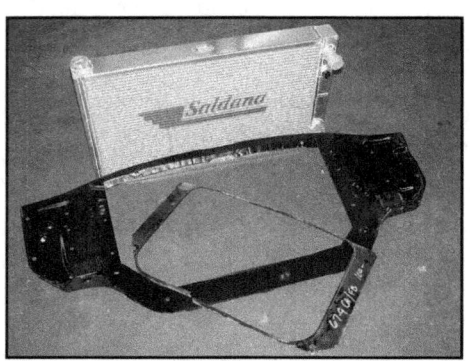

A new universal-fit dual-pass Saldana radiator (notice there are no brackets on the tanks) was chosen for the installation. The Meziere WP362 water pump requires a special mounting plate welded to the radiator, so Saldana installed the plate for me. A reproduction radiator support was modified for the huge radiator that barely fit between the frame rails. A narrower radiator would have been a better choice.

I had Jeff Silvera from Campbell Auto Restoration Services tig weld some mounting brackets to the side of the radiator tanks. I drilled holes in the brackets, and corresponding larger holes in the core support so I could use Wellnuts for mounting. The Wellnuts are made of rubber with a captured nut on the end. When tightening the Wellnut, the tip of it expands to hold the accessory, and still allows for vibration and expansion. Radiators expand, especially aluminum ones, so mounting should allow for some movement.

The pump is mounted to the back plate with more Allen bolts lubricated with anti-seize. The pump was a close fit, due to my choice of radiator to cool the "Millennium Falcon." I chose –16AN fittings coming out of the pump and off the engine block. I used XRP fittings to fully plumb the electric water pump. Keep engine movement in mind when installing the fittings and hose.

Mr. Gasket offer the Robertshaw Thermostat (left), which is the highest flowing thermostat on the market. A Stant unit is shown on the right. If you're not running a bypass in your cooling system, air bubbles can get trapped under the thermostat, and it won't open until it's too late. To solve this, two 1/8-inch holes were drilled in the Stant to bleed trapped air. The Robertshaw has one bleed hole built in (pointer), but I drilled one more hole for extra relief.

Thermostats

The engine operating temperature is regulated by the thermostat. Every thermostat has a temperature rating. The ratings typically range from 160 to 190 degrees. The rating is the temperature at which the thermostat opens. For instance, a 160-degree thermostat will stay closed until the coolant behind it reaches 160 degrees. When the thermostat opens, hot coolant flows through it. Once the coolant flowing through it drops below 160 degrees, the thermostat closes so the coolant can reach 160 degrees again.

Drag-racing applications can benefit from replacing the thermostat with a restrictor plate, since the cooling system only needs to operate for short bursts of time. Pro-Touring cars should be running a thermostat. With the exception of extreme Pro-Touring cars, our cars will probably be driven on the street on a regular basis. Street driving conditions are much different than drag racing conditions. The thermostat is necessary for bringing the car up to operating temperature. It traps water in the engine until it is hot enough to open. A cold running engine will not operate efficiently. Most people think a cool running engine makes more power, since the colder the air-fuel mixture is, the better it burns. This is correct for the intake system on a car. The intake system consists of the carburetor or throttle body, the intake manifold, and the intake system of the cylinder heads. The block and reciprocating assemblies operate better and wear less when the temperature is in the range of 190 to 210 degrees Fahrenheit.

Cooling system experts choose Robertshaw thermostats and Stant Superstats. The Robertshaw is available from many manufacturers, including Mr. Gasket and Flow Kooler. It is the most desirable thermostat since it's the least restrictive when fully open.

Cooling experts suggest drilling two small holes in the outer ring of the thermostat if your cooling system does not have a bypass system. Without a bypass system, air pockets can form under the thermostat. The hot air does effectively heat the thermostat to its temperature rating, so the thermostat will not open. If this happens, your system will fail and your engine will overheat in a hurry. The two small holes help eliminate the build up of hot air under the thermostat.

Radiator

The cooling system is made up of many important components. The radiator is the key to dissipating heat. The radiator is made of tanks, tubes, and fins. Hot coolant flows into one of the radiator tanks. The coolant is pushed through tubes on its way to the tank on the opposite side. In this movement, the heat transfers to the tubes, then the heat transfers from the tubes to the cooling fins, since the tube surface does not dissipate heat effectively. The fins are cooled by air flowing through them, which allows more heat to be transferred from the tubes.

Until the mid 1980s, most production radiators were constructed of copper-brass materials. When manufacturers started trying to make their systems more efficient, the copper brass tube thickness was causing radiators to weigh too much. They had to find alternative material to make radiators lighter, without losing strength. Instead of running four half-inch copper brass tubes .015-inch thick, radiators could be constructed of two one-inch aluminum tubes .016-inch thick, with half the weight and better cooling capacity. If you are trying to lighten up the front of your car, you may want to take into consideration that an aluminum radiator may weigh less in materials, but the bigger tubes hold more coolant. The more coolant, the more weight you will be adding. In Pro-Touring applications, cooling properties should be a higher goal than saving a few pounds of coolant by purchasing a radiator that is too small.

Griffin Radiator, BeCool, C&R Racing Inc, and Saldana Racing Products are just a few companies offering aftermarket aluminum radiators. Each company has a different construction process, and some may not offer direct bolt-in units for your application. Some manufacturers use special epoxy to attach their tubes to the tanks, while some are completely welded. If you want a direct bolt-in radiator for your '67 Pontiac GTO, you may be limited to one or two radiator companies. The bolt-in versions utilize original mounting brackets and correct radiator inlet and outlet sizes and locations. If you are building a custom cooling system and don't require a bolt-in radiator, universal radiators are available from most companies. The universal radiators are usually cheaper, but since they don't have any mounting provisions, some custom mounting and fabrication skill is required. Universals are sold by overall width and height, and are not always offered with different size inlets and outlets.

Custom radiators are available in singe- and dual-pass versions. A single-pass radiator is most common. The hot coolant is forced into the left tank, at the upper left corner of the radiator, where it works its way to the tank on the right side of the radiator and flows back into the engine through the lower right corner. The dual-pass radiator is essentially two single-pass radiators stacked on top of each other. A typical dual-pass design will have the hot coolant enter the upper right corner of the upper right tank. The coolant is forced across the upper section of the radiator to the left tank, where it travels down the left side tank into the lower half of the radiator. The coolant then has to pass from the left side to the lower right side of the tank, where it enters the engine.

Flex-a-Lite offers huge dual electric fans for cars and trucks. This setup consists of two 13.5-inch shrouded electric fans and fits many early GM radiators. It moves a whopping 5500 cfm. There are rubber flaps in the upper right and lower left corners, which help vent air when driving at high speed, but seal up when sitting in traffic for better cooling. The shroud hangs over the edge of this radiator, but could be sealed up with an aluminum filler panel to help seal the face.

Cooling Fans

The cooling system is put to the ultimate test in traffic and road-course racing. The system builds heat in the engine as usual, but the heat is trapped under the hood, where it heat-soaks the engine compartment. The worst part of traffic is not getting flow through the radiator.

I was once told, "If your car overheats in traffic, but runs cool at 60 miles per hour, your radiator is big enough, but you are not getting enough flow through your radiator." There are a couple more factors to this answer. The cooling fans may not flow enough cfm, or you may need a fan shroud to effectively direct air through the entire radiator.

Stock flex fans, like stock clutch fans, are great for stock to moderate performance engines. There are a few aftermarket companies making high-performance flex fans. The aftermarket flex fan is less reciprocating weight compared to stock solid and flex fans. Not all flex fans are created equal. Flex fans are typically rated between 6000 to 8000 rpm, and a few are even higher. They are rated for 4-, 6-, and 8-cylinder engines.

Flex fans have flexible steel fan blades. At low RPM, the blades keep their pre-formed curves, so they can pull as much air through the radiator as possible. This is great for when you are idling in traffic. At high RPM, the blades lose their curve and flatten out. The flat fan blade has less drag on the engine, which, along with their lighter weight, increases power output. This is great for racing, since your car will be moving when your engine is at high RPM, so the fan doesn't need to feed the radiator with air.

When using a stock or aftermarket flex fan, make sure you periodically check the fan blades for defects and cracks. Since the blades flex back and forth constantly, the metal can get fatigued and crack. Think of bending or twisting an aluminum can for a few minutes. It will eventually crack and break. I'm not saying flex fans break a lot, but if they do, they can be very dangerous. I had a stock flex fan break at about 4000 rpm on my '73 Camaro. The fan blade went through the layers of metal in my hood. I never found the blade. Minutes before that, a friend was leaning over my engine, revving the engine after he tuned my carburetor. Be aware of the state of your car and its parts.

Electric Fans

Deciding on what electric fan setup to run can be overwhelming if you don't know what to look for. Besides looking for a fan that will fit in the space you have for a fan setup, the most important thing to look at is the amount of air a fan moves. For instance, a single 15-inch diameter electric fan can move 2800 cfm and a 14.45-inch diameter fan from another company can move 1350 cfm. That is a big difference. Another feature to look for is the amperage that the fan draws. Of those two fans, the 15-inch model draws 13.9 amps, and the 14.45-inch model draws 10.5 amps. The higher the draw, the more power your alternator will need to generate.

Each company offers a variety of single- and dual-fan setups, with different widths, heights, and depths, along with cfm and amperage differences. In some instances, you may get stuck with a lesser-performing fan due to a cramped space. If your car heats up driving around town but stays cool on the freeway, you may need a fan that moves more cfm. Three inches of clearance between your water pump pulley and the radiator may get you stuck with a fan setup that moves half the cfm that a setup would with 4-1/2 inches of clearance. It could cost more money, but if clearance is your problem and you have a long water pump, you could switch to a short water pump or electric remote water pump setup. Driving around with an inferior setup that overheats in normal driving conditions can be unnerving and embarrassing.

You can mount electric fans directly to the radiator, to brackets, or to a fan shroud. Mounting fans to the radiator can be done by using plastic or metal rod kits that slide through the radiator cooling fins. The rod kits come with little locks to hold them from coming loose and causing the fan assembly to fall into the engine. When you cut the excess rod off, leave about 3/8 inch of rod sticking out. The excess rod sticking out is very dangerous cutting hazard, especially if it's metal. Go to your local hardware store and get some rubber screw caps, or some small engine vacuum caps to slip over the protruding rod tips. The first time you are working on your car and rub on one of those caps, you will be thankful you took a little time to do this right. Some fans or integrated fan and shroud systems can be mounted to metal or aluminum straps specifically for the job, or you can fabricate your own. They can be attached with rod kits through the radiator fins, or they might reach far enough to mount to the top or bottom straps of the radiator.

Fans come as pushers and pullers. A pusher fan will need to go in front of the radiator, so it can push air into the radiator. A puller fan needs to be mounted in the rear of the radiator so it can pull air through the radiator. Most electric fans with integral fan shrouds are puller types, since if it were mounted in front of the radiator, then the fan shroud would block the path of airflow. Pusher fans are good for a booster fan if you are running a mechanical fan and need some extra help cooling, and for custom applications without clearance between the radiator and engine.

High-output Pro-Touring cars need at least one electric fan pulling 2800 cfm. I have seen 550 horsepower small-block Chevy engines get by with a single 15-inch puller that moves 2800 cfm. I've also seen 480 horsepower big block cars have lots of issues with dual 12-inch electric fans pulling 2500 cfm. An engine that is out of tune can run hotter, and big-block Chevy engines historically run hotter than small blocks. Cooling systems on moderate to high-horsepower engines in hotter climates would be much happier with at least 3600 cfm. Getting too much cfm is almost impossible, unless you are Tim "The Tool Man" Taylor.

Factory production cars are another good source for electric fan setups. For instance, fourth-generation V-8 F-bodies came equipped from the factory with a dual electric fan setup. It's a complete package of dual 14-inch fans and a fan shroud. The setup measures to be approximately 28x18x5-inches. I have heard this setup moves 3600 cfm. There are plenty of other newer high-output factory electric fan setups that might work with your specific application. You can look at Ford, Dodge, and GM products.

Electric fans can be powered by a manual switch on your dashboard, or by a thermostatic switch. Fixed-range thermostatic switches screw into a water port on the engine or the radiator and have an operating range of 10 to 15 degrees. They can be purchased for whatever range you determine is best for your application. Adjustable thermostatic switches have a probe that either screws into a water port in the cooling system, or they have a probe that pushes into radiator fins near the inlet where the heated water enters. Either way, electric fans draw enough amperage that powering them without a relay can cause enough resistance in the wire to get it real hot. In some cases, the wire can get hot enough to drop the speed of your fans after 15 minutes of

A fan shroud has an inlet and an outlet. The inlet is the area closest to the radiator. The outlet is the section closest to the engine. The inlet is most effective when it is close to the same size as the radiator core. This stock fan shroud seals to the radiator all the way around. Here you can see the tight fit to the top of the radiator. GM knew what they were doing.

Engines

This electric fan will help cool, but the only section of the radiator getting cooled is the diameter of the fan itself. A fan with a shroud would help pull air through a larger section of the radiator. The area of the radiator not covered by the fan does not get airflow while the car is sitting still, when it needs more air to cool the engine.

runtime, or cause the insulation to melt off the wire causing serious problems. A relay mounted close to the fans will run the load-bearing hot wire a much shorter distance, for a much safer connection. If you connect the fan relay with a constant hot, the fans will run after the key is turned off. They will turn off after the engine temperature drops below the switches operating temperature. The companies will tell you not to wire it like this because there is a possibility the fans will run on and drain your battery. They instruct you to run a "keyed" hotwire to the fan relay, so the power is cut off when the ignition key is turned off.

Fan Shrouds

A fan shroud is an important part of getting optimum performance out of your manual or electric cooling fan. The shroud helps channel the airflow through the radiator for optimum cooling. Without a shroud, an electric fan will draw air through a limited section of the radiator. It is less than optimum to pull air through a 12-inch round section of the radiator when using a 12-inch fan. A shroud will help pull air through a larger section of the radiator. A lack of cool air flowing through the cooling surface of the radiator is inefficient and can result in overheating problems.

Running a manual fan without a shroud can produce similar cooling issues. A manual fan is driven by the engine, so it is not as close to the radiator as most electric units. Running a manual fan without a shroud will allow the fan to whip the air around in the engine compartment instead of pulling it through the radiator effectively. The air that does get pulled through the radiator only comes through an area about the same diameter as the fan. Increasing the shroud inlet size increases the cooling area. The best design would have the inlet of the shroud be the same size as the radiator core. The fan diameter should be about one inch less than the diameter of the outlet opening of the fan shroud.

People like to take the shroud off and throw it away. This is a bad idea because along with helping airflow, the shroud also helps keep the engine compartment safer while the engine is running. The fan, weather it's electric or manual, can be dangerous when you are working on your engine. Electric fans wired to engage solely by a thermostatic temperature sensor can turn on at anytime. Fingers or loose clothing pose a safety hazard if the fan kicks on when you least expect it. Fingers and loose clothing pose the same hazards for manual fans while the engine is running. The fan shroud doesn't eliminate the danger, but it helps.

Radiator Air Ducting

Street driven cars at normal driving speeds can get away without adding any additional ducting to keep the air traveling through the radiator, instead of all the other places it could go. If you're adding additional coolers or an air conditioning condenser, make sure you are getting enough air to these accessories and the radiator.

Oiling System

The engine oiling system consists of oil, oil pump, pump pickup, oil pan, oil filter, and the engine block's oil passages.

The oil system capacity is determined by how much oil the oil-pan sump will hold. Adding external filters and hoses adds the need for more oil in the system, but does not change the amount of oil in the oil pan. If a high-volume oil pump is used in a small-block Chevy that pumps 5 quarts of oil out of a stock pan into the valve covers at high RPM, the pan will be empty — even if you have two more quarts of oil in relocated oil filters and an external oil cooler. Some builders will put oil restrictors in the block to allow less oil to get to the top end of the engine. This helps, but adding a higher capacity oil pan will help even more. That is why some engine builders prefer to use high-pressure oil pumps in engines with stock-size pans. It will increase oil pressure, but will not suck a stock pan dry like a high-volume oil pump will in the right conditions.

There are two types of oil systems available for engines: wet-sump and dry-sump systems. Of the two systems, I will be covering wet-sump systems more than dry sumps, since the latter is very uncommon on street-driven cars.

A wet-sump system is the most common and holds the majority of its oil in the oil pan sump, hence the term "wet sump." All GM production cars run wet-sump systems. They are cheaper to build and maintain. Wet-sump systems are self-contained, with an internal oil pump (indirectly driven by the camshaft, or the crankshaft on the Gen-III small block) and a pickup in the oil pan. Until recent years, GM production vehicles did not have external oil lines.

Dry-sump systems hold the majority of their oil in an external oil tank, not in the sump of the oil pan, hence the term "dry sump." Dry-sump systems require an external pump turned by the camshaft or a crank-driven belt. Any problem with the drive system or hose failure will cause serious engine failure. Dry-sump systems are more expensive than wet-sump systems, due to the added components and plumbing. A dry-sump system is the safest way to keep your engine pressurized with oil. Oil is continuously pumped by one chamber of the pump into the external oil tank, where a constant supply of oil is available for another cham-

Chapter 5

ber of the pump to feed the engine. Depending upon the application, the available capacities range from 4 to 14 quarts. Under harsh acceleration, braking, and cornering, the pickups in the oil pan will be sucking air, which could cause damage to the engine with a wet-sump system. They allow for a very low-profile oil pan, which allow racers to set the engine closer to the ground for a lower center of gravity. The dry-sump pump removes the oil from the pan to eliminate it from sloshing up during extreme conditions and hitting the crankshaft and rods, where it robs power from the engine.

Oil Filters

Not all oil filters are created equal. There are many different oil filters on the market. Only a few of them are suited for performance applications. If you are going to drive your car hard, you should get a performance filter. Performance-oriented filters have better filtering media and thicker cases to increase the burst pressure to at least 500 psi to protect against rock and stone damage. Wix Racing filters with an "R" after the part number to denote the racing filter series, which are individually wrapped to keep out contaminants. K&N Filters offers Performance Gold filters that have an additional one-inch wrench nut on the end with a provision for safety wiring. Fram also offers Racing series filters for performance applications.

Windage Tray

During harsh driving conditions, oil sloshes around enough in the oil pan, that it can come into contact with the crankshaft. This contact can rob power from the engine. A windage tray is basically a shield located between the crankshaft and the oil. It not only keeps the oil off the rotating assembly, but it also keeps it in the pan, so the pickup does not become uncovered and suck air into the oil pump and the system.

Many aftermarket manufacturers offer their own versions of windage trays. Milodon is one of those companies. They offer two types of windage

This is a Milodon Diamond Stripper screen-type windage tray. The screen openings are positioned so the slinging oil will travel through but not splash back. Since the screen is curved, it can scavenge oil from the crank better than the flat tray. The screen is not bolted down.

trays: louvered trays and screen trays. Their testing of these trays has shown real-world gains on 400 horsepower engines. The louvered trays have shown up to 12- to 15-horsepower increases, and their screen trays have shown up to a 25-horsepower gain. The louvers allow oil to fly off the crank into the pan, where the tray is able to keep the oil. With the right screen trays, they do this job even better, by allowing more holes for the oil to travel into the pan at a higher rate. The screens are built with the pattern going in the optimum direction to let all the oil pass through when flung from the crankshaft, but not fly back up to the rotating assembly.

Windage trays are connected to the oil pan, or they are bolted to crankshaft main studs and the oil-pump bolt or stud. If your frame and suspension limits your oil pan clearance, you can use a stock or stock shaped aftermarket oil pan. Some of these oil pans have windage trays welded inside near the top of the sump. The bolt-in windage trays require a windage tray install kit, which includes main studs that feature extra threads on the ends for tray height adjustment. Milodon says you can adjust the windage tray to no closer than .100 inch of clearance to the rotating assembly (crankshaft and rods). These studs typically have an extended length of 5/16-inch threaded stud on the end of

Using an old sheetmetal brake, we were able to modify the screen to fit over the mains, while allowing the oil pan to fit correctly. It would have taken more time if we had to use a hammer and some wood to bend the tray, but this is very doable. The screen can be adjusted close (a minimum of .10 inch) to the rotating assembly for extra pan clearance. Rotate the crank at least one revolution in each direction to ensure clearance. You can see the stud extension with the two nuts holding the tray.

the main stud. The extra length of stud should be left as long as possible (without interfering with the oil pan), just in case you eventually want to switch the style of tray or spend some more money on getting a stroker upgrade. Replacing the main studs on your second buildup, because the studs were cut 1/2 inch too short, is an unnecessary expense.

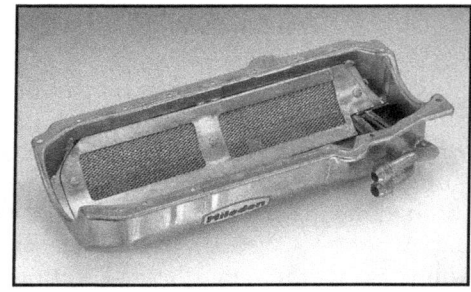

This Milodon dry-sump oil pan obviously lacks a large reservoir like a wet-sump pan. A dry-sump pump would suck the pan dry through the two pipes shown. This dry-sump pan has a windage screen to assist oil scavenging. (Photo courtesy of Milodon)

Engines

This is called a trap door. Behind this trap door is a hole in the baffle wall. Oil on the other side of this baffle can push through this door during a hard right hand corner, so it can keep the oil-pump pickup covered. The wire on the hinge will only allow it to move up a limited amount.

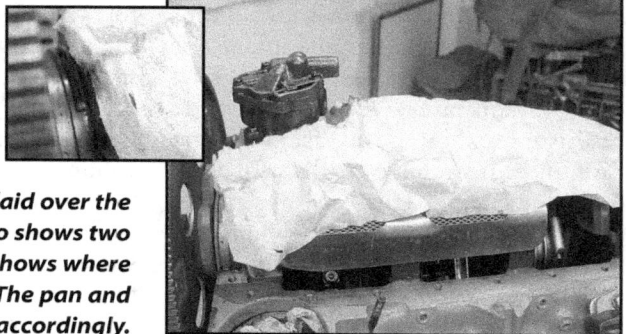

With my new Milodon Diamond Stripper windage tray installed, the oil pan was test fitted. There was a little interference, so the oil pan was test fit with clean paper towels laid over the windage tray. The inset photo shows two small cuts in the towel. This shows where the interference was. The pan and windage tray were adjusted accordingly.

Even after flattening the back of the oil pickup, the pan had to be dimpled outward with a ball-peen hammer in order to clear the Melling oil pump's pickup. Apparently Melling changed their design a few times in the past, but Milodon makes sure all their pumps are the same. If I had bought a Milodon pump, it would have fit without modification.

A tip for installing any part is to get all the bolts started before tightening any of them. The gasket kept the pan up a little bit. After a little work, the gasket compressed enough to start all the bolts. Maybe Milodon's gasket would work better with their pan. In case you wonder what the bungs on the side of the pan are for, I had the pan modified for a custom oil system.

With the engine tilted up all the way, it would not fit into place. The frame stands were keeping the engine from going into place. The arrow points to the frame stand that we unbolted from the frame. Once the stand was out of the way, the engine slid right in. Once the engine was in place, we reinstalled the stand and slid the steering rack in from the left side of the car.

Dry-Sump Oil Pans

Since very few Pro-Touring cars will have dry-sump systems, I will be covering them very briefly. They are very low profile. They usually only have about one inch of clearance between the rotating assembly and the bottom of the oil pan. They have pickup tubes that run the length of the pan with little inertia-baffles, or they have multiple pickups so the oil can be picked up during hard acceleration, braking, and cornering. Since the dry-sump system does not rely on the pan for its oil supply, a little air sucked up by the pan pickup won't kill the engine. As with most parts, dry-sump oil pans are designed differently for road racing, circle tracking, and drag racing. Make sure you buy the right pan for your application.

Wet-Sump Oil Pans

Since Pro-Touring cars are meant to be driven fast around corners, a stock pan might not be adequate for your application. Stock pans don't hold much oil compared to aftermarket oil pans, and are barely suited for mild performance engines and/or road-course driving. Aftermarket street/strip pans are designed to control the oil from front to rear, and the oil pickup can get uncovered. The engine's reciprocating parts don't work well without oil. They typically hold 2 to 2.5 quarts more oil than a stock pan. They also hang down, limiting your ground clearance. When you are building a Pro-Touring car, a step to getting better handling is to lower the car for better center of gravity, so ground clearance is a common issue.

A road-race pan has trap doors to control the oil from moving in every direction. This keeps the oil pickup covered with oil so the engine components will stay happy. Installing a street/strip pan is adequate for mild performance driving on a road course. When you dial in your suspension, have extremely good brakes, and sticky tires on a road course, you will need an oil pan designed for road racing. Road-race pans have a wider sump than street/strip pans, so they can hold as much oil or more. They are typically shallower than street/strip pans, so ground clearance can be even better, while still increasing the oil capacity.

Since road-race pans bigger sumps, it is hard to find one that fits your application. They can interfere with headers, or at least get close enough to heat up your oil without a thermal barrier. The biggest hurdle to jump is possible interference with steering linkage, especially if you're working with a first-generation F-body or a first- or second-generation X-body. Some interference problems can be overcome with the right combination of steering components from correctly optioned models. For instance, '67 Camaro manual steering idler and pitman arms are longer than '68 and '69 power steering idler and pitman arms. I'm not sure they will help your steering geometry and steering ratio, but the longer arms will net about a half-inch of clearance between the pan and the steering linkage. Cars that are front steer may not have any steering interference issues. Consult the manufacturer's technical department about your engine size and chassis type for the correct road-race pan before laying down money for one.

When upgrading to a new oil pan, you will need to buy the proper oil pump pickup for it. Each pickup is designed specifically for each pan. In fact they are also designed around specific oil pumps too. Oil pump companies don't have any kind of standard. So, it is a good idea to purchase your oil pump and oil pump pickup from the same company you purchase your oil pan from. That way you know the pan, pump, and pickup will all fit when you go to bolt them up. It's pretty frustrating to buy a pan and pickup and hope to bolt it all on over a weekend, to only find out they don't fit. You may later find out your oil pump was made by a manufacturer that changed the pump design four times within a couple of years. A 3/8-inch change is huge when you are working with tight tolerances in the oil pan. The oil pump pickup is supposed to be 3/8 of an inch from the bottom of the oil pan. If it is too far from the bottom of the pan, it could starve easily under hard driving conditions. If the pickup is too close to the bottom of the pan, it will be too restricted and not be able to feed enough oil to the engine. Or it could cause so much suction it will pull the pan in and out at different RPM and eventually cause the bottom of the pan to fail from fatigue.

GM's stock oil-pump pickups are pressed into the oil pump, with few exceptions. It takes a special tool to help drive the pickup onto the pump. Good aftermarket pickups are an interference fit with the oil pump, like the stock pickup, but also have a tab with a hole. That extra tab mounts under one of the screws that hold the bottom cover on the oil pump. Having that extra positive locking mechanism is great insurance. It's a huge headache if your oil pump pickup falls off your pump, and it can cost you a lot of money. It doesn't take much to suck the oil down far enough to uncover the oil pump's suction port when the pickup is swimming around in your pan.

All this information about oil pans, pumps, and pickups is not just a scare tactic — it is written from personal experience. These problems can happen to anyone. So, the moral to all this is: Don't mess around with your oil system. The oiling system is very fickle and it doesn't take much to cause expensive problems.

Oil Cooling

When driving your Pro-Touring car hard at a road course, your engine oil temperature will climb higher than you have ever imagined it could. On a road course, you keep the RPM up and the engine working harder than any other type of driving you do. The water-cooling system is usually hotter too. All the components under the hood are hot from trapped air under the hood. Your engine oil can climb to 260 degrees or more. There are a few ways to cool the engine oil. You can run an external cooler in front of your radiator or a cooler built into the radiator. The other way is to run a heat exchanger.

Aftermarket radiators are available for serious performance applications with oil coolers built directly into the radiator. This helps keep the oil cooler, but at the same time, it heats up your coolant. Think of your engine oil running about 265 degrees, and your engine coolant running about 215 degrees. The oil will be trying to dissipate heat to the coolant, and since the water is considerably cooler, it will cool the oil. This can be a happy relationship if your coolant system is extremely efficient. The oil cooler in the radiator can also work in the opposite way during normal day-to-day driving conditions. The engine could take forever to heat up to operating temperatures. The water could cool the oil too much to effectively protect your engine.

An external oil cooler in front of the radiator will transfer less heat to the cooling system directly, but since there will be hot air flowing through the oil cooler into the radiator, you will get some extra heating in the coolant system. The best external coolers on the market are Setrab coolers. They are known worldwide and supply many manufacturers. They are stacked plate design and are durable in racing environments. There are a few companies offering copies of lesser quality, and there are a few companies re-labeling Setrab coolers as their own. Check with your vendor if you care to get the best cooler on the market.

A heat exchanger works as an oil cooler. Coolant runs through plumbing that runs through the oil system. This allows the heat from the oil to transfer to the cooling system and vice versa. This helps equalize the two temperatures for better performance and longevity. GM has been using a small heat exchanger on its trucks for a few years. It is plumbed through a sandwich adapter located between the oil filter and the engine block. I've been told by a heat-exchanger company that the GM truck system is good up to about 450 horsepower. A larger external heat exchanger is good enough for higher horsepower levels, depending on the system. Typically you will only find heat exchangers on high-dollar race cars. They use bypass systems that close off the oil going to the exchanger until oil operating temperatures have been met. This combats the problem of getting engine fluids up to proper operating temperature. This allows for faster warm-up times and better (less) engine wear.

Engines

Induction and Fuel Systems

The most important elements in making power are air and fuel. Getting the correct air/fuel ratio into and out of the combustion chamber is the key to making power. There are a few ways to get them into the engine. Natural aspiration through a carburetor is the oldest way to feed an engine. Fuel injection can be more efficient if it's tuned properly. To increase power, you can cram more air and fuel into the engine by bolting on a turbocharger or supercharger. Of course, don't forget, first you have to get the fuel to the carburetor or fuel injection system.

There are at least a few separate books for each one of the subjects covered in this chapter. There is too much information out there to fit it all into this section, so they will be covered briefly.

Carburetors

Carburetors are rated by how many cubic feet per minute (cfm) they flow. This rating is helpful in choosing a carburetor depending on the number of cubic inches or potential hp output of an engine. You can over-carburete an engine. Bolting a big 750-cfm carb on a stock small-block 350 is overkill, and the engine will not operate at its optimum potential. If you bolt a little 600-cfm carb on a 427-ci Chevrolet built for high-RPM potential, it will not run correctly. There are charts and information to help find the carb for your application, but it's best to consult an experienced professional on your application, because charts and suggested cfm ratings can differ from one manufacturer to another. So it's best to consult a knowledgeable professional, such as a technician form the carb company, or an experienced carburetor guy at a speed shop. If you get the wrong size carb, your performance potential can be limited by over carbureting and running too rich, or by under carbureting and running too lean. In extreme cases, running excessively rich can cause fuel contamination in the oil, which thins the oil and can lead to internal engine failure. Running too lean can cause overheating and possibly piston failure. These conditions can happen with the correct sized carb that is seriously out of tune, so if you don't know what you are doing, be sure to consult a professional who does.

Before choosing a carburetor size, choose your carburetor company. There are a few common ones on the market today. Each one has its benefits for different applications. Some carburetors are better for trouble-free street driving, some are best for street/strip driving, and some are better for performance driving, such as road-course racing. The well-known aftermarket carburetor companies include Holley, Barry Grant Demon Carbs, Carter, and Edelbrock. Factory remanufactured replacement Rochester carbs are also available from a few companies. There are also shops that rebuild and power tune factory and aftermarket carburetors. The best way to tune a carburetor for optimum fuel efficiency and power is to take your car to a shop equipped with a dynamometer, where an air-fuel meter can be connected to the exhaust with an oxygen sensor. With this equipment, the shop can fine tune your car's fuel system while putting the entire mechanical drivetrain under load.

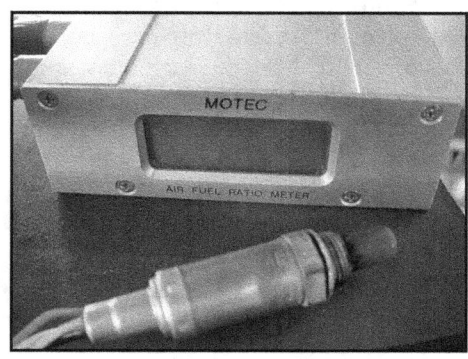

This MoTeC air/fuel ratio meter is used to help tune the carburetor or fuel injection. By installing an oxygen sensor in the exhaust system shortly after the header collector, you can correctly read the air/fuel mixture. The MoTeC meter shows the mixture ratio in an easy-to-read digital display that reads to two decimal points. It is an indispensable tool for fuel-injection tuning. By checking the readout, you can easily tell if you are getting lean or rich conditions anywhere in the entire RPM range.

Fuel injectors are fed and held to the runner by way of a fuel rail. You see the fuel pressure regulator mounted on the fuel rail (far right). Some systems have a fuel balance tube that connects the rails. This system on Stan Davis's Buick V-6 has a regulator on each rail. (Photo courtesy Joe Pettitt)

Fuel Injection

If you are tired of tuning your carburetor, you can step up to a fuel-injection system. Compared to carburetors, fuel-injection systems are completely tunable, and the torque curve is usually more level and kicks in earlier in the RPM range. There are throttle-body injection (TBI) systems and direct-point fuel-injection (DPFI) systems. Throttle-body injection has a single point of injection (one area, on top of the intake manifold), where port injection has multiple ports (injectors). DPFI has many other commonly known names, such as: direct-port fuel injection, direct fuel injection, multi-port fuel injection, port fuel injection, and more. These are available from factory donor vehicles and aftermarket companies. Mechanical fuel injection is far from fuel efficient, so it will not be written about in this book.

Fuel-injection systems are built from two types of components: electronics and hardware. Electronic components include the ECM, wire harness, and sensors. The hardware components are: the manifold, throttle body, injectors, fuel rails, fuel pressure regulator, and fuel pump.

Fuel-injection systems come in many different configurations and manifold designs. Direct-port fuel-injection (DPFI) systems are superior to throttle-body injection (TBI) systems and are the

Chapter 5

Each of the eight runners on this Accel SuperRam intake manifold share a common plenum. The large open plenum on the top feeds all eight intake runners.

Each runner on this Mark Stielow-built intake manifold operates individually. They don't share a plenum or any airflow. This intake manifold is on Charley Lillard's Mule.

This is the dual-plane Tri-Power fuel-injection manifold on Joe Sura's '67 Pontiac GTO. It's actually a form of a common plenum manifold, but the dividers under the carburetors were removed. The carburetors have also been converted to throttle bodies.

only systems we will be considering for Pro-Touring use. TBI systems were used early on in General Motor's quest for fuel-injection performance. TBI systems are not generally thought of as much of a performance upgrade over a good carburetor setup, and therefore are not going to be recommended.

Do not get the term "throttle body" confused with TBI injection. A throttle body of some kind is also used on all DPFI systems. The difference is that in a TBI system, the throttle body actually contains two fuel injectors. Since the air and fuel all flow into the manifold at a single point, a TBI system still utilizes the intake manifold to try and distribute the air-fuel mixture evenly to all the cylinders.

All manifolds and throttle bodies in DPFI systems deliver air only. In almost every configuration, fuel is injected at the base of the intake manifold directly into the runner of the cylinder head. Therefore, there must be an injector for every cylinder. There are two distinct styles of intake manifold designs: plenum-style manifolds, and individual-runner manifolds. Plenum-style manifolds have central throttle body that feeds into a central common plenum. This plenum branches off into individual runners that flow to each intake port in the heads. Individual-runner manifolds do not share any common area, and have individual throttle bodies and injectors for each runner.

Examples of plenum-style systems are GM tuned port (TPI), GM LT1/LT4, Accel SuperRam, GM Ramjet, and converted single-plane or open-plenum carbureted manifolds. Examples of individual-runner systems are converted stack or ram injector intakes like ones available from Hilborn or Crower, or Weber-style manifolds with throttle body replacements made to replace the Weber carburetors.

One of the fun things about fuel-injection conversions is the fact that almost any manifold and throttle body combo that will deliver air can be made to work as a fuel-injection intake. With some creative thinking, some builders have merged vintage intake styles with updated electronic fuel injection. An original intake manifold can be modified to accept fuel injectors, and even vintage-looking carburetors can be altered to serve as throttle bodies, making for a nice blend of performance and looks.

Fuel Feed Systems

The fuel has to get to the carburetor or fuel injection system from the fuel tank. The feed system consists of the fuel, tank, pickup, filter, pump, and line. If this system is not upgraded when you upgrade your engine and its induction system, you won't be able to optimize the performance. In some cases, you can damage the engine from starving the induction system and running lean.

Fuel Tanks

In the past, fuel tanks were not designed very well. Fuel tanks in cars built after the mid 1980s are designed with baffles around the fuel pump and pickup. Flaws in older designs first became evident to drag racers. During straight-line acceleration, the fuel would rush to the rear of the fuel tank, leaving the fuel pickup uncovered. Without fuel covering the pickup, the pump could not suck fuel from the tank. The fuel in the system would feed the carb until the line ran dry, which could happen in a matter of a few seconds. Once the car stumbled and slowed down from running out of fuel, the fuel would slosh towards the front of the tank, where the pickup could suck fuel again, instead of fumes.

Pro-Touring cars have the same problem, but not from straight-line acceleration. The pickup gets uncovered by turning left and right. Drag racers found resolution by putting a sump in the rear of the tank, where the fuel is during straight-line acceleration. Although this move not common for Pro-Touring builders, they can gain some resolution by installing a sump in the rear, as long as it's baffled. A non-baffled lower sump will not help contain the sloshing fuel during cornering. A few companies offer fuel tanks for older cars with built-in baffles to keep the fuel trapped around the fuel pump pickup. Aeromotive offers a tank with a baffled rear sump that is a direct replacement for many popular GM cars. Rock Valley Antique Auto Parts offers replacement fuel tanks built out of stainless steel with internal baffling (without lower rear sump). They also have options for internal fuel injection pumps, and offer tanks for selected GM cars from 1931 to 1969.

If you are building a Pro-Touring car or racer and don't have constraints of using a stock fuel tank, you can step up to a fuel cell. They come in different forms. The less expensive fuel cells are typically a polyethylene outer shell with aviation foam inside to assist in baffling. The safer and more expensive fuel cells have a metal outer shell with an inner bladder filled with internal fuel strainers and foam baffles. The inner bladder is the wearing part. If you are purchasing a fuel cell for a long-term project car, make sure to check the company's fuel cell warranty. If the warranty is for five years or less, and your car doesn't get running for 2 years, you will be limiting the lifespan of the bladder. So you may want to purchase your fuel cell towards the end of your project.

Fuel Pumps

There are performance mechanical and electric fuel pumps available for all power ranges. All fuel pumps are rated by gallons per hour (gph) and how many psi they maintain. For a carbureted engine, you need 6.5 to 7.5 psi. Any more than that, and the fuel will push past the needle and seat in the carburetor and cause a rich running condition or flooding, depending on severity. If you install a pump with more psi, a fuel pressure regulator is necessary between the fuel pump and carburetor. Mechanical fuel pumps are pretty basic, since they all have a specific place they mount on the block. They are available up to 130 gph and 15 psi for high-revving engines.

Most builders prefer to have their higher-output engines fed by electric fuel pumps, since it does away with the stock style mechanical pump, which robs a little power from the engine. Since the pump is mounted on the side of the engine, it transfers heat to the fuel as it passes through the pump. For standard applications, electric fuel pumps mount in two places, either in the fuel tank or outside of it. In-tank pumps are mounted inside the fuel tank and are immersed in the fuel. Ninety-nine percent of externally mounted electric fuel pumps are "pushers," which means they push fuel better than they suck it from the tank. Pushers need to be mounted as close to the tank and its fuel pump pickup as possible. Electric fuel pump companies suggest mounting the fuel pump within 12 inches from the tank. If you mount the fuel pump ten feet from the fuel tank, the pump will not be running at optimum performance. It will not be able to supply the engine with enough fuel and your car will be plagued with driveability problems.

This Aeromotive 11101 fuel pump has a large aluminum body and a nice flat mounting flange. It requires O-ring-sealed –10AN fittings, not pipe-thread fittings. Do not use any type of sealant on the threads. For ease of mounting, their fuel filter can be threaded right into the fuel pump using the fitting shown.

The Fuel System Solutions Power Pickup is installed in conjunction with your fuel system. It allows stock fuel tanks to be run within 1/8th of a tank without letting your engine run out of gas. Fuel cells can be run almost bone dry without letting the engine skip a beat. This is a big help when running fuel injection with a stock tank, but it even works great when used in conjunction with fuel cells and carbureted systems.

Not all fittings are created equal. As you can see, the fitting on the left has a huge step on its inlet. The XRP fitting on the right is "flowed" much better and has a gradual inlet. With fuel- and oil-system plumbing, restrictions like the one on the left can add up fast and really hurt your flow.

This Aeromotive fuel pressure regulator, part number 13204, is used with carbureted applications. It is a bypass-style regulator that requires a –8AN return line. It is adjustable from 3 to 14 psi. It requires AN fittings with O-rings, not pipe-thread fittings. Don't use any thread sealer. Using 90-degree fittings to feed the carburetor can be a little restrictive, so fittings no a bend no larger than 45 degrees should be used for better flow. The 1/8-inch plug is a provision to mount a pressure gauge.

Regulators

Fuel pressure regulators do as their name suggests. Performance fuel pumps push more pressure than the carburetor or fuel injection can handle. This is necessary to keep fuel flowing to the engine under load when it demands more. The regulator regulates the pressure to the predetermined amount (on nonadjustable versions) or the pressure you designate yourself (on adjustable versions). Each regulator is designed for a specific job. High-performance regulators are designed to operate at full potential with a specific fuel pump, so if you are running an Aeromotive fuel pump, you should get the properly matched regulator. Some are also designed specifically for turbocharged and supercharged boost demands, with a vacuum boost port that increases fuel pressure during boost conditions.

They should be mounted as the manufacturer suggests. The regulator is typically mounted within 12 inches of the carburetor or fuel injection. Some racetracks won't let you race if your fuel pressure regulator is mounted on the firewall, since it would be in the path of the flywheel and clutch, if either were to fail and scatter. It is better to mount the regulator in a place that is not too close to a heat source, unless it's shielded.

Some regulators work without a return line to the fuel tank (called a static or dead-head system). Dead-head systems require the fuel pump to cavitate, since the pump has to pressurize the feed line up to the regulator. It holds the fuel in the feed line and only allows (for instance) 7.5 psi to flow past the regulator to the carburetor. The feed line is kept at a higher pressure, and the pump just sits there and cavitates. Some dead-head regulators make loud knocking noises, caused by the piston or ball cavitating while the pump keeps higher pressure against it. This cavitation can also cause the regulator to not supply enough fuel when the engine demands it, which can cause engine damage if it runs lean.

A carbureted system with a fuel return line has a feed line plumbed into the regulator from the fuel tank and a line that returns all fuel over 7.5 psi back to the fuel tank. Fuel pressure regulators on injection systems mount after the fuel rail, which allows the fuel to come from the tank, pass through the fuel rails to the injectors, then the regulator returns the excess fuel to the tank. The fuel return system allows the fuel pump to constantly flow at its full potential while the regulator keeps only the necessary fuel where your engine needs it.

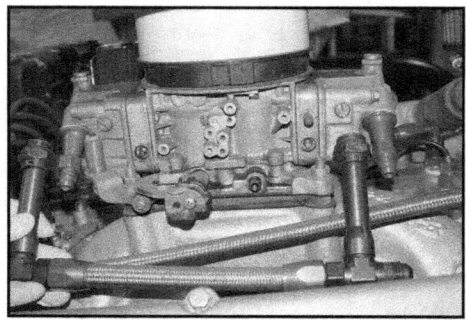

Fuel inlet lines are important. The fuel line held up has 90-degree fittings that can restrict flow to the carburetor. The Johns Fuel Systems –6 high-flow fuel inlet fittings are shown threaded into the fuel bowls. (Photo courtesy JFS)

Fuel Line

High-performance engines demand more fuel. You can upgrade all the components of your fuel system, but you will be limiting the system's potential if you don't upgrade the fuel line from the rear of the car to the front. For instance, a '68 Camaro equipped with a 6-cylinder had a 5/16-inch fuel line that ran from the tank to the fuel pump. This fuel line will not support the small-block Chevy, let alone a big-block Chevy V-8. The higher-output small-block V-8 '68 Camaros had a 3/8-inch fuel line running from front to rear. This is great for big and small blocks, up to the 400-horsepower range, but is not sufficient for much more than that. Once you move into the moderate performance levels (400 + horsepower), you need to upgrade to a larger fuel line. Better fuel system performance companies will be able to answer questions about what size fuel lines should be run with your specific application. For instance, Aeromotive Inc. suggests running a –10-AN (5/8-inch) feed line and a –8-AN (1/2-inch) return line with a 480-hp 433-ci big block built for street and road-course racing. A 5/8-inch fuel line might seem like a lot, but if you spend the money on the pump and regulator, you should listen to what the company suggests. They know their products better than anyone else. High-performance engines are demanding at high RPM, and the fuel line sizes need to be stepped up. It's very annoying to spin the motor up and have it cut out because the fuel pump just can't get the volume to the engine.

The other fuel lines need to be upgraded too. Sucking fuel out of the tank through a stock 3/8-inch fuel pump pickup will defeat the purpose of upgrading the size of the fuel feed line. Make sure your fuel hoses and fuel fittings are not too restrictive. Running a 5/8-inch feed line into a –6-AN (3/8-inch) fuel filter creates a bottleneck and defeats the purpose of running a large feed line. Be careful when using fuel fittings. Bent fittings come in two different types. There is a "forged" style and a less restrictive "tube" style. Every 90-degree forged fitting decreases the flow. Some companies offer fittings that are "flowed" better than others. A few restrictive fittings will hurt the engine's performance potential.

When running feed and return lines, I have found Moroso aluminum fuel line to be the easiest to use. It can easily be bent by hand. But be careful, because you can kink it if you bend it too far. Before installing the aluminum hard line, take a few items into consideration. Don't run fuel line (or any line that carries important or flammable liquid) in the transmission tunnel, because if you ever break a universal joint or a driveshaft, the flying parts can possibly damage the lines within reach. The lines should not be the lowest hanging part of the underside of your car. They should not be in a position to be ripped from the car if you were to drive off the road course or pull off the highway on a soft or uneven shoulder. Every 90-degree bend is another restriction in the system; so if a 90-degree bend is necessary, try to make it a sweeping bend, rather than a tight bend. With the aluminum hard line, you can use tube nuts so you can use fittings to connect it to accessories. Otherwise you will need to run a short section of hose between the hard line and the accessory.

Engines

All fuel systems require a fuel filter installed before the pump. Fuel-injection systems should have an additional filter between the pump and the fuel injection. This Aeromotive fuel filter is 5 inches long and 2 inches in diameter, and has a cleanable stainless-steel 100-micron filter media. O-ring style -10AN fittings are required to plumb it into the fuel system.

Fuel Filters

On carbureted systems, at least one filter should be mounted between the tank and the pump. Some pumps have such tight tolerances that a small piece of debris will cause the pump to jam. On fuel-injection systems, filtering is even more important. The injectors are much more susceptible to getting clogged than a fuel pump, because the injector clearances are so precise. A clogged injector has the potential to lean burn a hole in your piston. That is why it is suggested to run a filter between the tank and the pump, and another between the pump and the fuel rails, just for an extra point of filtering protection.

Turbocharging

Turbocharged street cars have become more common in the last few years than ever before. With the introduction of computer-controlled fuel-injection systems and new turbo technology, some of the turbo woes of the past have diminished. One of the problems that still exists is that the boost kicks in sooner than with a supercharger, which makes it harder to modulate on a road racing setup.

Running an intercooler is more effective on a system running above 6 to 7 pounds of boost. Intercoolers come in two types: air-to-air and air-to-liquid/water. If you have a way to feed a steady supply of cooled water to the intercooler, the air-to-liquid units are more efficient. They just require more plumbing and weigh more due to the liquid and extra equipment necessary to cool it.

Supercharging

There are a few types of superchargers available. The two most common superchargers are the Roots-type and the centrifugal. The most popular type in the 1980s was the Roots-type supercharger. It was really cool to have a big 6-71 or 8-71 Roots blower sticking out of your hood with the carbs and air cleaner sitting as high as the roofline of your car. These big Roots-type superchargers are not fuel-efficient, they generate lots of heat, they obstruct the driver's vision, and they make a lot of noise. Every once in a while, auto manufacturers play around with blowers and offer them to the public on special-option vehicles. In 1995, GM started introducing smaller Roots-type blowers on production vehicles. These Roots-type blowers are starting to be more common on production cars, but they are smaller and quieter than the 6-71.

Hot rodders in the 1990s have changed their building ideas to being a little more subtle. They were building more hot rods with all the performance parts under uncut hoods. Car guys still want big power, but they don't want their source of power to be obvious to everyone, including local authorities; so people started moving to centrifugal superchargers. Centrifugal superchargers had been around for at least 70 years in one form or another, but are getting more popular. These units had previously been very noisy, but a drive design change in the early 1990s made them more bearable on the ears. By the late 1990s, centrifugal supercharger technology had vastly improved. The newer centrifugal units are better built, more suited for fuel-injection systems, available for more applications, and some even include a warranty. The most popular centrifugal supercharger companies are Vortech Engineering, Accessible Technologies Inc (ATI), and Paxton Automotive.

Designing a twin-turbo setup on an early-model car is a huge undertaking, unless you can adapt a kit made for a late-model car. Vince Asaro spent hundreds of hours designing this setup to fit within the constraints of his El Camino's engine compartment. Turbos are becoming more popular, especially since the new computer-controlled fuel injection allows you to tune for optimum performance, fuel mileage, and driveability.

Some people prefer to advertise their engine combinations a little less than others. This is part of the reason that centrifugal superchargers are becoming more popular than Roots-type units, since they are easier to fit inside the engine compartment. Tony Laruffa installed this D-2 ATI Procharger in his 461-ci big-block-powered '81 Chevy Malibu. It sucks in cool air through a modified cowl-induction hood and custom air box. The engine is fed by a throttle body and port fuel injection. (Photo courtesy of Tony Laruffa)

How to Build GM Pro-Touring Street Machines

Chapter 5

Mike Face's '70 Chevelle Extreme Pro-Touring

Most Pro-Touring Chevelles have the usual bolt on suspension components and lowered stance. Mike Face's '70 SS454 Chevelle steps over the line of Pro-Touring to the extreme Pro-Touring category. That line is crossed when the custom built parts outweigh the amount of bolt-on parts and the car is on the edge of what most would consider unstreetable, due to its lack of creature comforts and obscene amounts of power.

Extreme cars don't have to be equipped with a fully fabricated rectangular tube frame attached to a NASCAR-influenced cage made of 1.75-inch diameter tubing with 0.090-inch wall thickness. Every inch of the original floorpan doesn't have to be removed and replaced with all new custom panels. But that's part of what Mike had in mind when he started this project. He wanted to build the '70 so he could race it in one of the high-speed open-road racing events, but

Mike Face's '70 Chevelle is modified enough to make a classification called extreme Pro-Touring. The only stock parts on this bruiser are some of the body panels. (Photo courtesy Mike Face)

still drive it on the street. Mike knew using the stock frame and suspension would not get the stance and performance he was looking for. He is a talented body man by trade, with connections in a couple different industries. One of those connections is the high-echelon circle track industry. That made it easier for Mike to build this extreme Chevelle based on knowledge and skill.

The Chevelle has a three-link rear suspension setup with a panhard bar that Mike can raise and lower from inside the trunk. This setup keeps the 3.40:1 Richmond-geared Speedway Engineering 9-inch full-floater rear end in place. The front suspension is built from a plethora of circle-track parts. A Wilwood master cylinder pedal assembly operates the Wilwood brakes front and rear. Part of the amazing engineering on the '70, is the front and rear tire and wheel sizes that accentuate the perfect stance. The Jongbloed wheels are spun aluminum with magnesium centers. The front wheels are 17x11-inch with 275/40ZR17 tires, and the rears are 17x12-inch with 315/35ZR17s.

Power to the wheels comes from a big-block Chevy 502-ci rat that pumps out 682 hp at 5200 rpm and 698 ft-lbs of torque at 3200 rpm. Jim Vangordon of Vangordon Racing in Upland, California, is responsible for this magnificent power plant. The engine is comprised of a Bowtie iron

The adjustable rear wing was installed for when Mike took the car out to the Pony Express open-road race. Along with the wing, the fuel cell and 315s in the rear give a glimpse of what most people see. The third brake light on the license plate is a nice touch. (Photo courtesy Mike Face)

Mike Face's '70 Chevelle Extreme Pro-Touring (Continued)

block, a GM nitrided steel crank, JE 9.7:1 forged pistons, GM iron rectangle-port heads (with the "works"), a custom-ground mechanical roller cam, and a Dart intake topped with a 1000-cfm HP series Holley carb. The engine is lubricated by way of a complete dry-sump system. The external parts consist of K&N carbon-fiber valve covers, carbon fiber cold-air inlet box, and a bunch of circle-track gear. Behind the 502 is a multi-disc Tilton clutch assembly and a Richmond 6-speed transmission. The low profile exhaust is definitely NASCAR-esque with BSR oval tubing, Spin Tech mufflers, and boom tubes that exit the body in front of the rear tires.

The body got special treatment, since Mike is especially talented in that area. For speed and styling, he shaved the drip rails, added a little bit of a ground-effect to the rocker panels, and installed a custom adjustable deck lid mounted wing, so he could tune downforce for high-speed stability for open road racing. He set the engine back a few inches and made a custom firewall, because the stock one would not allow him to accomplish the look he was going for. The body was covered in Flex Products ChromaFlair Color Shift Burnt Fire paint.

The interior sports a bunch of AutoMeter instruments stuffed in an aluminum dash, also built by Mike. The Chevelle also features a quick-release steering wheel, which is a must for entering and exiting a car with high door bars. The Kirkey aluminum race seats and Crow harnesses sit amid endless well-built, reinforced sheet-metal interior and accent panels.

With all the pure-race parts and construction, Mike's Chevelle exudes extreme Pro-Touring. When he isn't too busy with work, he takes some time to put the "Touring" in his Chevelle by driving it to a local car show or terrorizing the streets a little. That would be quite a scene.

The interior is race-bred. The seats and door panels are the only upholstered parts. The Custom aluminum dash houses full AutoMeter instrumentation. The removable steering wheel makes it easier to get in and out of the car. (Photo courtesy Mike Face)

With the hood up, you can see all the stock-car-style suspension pieces. Tucked under all the chassis tubing is a 502-ci big-block Chevy that pumps out a whopping 682 hp and 698 ft-lbs of torque. (Photo courtesy Mike Face)

CHAPTER 6

DRIVETRAIN

For better fuel economy and all around performance driving, most Pro-Tourers swap in late-model transmissions with extra gears or overdrives. This section will cover the most popular manual and automatic transmission swapping info, where to get the parts, and who offers what. Picking a transmission to run in your car is determined by a few factors, including but not limited to: your everyday driving style/frequency; the condition of your clutch knee; whether or not you want to cut a hole in your floorpan; whether you drag race, road race, or both; and the size of your wallet.

If you decide on a stick shift, do you want a smoother shift of an internal-rail shifted Tremec TKO or T-56? Would you rather have more gear ratio selections like a Richmond 6-speed? If you pick an automatic overdrive, do you want to have it manually controlled like the 700R4, or do you want to fork out the extra dough for the computer controller so you can use a 4L60E transmission?

New transmissions might come out later that might work even better for you. Maybe GM will come out with newer and stronger transmissions, like a 7-speed manual, or maybe a 6-speed automatic.

Manual Transmissions

Tremec TKO 5-speed

TKO 500
Gear Ratios:
    First   3.27:1
    Second   1.98:1
    Third   1.34:1
    Fourth   1.00:1
    Fifth   0.68:1
    Reverse 3.00:1
    Design Torque Rating: 500 ft-lbs

TKO 600
Gear Ratios:
    First   2.87:1
    Second   1.98:1
    Third   1.28:1
    Fourth   1.00:1
    Fifth   0.64:1
    Reverse 3.00:1
    Design Torque Rating: 650 ft-lbs

Keisler Automotive Engineering

The TKO 5-speed transmission is available in two different versions from Keisler Automotive Engineering. They offer the TKO 500 and 600, which have a different fifth gear and have different torque capacities. They offer them with numerous shifter locations to allow the use of a stock console in most GM floorpans and consoles without body or frame alteration. They even offer stock shifter placement for early Corvettes. They offer full kits to make this a bolt-on conversion, which includes a crossmember and custom driveshaft made to your measurements. The TKO bolts to an adapter bellhousing available from McLeod Industries. The tip of the input shaft is a little larger and shorter than the GM input shafts, so a special pilot bearing is

The Tremec TKO 5-speed manual transmission is available in two versions. They have different gear ratios and torque ratings. The TKO has a distinctive, bulky counterweight under the tail-shaft housing. Most people remove them. The one in the picture has had its tail shaft modified already. Crossmember modifications are necessary. For positive retention, the rubber crossmember mount has been replaced with a polyurethane Prothane Mustang mount.

Drivetrain

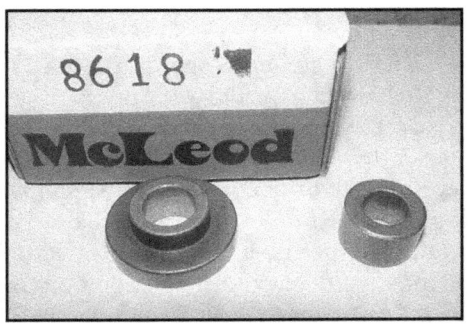

The TKO swap requires a special pilot bearing or bushing. The TKO input shaft is shorter and has a larger diameter than the GM unit. The McLeod TKO pilot bushing is on the left. The standard early model GM pilot bearing is on the right. When installing the McLeod bushing in the end of the crankshaft, put the smaller step towards the crankshaft, leaving the larger flat surface facing the transmission.

required to mate the input shaft to the end of the crankshaft. The TKO requires a late-model Mustang transmission mount.

Tremec T-56

The Tremec T-56 (formerly Borg-Warner T-56) has been a huge help with the Pro-Touring crowd. It has two more gears than the usual Pro-Touring cars' stock 4-speed transmission, which allows higher fuel mileage numbers and higher top speed. The GM T-56 has three different versions. Due to torque capacity and gear ratios offered (shown below), the 1994 and newer GM T-56 transmissions are preferred. Upgrading to a T-56 transmission will require a custom length driveshaft.

1969 Muncie (for comparison)

M20 Gear Ratios:
First	2.52:1
Second	1.88:1
Third	1.46:1
Fourth	1.00:1

M21 Gear Ratios:
First	2.20:1
Second	1.64:1
Third	1.28:1
Fourth	1.00:1

GM T-56

1993 Gear Ratios:
First	2.97:1
Second	2.07:1
Third	1.43:1
Fourth	1.00:1
Fifth	0.80:1
Sixth	0.62:1
Reverse	3.28:1

Design Torque Rating: 400 ft-lbs

1994 through 1997 Gear ratios:
First	2.66:1
Second	1.78:1
Third	1.30:1
Fourth	1.00:1
Fifth	.74:1
Sixth	.50:1
Reverse	3.28:1

Torque capacity: 450 ft-lbs

1998 to present (2003)

In 1998 the T-56 was changed to fit the Gen-III small block (LS1).

Gear ratios:
First	2.66:1
Second	1.78:1
Third	1.30:1
Fourth	1.00:1
Fifth	.74:1
Sixth	.50:1
Reverse	3.28:1

Torque capacity: 450 ft-lbs

Campbell Auto Restoration

Campbell Auto Restoration offers T-56 transmissions in a couple of different configurations. They offer the Retrofit version, stock replacement models, and a modified Viper T-56.

The Retrofit T-56 was produced for bolting into T-5 equipped third-generation F-bodies. They are only offered built from the 1993 T-56, so they are rated up to 400 ft-lbs of torque. It has a special tail-shaft housing that moves the shifter forward about 2 inches from the standard T-56, which is about 2 inches farther rearward than on a Muncie 4-speed. The housing also allows you to use a mechanical speedometer, instead of the stock electric speedometer sensor. With a supplied 3/4-inch thick adapter plate, it mounts to stock T-5 bellhousings that are 18 degrees counter-clockwise from vertical. The adapter is also drilled for the standard early GM transmission bellhousing or an early style heavy-duty scatter shield. Attached to the adapter is a T-5 front bearing retainer. The input shaft is the standard 26 spline, and it fits in the standard GM pilot bearing. It also uses the earlier-style clutch and pressure plate, as well as all the stock manual clutch linkage.

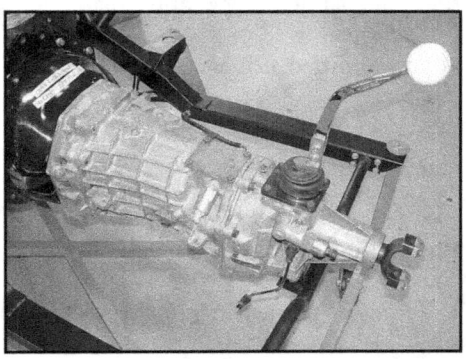

Compared to the F-body T-56, the Viper model has a larger 30-spline output shaft. The Viper T-56 is rated up to 550 ft-lbs of torque, compared to the F-body's 450 ft-lbs. Some companies offer the Viper unit with a modified input shaft, but Campbell Auto Restoration leaves well enough alone, so service parts are easier to find.

Campbell Auto Restoration offers this cool converter box. The pulse signal from the transmission goes into the box, which converts the signal to an electrical motor that accepts and drives the standard GM mechanical speedo cable. It is fully programmable for different gear ratios and tire diameters.

How to Build GM Pro-Touring Street Machines

The standard T-56 is the 1994 through 1997 version, which is rated for 450 ft-lbs of torque. They offer it with the bellhousing adapter, like the one offered on the Retrofit T-56 version. It utilizes the standard T-56 tail-shaft housing, so the shifter is located about 4 inches farther rearward than the standard Muncie 4-speed shifter. It also uses the electronic speedometer.

They offer a Viper T-56 that is rated at 550 ft-lbs of torque. It's offered with the same bellhousing adapter plate mentioned with the Retrofit T-56. They use an unmodified Viper input shaft and custom-made pilot bushing. It utilizes the larger 30-spline output shaft, instead of the GM versions' 27-spline, so it's much stronger. This also makes it necessary to get a Viper slip yoke. This version uses an electronic speedometer.

Keisler Automotive Engineering

The T-56 offered by Keisler Automotive Engineering has a few different shifter locations, so depending on your application, you may be able to use the stock shifter location without modifying the floorpan. Their transmission uses an adapter plate to bolt to the earlier Muncie-style bellhousing. They offer bolt-in kits that include all the parts necessary to bolt everything in, including the crossmember.

D&D Performance

The D&D Performance T-56 starts life as a Viper model, and is rated at 550 ft-lbs of torque. The longer 26-spline input shaft is machined down, welded up, and machined again for a precise fit using the early-style pilot bushing or bearing. They supply an adapter plate for bolting to an early-model Muncie-style bellhousing. A T-5 bearing retainer collar is bolted to the adapter plate. You supply the pressure plate and fine-spline clutch disc. The output shaft housing is custom cast to move the shifter about 2 inches forward from the stock GM location, which means it is about 2 inches rearward of an original 4-speed shifter attached to a Muncie. The housing also allows the use of a standard GM transmission mount. It also has provisions for running a standard 4-speed-style mechanical speedometer gear that is driven by a custom seven-tooth gear on the output shaft. The large 30-spline Viper output shaft requires the use of a Viper slip yoke.

ATS

If you have a 1993 through 1997 GM LT1 T-56 and want to bolt it to your Gen-I or -II small-block Chevy or a big-block Chevy engine, Auto Touring Specialties (ATS) has a kit for you. They have done all the work for you to make their kits easy to install. Their kit is designed for using the stock 1993 through 1997 bellhousing. If you have a 1998 and up Gen-III (LS1) T-56, ATS has an adapter that allows you to use your transmission on the back of Gen-I and -II non-LS1 engines. The kit includes a well-engineered three-piece transmission crossmember, which once installed, is designed to drop straight down instead of sliding out like the original. It also includes an adjustable-length GM 1996 F-body hydraulic clutch actuator and slave assembly, and a laser cut firewall adapter bracket that attaches the hydraulic actuator to the original pedal assembly.

To complete the conversion, you supply the T-56 transmission with clutch fork, the flywheel, clutch, stock stick-shift brake and clutch pedals, driveshaft with TH-350 slip yoke (modified to length measured after the transmission is installed), shifter, polyurethane transmission mount, flywheel hardware, clutch hardware, pilot bearing, synthetic trans fluid, brake fluid, clutch alignment tool, shifter boot, shift knob, and fluid pump.

When using a big-block or Gen-I small-block Chevy, you need a McLeod or Lakewood flywheel that uses the LT1-style pull-off clutch. One-piece rear main seal engines can use the LT1 flywheel. An LT1-style clutch and pressure-plate assembly are required.

Richmond Performance Products

Richmond Performance Products offers ring-and-pinion gears and transmissions. Their line includes 2-speeds, 4-speeds, 5-speeds (street and road-race versions), and 6-speeds. Since I can't remember the last time I saw someone swapping in a Richmond 5-speed, I will only be covering their 6-speed.

The Richmond 6-speed (aka ROD — Richmond OverDrive) is put together using NASCAR proven technology. Its shifter has external arms and side levers. They offer coarse and fine-spline input shaft. It bolts directly to the early Muncie 4-speed bellhousing without an adapter plate. The transmission mount is located 4 inches rearward of the standard Muncie 4-speed, so the crossmember will have to be modified. The centerline of the shifter location is within an inch rearward of most GM stock 4-speed shifters. The transmission tunnel requires modification for the shifter location. The overall length is within 1/2 inch of the 1963 through 1970 Muncie, which makes it one of the easiest 6-speeds to swap in.

The Richmond overdrive 6-speed transmission is available with plenty of different gear ratios to meet your needs. They used NASCAR-proven technology from their Super T-10 racing transmissions to aid in its initial design. This is a cutaway display model that shows the gears, syncros, and other internal parts. The shifter location and overall length are close to the dimensions of some early Muncie 4-speeds, but the transmission mount is 4 inches farther rearward than the mount on those same Muncies.

Richmond 6-speeds are available with two different drive ratios.

1.682 drive ratio:
First	4.41:1 thru 3.04:1
Second & Third	2.75:1 thru 1.57:1
Fourth	1.24:1 and 1.74:1
Fifth	1.00:1
Sixth	0.76:1 thru 0.91:1

Drivetrain

1.148 drive ratio:
- First   3.01:1 thru 2.08:1
- Second & Third   1.88:1 thru 1.07:1
- Fourth   0.84:1 and 1.19:1
- Fifth   1.00:1
- Sixth   0.52:1 thru 0.62:1

T-56 Speedometer

You will need a speedometer to know how fast you're going. There are two types of speedometers: electronic and mechanical. Some modified T-56s are offered with a mechanical speedometer. The factory T-56 is equipped with an electronic speedometer that reads a signal from the reluctor ring on the output shaft in the tail-shaft housing. To pick up this signal, you have to get a factory vehicle speed sensor (VSS) that attaches to the transmission. There are aftermarket speedometers that read this signal and convert it to operate the indicator needle. If you want to keep the stock mechanical speedo or use an aftermarket mechanical unit, but don't have a mechanical speedo-cable receiver on the tail-shaft housing, you are in luck. There is a little black box on the market that converts the pulse signal to an electric drive motor that accepts the mechanical speedo cable. By moving some simple dip switches, you can program the output for different rear-end gear ratios and tire diameters.

If you would rather have a mechanical speedo gear straight out of the transmission, you can pick up a modified tail-shaft housing from Jags That Run (JTR). They also offer services to put in a mechanical speedometer and relocate the VSS and install a reluctor ring. Having a mechanical speedometer and a VSS at the same time would be necessary if you have a mechanical speedometer and a computer-controlled fuel-injection system that requires a VSS signal to operate.

Bellhousing Setups

When bolting on any stock or aftermarket bellhousing with a centering hole that locates the transmission front bearing retainer, you need to check some critical measurements. If you just bolt one on your car and throw in a transmission, you run a high probability of destroying your pilot bearing, input shaft bearing, input shaft, and other internal parts. The symptoms can be extreme clutch chatter, engagement problems, and erratic clutch operation. The aftermarket companies typically have a maximum specified run-out of .010 inch. Check with the manufacturer of your bellhousing for exact measurements and instructions. There are two bellhousing alignments to check. First, check the run-out on the inside circumference of the pilot hole compared to concentricity of the crankshaft centerline. You do this by mounting a dial indicator on the end of a stand with a magnetic base centered on the end of the crankshaft. Turn the crankshaft and check for a minimum of .010 inch. The second measurement to check is the mounting surface of the bellhousing. It should be within the same .010 inch from top-to-bottom and side-to-side. Mount the dial indicator to an extended arm that places the dial indicator on the mounting face, and then turn the crankshaft. If you have anything over the .010-inch measurement on either location, then you will need to adjust the bellhousing with offset dowel pins or other methods suggested by the manufacturer.

The transmission pilot hole must be within .010-inch of the concentricity of the crankshaft. You can measure the run-out with a dial indicator by turning the crankshaft. The dial indicator must be connected to an extended magnetic base centered on the end of the crankshaft. Without ensuring the correct run-out on the pilot hole and mounting face, you will severely shorten the life of your transmission.

The transmission mounting face is as important as the pilot-hole run-out. With an extension, place the dial indicator on the face with the magnetic base connected to the end of the crankshaft. Then check the side-to-side and top-to-bottom run-out. The dial indicator should spin around the outside of the pilot hole and not have more than .010 inch of run-out.

McLeod Industries

McLeod Industries is one of the major companies in the clutches, flywheels, and bellhousings.

Clutches

They offer street and racing clutches in both single- and dual-disc setups. They also offer multi-disc clutches for serious racing applications. One of their popular heavy-duty clutches for Pro-Touring cars is their Street Twin clutch setup. It is available with a steel or a lightweight aluminum flywheel. If you want a clutch that's bulletproof, you can get their oval-track, road-race, and dry-lakes clutches. Their non-strapped single clutch setup holds up to 500 ft-lbs of torque, the dual-disc model holds up to 900 ft-lbs of torque. If you are serious about your power, you can step up to the triple-disc setup that is rated at 1500 ft-lbs. McLeod offers these road-race clutches in a strapped version to limit the chatter. The strapped single- and dual-disk setups have the same torque capacity ratings as their non-strapped models. They don't offer a strapped triple disc setup. The strapped clutches are only available with a lightweight aluminum flywheel.

Chapter 6

The McLeod Road Race clutch is for serious high-horsepower applications. This one has the lightweight aluminum flywheel. It is available in double- and triple-disc setups. The triple-disc unit is rated up to 1500 ft-lbs of torque.

Bellhousings and Adapters

McLeod makes heavy-duty bellhousings for just about any make and model. For those of you wishing to bolt a T-56 to your Buick/Olds/Pontiac (BOP) engines, McLeod has come out with the ultimate in bellhousings. It's a modular heavy-duty multi-pattern bellhousing that bolts to most GM engines from 1955 on up, excluding metric V-6 engines, but including the Buick/Olds/Pontiac & Cadillac (BOP) V-6 and V-8 patterns. It features starter pockets on both sides of the block. This is great news for BOP owners wanting to run a T-56, or any other transmission for that matter. Since each transmission has a different length input shaft, there are adapter rings to space out the transmission-mounting surface. The spacer rings are available in five different thicknesses, ranging from .25 to 1.9 inch.

McLeod also offers the adapter plate to mount a stock Chevy T-56 to a conventional Chevy bellhousing.

Weir Hotrod Products

If you have a '93 through '02 F-body T-56 and want to bolt it to your Chevy, Buick, Olds, Pontiac, or Cadillac, you can always get a Weir Hotrod

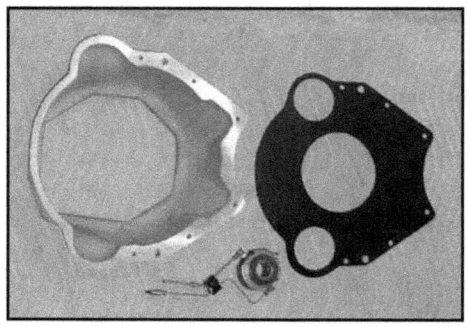

This is a Buick/Olds/Pontiac/Cadillac version of the Weir Hot Rod Products aluminum bellhousing. The kit includes dual starter patterns, backing plate, and hydraulic release bearing. Weir has bellhousings to adapt the T-56 to almost any GM V-8 engine. (Photo courtesy Weir Hot Rod Products)

Products adapter bellhousing. They are made of heat-treated 356 cast aluminum. The stock '93 through '97 F-body T-56 bellhousing fit on the Chevy small and big blocks, but they limit the use of a larger flywheel and pull-style small-diameter clutch setups. The Weir bellhousing allows the use of the larger 168-tooth flywheel. You can also use a heavier-duty 11-inch clutch with the included Weir self-adjusting hydraulic release bearing. They also offer custom crossmembers.

Automatics

There are a few good automatics on the market for swapping into GM cars. I will be covering overdrive transmissions in this section, since Pro-Touring is about driving hard, but keeping an eye on driveability. Questions have been asked whether automatic transmissions are good for road-racing and open-track events, so I asked Phoenix Transmissions in Texas about this issue. I have personally beaten the living snot out of my 700R4 (behind a stout big-block Chevy) on an occasional open-track day. It was a Phoenix-built transmission and it held up, so they must know something about building them strong. They said there are helical gears in the transmission that have a thrust bearing to hold the internals during acceleration. But, there isn't a thrust bearing to contain the internals when they slide forward during hard decelerating downshifts. There is only a ring on a shaft to take the brunt of the shock. If a builder sets the clearances too loose, the internals can slide forward and destroy the ring and everything in the transmission. It's a matter of setting up the transmission correctly. He also added that using the transmission (stick or automatic) is not the best way to slow your car down anyway. Downshifting unloads the rear suspension and causes the car to get loose. It also causes the tires to break traction during the downshift, which is also bad for handling. I have also talked to professional racers who say it is better to use your brakes to slow down, rather than the transmission. This is just another reason to upgrade your brakes.

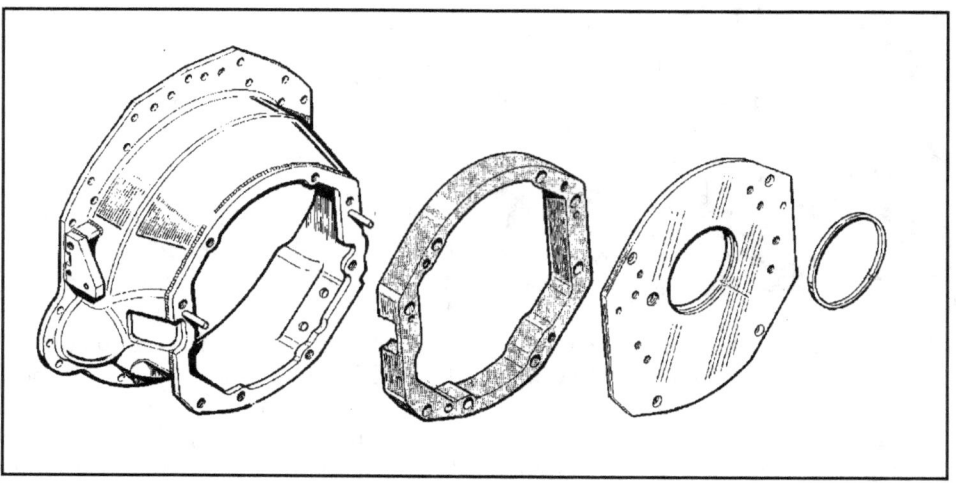

The McLeod modular bellhousing is a huge step in making just about any transmission bolt to all the GM V-8s (except the Cadillac Northstar). You could easily bolt a T-56 to any early Buick, Olds, or Pontiac (BOP) engine. It utilizes rings of varying in thickness in order to be truly universal.

Drivetrain

Chris Kerr's '68 Camaro Pro-Touring Extreme

Chris Kerr's '68 Camaro was removed from the street for racing only, and then it came back as a street-driven race car. The front wheel openings were raised and widened to clear the huge front rollers. (Photo courtesy Chris Kerr)

Typically, when a street car is taken off the street to be strictly used as a race car, it doesn't make it back to the street. Chris Kerr is one of a handful of extreme Pro-Touring builders. His '68 CP Autocross Camaro SS pushes the envelope with streetability and all-out racing ability.

Along with the car's life on the street, racing, and then back to the street again, Chris has taken the car through many different complete rebuilds since he bought it in 1986. The only stock parts of the frame are the front subframe side rails. The rest of the frame and subframe have been replaced with a 22-point cage and new frame of an array of square, rectangular, and round tubing. The rear suspension is a custom three-link system with an adjustable rear sway bar, controlled by Koni coilovers wearing 225-lb springs. The rear axle is a narrowed Ford 9-inch with 3.50:1 gears and Moser 31-spline spline axles. The front suspension includes '85 Vette spindles, Afco upper control arms, Afco lower strut rods, Koni coilovers with 650-lb springs, adjustable 1-inch high-mounted circle-track sway bar, and a front steer 21-inch BRT 12:1 power steering rack. The brakes are Baer PBR 13-inch Track kit in the front and a GM 11-inch system in the rear. The brakes are controlled by dual Afco masters, mounted to a pedal assembly with an adjustable balance-bar. To assist in braking and handling, Chris chose Budnick 11x17-inch and 13x17-inch wheels, wrapped with 275/40ZR17s and 315/45ZR17s.

Instead of picking tires and wheels to fit within the confines of the stock fender openings, Chris raised and widened the front fender openings to fit the desired tire size. He installed a VFN fiberglass cowl hood and trunk lid. The body was covered in DuPont maroon urethane paint by Weight Autobody in Neselm, Illinois. Chris moved the engine back four inches into the passenger compartment for better balance and distribution. He also closed the floor and covered the rear cage area with custom sheetmetal. Within the confines of the well-padded roll cage, Chris installed '93 Z28 seats covered in black and gray cloth by Auto Trim & Glass in Bourbonnais, Illinois. The dash is basically stock with the addition of a few AutoMeter gauges. For long road trips, such as the *Hot Rod* Power Tour, Chris installed a high-powered sound system, and he picked up a handy $6.00 cup holder at Wal-Mart. In the holder, he keeps his CDs, cell phone, tollbooth change, and Mountain Dew.

You can see the 454 has been set back a few inches for better weight distribution. For suspension tuning, Chris installed a high-mounted adjustable stock-car-style sway bar. (Photo courtesy Chris Kerr)

The rear suspension is of three-link persuasion. Chris built the cage so the car could be abused on a regular basis. For rigidity, Chris replaced the floor with tubing and custom sheetmetal floor panels. (Photo courtesy Chris Kerr)

The engine is a 1970 454-ci big-block Chevy built by Dan Keversan, in Millington, Michigan. It houses a Moldex crankshaft that has been internally balanced, GM LS6 rods and 10.0:1 pistons, Comp Cams camshaft, and Comp Cams valvetrain components. The block is capped with cast-iron oval-port heads with 2.19/1.88-inch valves and some port work. The intake is an Edelbrock Victor Jr. topped with a Holley 750-cfm double pumper. Ignition is handled by Accel, and the oil is controlled by a Milodon oil pan. Exhaust exits through modified Hooker headers, 2.5-inch exhaust tubing, and Flowmaster mufflers. The shifting duties are done by a Muncie four-speed, coupled with a 10,000-rpm triple-disc Kevlar clutch and a Howe hydraulic throwout bearing.

Chris wanted to thank his mom and dad, Jack and Kathy Kerr, for letting him build the car in their garage for its first 5 years, and wife Mary Kerr for support and understanding. He also wanted to thank friends Jeff Dellamater, Pat Glenn, Bob Thrash, Larry Cheffer, Jeff St.Aubin, and Mike close for project help and support.

Even though the design has totally changed a few times, the Camaro design has been well executed, with a total weight of 2825 lbs and a distribution of 50.5% in front and 49.5% percent in the rear. The combination is perfect for Chris's all-around driving.

NOTE: The following horsepower ratings are given by Phoenix Transmission's highest tier custom-built transmissions. Numbers from other builders will differ. Phoenix dyno tests every transmission before it ships to ensure proper operation and to adjust shift points to your custom requirements.

200R4

The 200R4 transmission is good up to 350 horsepower when modified, and in some applications, it can be built to handle more. Compared to the 700R4, its first gear is not as deep and it is closer to the ratio of second gear. This means that when launching the car, you don't have to shift from first to second as fast. The 200R4 has a mechanical speedometer drive. Modifying the crossmember may be necessary to install the 200R4 in certain earlier cars, or you can purchase a custom-built crossmember. The 200R4 has the same block-face-to-mount distance as the Turbo-400, so if you have a crossmember meant for a TH400, it will work. The 200R4 is cast as a multi-pattern case that fits both Chevrolet and all other modern GM V-8 engines. Some early models were cast as Buick, Olds, Pontiac, and Cadillac only. A throttle valve cable is used to control line pressure and shift points in the 200R4. See 700R4 section for further details on this cable.

Gear ratios:
First   2.78:1
Second 1.57:1
Third   1.00:1
Fourth   .67:1
Horsepower capacity:
up to 350 hp.*

700R4

If you are running up to 575 hp and 600 ft-lbs of torque, you might want to upgrade to the stronger 700R4. It is strong for all-around racing and has a .70:1 fourth gear for freeway driving. It is setup for a mechanical speedometer cable. Installing a 700R4 in place of a TH400 requires notching the crossmember for pan clearance and lengthening the crossmember mounting pad. Or you could purchase a custom crossmember. The Caprice-style extension housing moves the mount from the case and places the rear mount very close to the TH400 location, and also lowers the trans from the floorpan for additional clearance. The 700R4 was never cast in any bellhousing configuration besides the Chevrolet style; however, there are numerous adapters on the market to adapt this transmission to most any V-8 engine. A cable-operated throttle valve controls the internal transmission pressure and shift points. Adjusting the throttle valve cable correctly is critical. If you leave it too loose you run the risk of destroying your clutches on the first drive. It isn't hard to adjust, but it is necessary. Ideally, the cable actuation should be a total of 1 1/8 inch of travel in a straight line, as the throttle travels from idle to full throttle. At full throttle, the cable should be "piano-wire" tight to ensure maximum line pressure under full engine power. Custom brackets are offered by a few different companies to help set the cable up with the correct travel and geometry for your carb or fuel-injection application. TH350 brackets can be modified for proper installation. Some custom brackets are flimsy and can break or bend under hard driving. Choose or build a strong bracket to ensure maximum pressure for your transmission.

Gear ratios:
First   3.06:1
Second 1.63:1
Third   1.00:1
Fourth   .70:1
Horsepower capacity:
up to 575 hp.*

4L60E

The 4L60E transmission is basically the same transmission as the 700R4, but it does not have a throttle valve cable or conventional valve body. A computer is used to perform governing functions. The 4L60E can be used in conjunction with a computer-controlled engine and transmission management system. If you don't have a computer controlling your engine management, or want the transmission to have a separate computer, you can purchase a stand-alone computer. The computerized controllers are available from a few different aftermarket companies and allow the user to tune shift points and firmness to your desire. If you like to get the maximum tuning out of your vehicle, these newer electronic transmissions can be very rewarding. The 4L60E stats are the same as the 700R4 stats.

4L80E

The 4L80E transmission was first used in 1991 in GM trucks and vans. Built correctly, it can handle up to 750 hp. Like the 4L60E, it is completely computer controlled. If you wish to purchase a Compushift computer controller, Phoenix Transmission Products will dyno it with your trans and converter and fully program it to your required specifications. When the customer receives the transmission, they only need to attach four or five simple wire connections and bolt it in. The Compushift can be fine-tuned by the user to get the very most out of this super-heavy-duty transmission.

The 4L80E was originally designed for truck applications and can be built to handle up to 750 hp. The 4L80E requires a computer like the one seen here to perform governing functions. (Photo courtesy Phoenix Transmissions)

Gear ratios:
First   2.48:1
Second 1.48:1
Third   1.00:1
Fourth   .75:1
Horsepower capacity:
up to 750 hp.*

Drivetrain

Rear Ends

Putting that power to the street is going to be tough unless you have a rear end that can handle it. In the GM world, there are two main OEM rear end choices — the 10-bolt and 12-bolt. There is also a somewhat surprising third choice — the Ford 9-inch.

The GM 10- and 12-bolt rear ends consist of a cast center housing, with the axle tubes pressed into the casting and attached with plug welds. A sheetmetal cover bolts on to the back of the housing; the gears and differential are accessed by removing this cover. Changing axles is fairly easy, but changing gears or differential is relatively difficult with this style of rear end. The axles are held into the differential with C-clips. To remove the axles, you have to drain the housing, remove the cover, and remove the C-clips — then the axles can be pulled.

The Ford rear end consists of a welded stamped steel housing. The differential and gear set are held inside a cast center section (usually referred to as a "pumpkin") that bolts to the housing. Retaining plates on the ends of the axle housing hold the bearings, which keep the axles in their respective places. Compared to the GM rear ends, axle and gear changes are relatively easy.

GM 10-Bolt

Depending on the year and application, most GM 10-bolt rear ends came with either an 8.2-inch or 8.5-inch ring gear. Most applications from 1964 to 1972 had the 8.2-inch ring gear (there are also slight differences between the Chevy rear ends and the Olds/Pontiac rear ends), and used 28-spline axles. The 8.5-inch 10-bolts started in Chevy applications in 1970, and ran through 1976 in most models, except for Camaros and Firebirds, which used this rear end through 1981. These rear ends used 30-spline axles, but aftermarket axles are available in 28, 30, and 33-spline sizes for use with spools, lockers, or aftermarket limited-slip differentials.

Aftermarket gear sets are available for most 10-bolts; 8.2-inch gear sets are available in ratios from 3.08:1 to 5.13:1 for the Chevy rears, and from 3.55:1 to 4.56:1 for the Olds/Pontiac rears. A wider range of gears are available for the 8.5-inch rear ends — from 3.08:1 to 5.57:1.

GM 12-Bolt

The GM 12-bolt rear end was one of the strongest rear ends GM ever built, and was used in most of the traditional full-size and mid-size muscle cars from 1965 to 1972. These rear ends used an 8-7/8-inch ring gear, 30-spline axles (33- and 35-spline axles are available through the aftermarket), and aftermarket gear ratios range from 3.08:1 all the way to a stump-pulling 6.14:1.

Ford 9-Inch

The Ford 9-inch, besides being easier to service and work with, has more gear ratios available than the GM choices. They are also more common than the GM 12-bolt, and while they're no longer produced by Ford, there are plenty in junkyards, and complete center sections, gear sets, differentials, and even complete housings are available through the aftermarket. Companies like Currie Enterprises and Moser Engineering build complete, new, 9-inch housings that will bolt right into just about any GM performance car — they come in the correct width and with all the necessary mounting brackets welded on. That makes the Ford 9-inch a very popular choice for Pro-Touring applications.

Limited-Slip Differentials

Chevy Posi-Traction, Ford's Equa-Lok and Traction-Lok, and aftermarket differentials like the Auburn, DAPCO No-Spin (also known as a Detroit Locker), and others, are almost a necessity for a high-performance Pro-Touring car. While they operate in different ways, all these differentials essentially keep both axles locked together when the car is traveling in a straight line, which improves traction. When the car turns, the outer wheel is allowed to turn faster, usually through a clutch or ratchet-type mechanism. New limited slips are available for GM and Ford rear ends from a number of aftermarket suppliers, such as Richmond Gear.

Gear Ratios

What gear ratio you choose depends on a number of variables — how much torque your car's engine produces and when, what kind of tranny gearing you have, and how tall your tires are. In general, an overdrive (OD) tranny (automatic or manual) will take a lower rear end gear (higher ratio), from 4.10:1 to 3.70:1. This will give your car good launches, good low-end pickup, and still maintain reasonable engine RPM at highway speeds.

If you're using a 4-speed (1:1 final drive ratio) or non-OD automatic transmission, and plan on a lot of highway use, you'll probably want a slightly higher gear (3.50:1 to 3.10:1) to keep the RPMs reasonable on the road. A healthy engine with good low-end torque will still let you get off the line okay if you choose this route. On the other hand, if you plan to use the car more on the track or for local cruising, a lower gear will do the job.

So What Rear End to Use?

If you're planning a relatively mild motor for mostly street use, and your car is equipped with a 10-bolt, you should be fine. 12-bolt rear ends can handle more horsepower and torque, and if your car is already equipped with one, consider yourself lucky.

If you decide that your 10-bolt won't be enough, however, you may want to upgrade. If you can find a 12-bolt that fits your application, great — but don't count on it. 12-bolt rear ends are no longer common, and the ones that are out there have often been thrashed either on the street or strip. You may be better off bypassing the 12-bolt entirely and going directly to a Ford 9-inch built for your car.

Likewise, if you're building something with a lot of horsepower, you may want to consider replacing a 12-bolt rear end with a purpose-built 9-inch. With the wealth of aftermarket support out there, the 9-inch can be built to handle just about any horsepower level.

Chapter 6

Stan Davis's '87 Buick T-Type

Pro-Touring cars come in different degrees. Some are sedate with mild modifications, and some go full-tilt and would be considered extreme Pro-Touring. There are a few standouts in the extreme sector. One of them is Stan Davis's '87 Buick T-type. He wanted to build the fastest street car, and he wanted to do it using tried-and-true Buick racing technology. You might remember that the late 1980s and early 1990s were filled with Buick V-6 powered Grand Nationals, GNXs, and T-Types. These cars were putting unsuspecting V-8 bigots to shame with the unheard-of power that Ken Duttweiler, Kenne-Bell, and others were extracting from these V-6s.

To ensure that no detail was overlooked, Stan had Ken Duttweiler work his magic on the Buick V-6. It was built around a 260-ci Stage II block. The rotating assembly consists of a Stage-II crankshaft and Duttweiler-spec forged JE pistons. An overall compression ratio of 8:1 was accomplished with Stage-II heads that were prepped by Chapman and Duttweiler. Intake air starts its journey through a large Walker Engineering flow-bench tested K&N air filter. From there, it travels through 4-inch ducts to the custom Turbonetics-built Garret turbocharger that was specifically designed to deliver the flow and power that Stan wanted. Stan built the intercooler that cools the air before it flows through a throttle body mount-

Late-model cars are not usually thought of as Pro-Touring candidates, but since Stan Davis's street-driven '87 Buick T-Type is heavily modified for handling and speed, it's definitely extreme Pro-Touring. (Photo courtesy Joe Pettitt)

ed to a modified Victor Jr. tunnel ram. A MoTeC engine-management/data-acquisition system was installed so Stan could keep tabs on the vitals. The fuel and spark components are: MSD 100-lb/hr injectors, two Paxton regulators, a Weldon fuel pump, an MSD Billet distributor, and an MSD 7AL box. The exhaust gas exits the engine and flows through custom stainless-steel headers on its way to the turbines. From there, the spent gasses then flow through a stainless exhaust system that exits between the passenger door and right rear tire.

The engine is coupled with an Autorite-built TH400 and a Continental converter, specially built for maximum performance at 200+ mph. The WenCo driveshaft transfers power to a Ford nine-inch housing filled with all the heavy-duty stuff. For high-speed open-road racing, Stan has a U.S. Gear 2.47:1 gear set. Since he was shooting for "fastest street car," Stan entered the T-Type in the Silver State Classic Challenge in September 1998. With Joe Pettitt as driver and Stan Davis as navigator (or in this case, pilot and co-pilot), they took first place in the unlimited category. The

The race-bred interior was designed for high-speed open-road racing. The AutoMeter gauges are in full view of the driver and navigator. Every part on this car was meticulously built and/or installed by Stan Davis. (Photo courtesy Joe Pettitt)

Drivetrain

Stan Davis's '87 Buick T-Type (Continued)

posted radar speed was 205.1 mph. That was taken from one location in the 90.348-mile course. The car realized its potential on its second time out, managing a 208-mph blast with only 15 of its 24 pounds of boost. At 24 lbs of boost on the dyno, the engine put out 925 hp and 685 ft-lbs of torque at 7100 rpm.

Stan spent painstaking hours being meticulous about every detail of the car. Joe Pettitt pointed out that Stan's attention to detail was evident on parts "where less effort would not be noticed." Stan wanted everything done correctly the first time. Nothing was simply done "good enough," since the car was built for speed. The body was lightened by installing 13-lb carbon-fiber doors, an 11-lb deck lid built by Mel at InterCoast design, and an Abstract fiberglass hood. All the parts were covered in purple. The interior is race-bred with some personalized touches. It has a custom aluminum dash with AutoMeter gauges, designed to be viewable by the driver or the passenger. A Personal steering wheel is mounted atop a collapsible Woodward steering column. A chrome-moly roll cage and other supports protect the passengers and help strengthen the

It's not everyday (for most people) that you see a full-tilt turbocharged Buick V-6 like this one. This engine produces 925 hp on 24 lbs of boost and has motivated the car to over 208 mph! On asphalt! (Photo courtesy Joe Pettitt)

chassis. Bill Osborn designed the SLA front suspension and 3-link rear suspension. All the best high-speed parts were used, which include large-bearing Speedway front hubs and a full-floater rear end. The brakes are Wilwood 6-piston calipers on 13-inch front rotors and Wilwood 4-piston calipers on the 11.75-inch rears. The big brakes require big wheels, and high speeds require correctly rated tires, so Stan purchased Pirelli P-Zero P265/40ZR17s for the front and P335/35ZR17s for the rear. They comfortably wrap around 3-piece Simmons wheels.

Overall, the complete package is blazingly fast on the open road (as mentioned earlier), with the 208-mph run on Nevada Highway 318 to its credit. With street tires and a 3000-rpm stall converter, the car runs 10.80s in the quarter mile. It has the capability to run in the 9-second range with a higher stall, a better rear gear, and slicks. All these numbers make Davis's street-driven/race-bred Buick T-Type stand out as an extreme Pro-Touring car.

For high-speed stability and safety, only the highest quality suspension parts were used. The brakes are Wilwood 6-piston units in front and 4-piston units in the rear. (Photo courtesy Joe Pettitt)

How to Build GM Pro-Touring Street Machines

Chapter 7

Body and Electrical

Pro-Touring is about doing something different, but making body modifications are not required. Sometimes the stock GM body just won't work with what we want to do with our car, so some changes might be in order.

Stock Body

There are a few benefits to using stock body panels. If you have stock front fenders and damage one in an accident, you can simply locate another stock fender, bolt it into place, and add some paint. That is much easier than replacing a front fender that had a custom fender flare or bodywork. The job becomes a lot bigger when you have to replace a part and modify it again.

Steel body parts are stronger when they are bolted together as the factory intended. For instance, a '68 Camaro came from the factory with steel inner fenderwells that bolt to the steel front fenders, steel front fender extensions, steel radiator core support, and the firewall. The inner fenderwells tie the entire front sheetmetal together. The front subframe has six large bolts that hold it in place. Two of those are bolted to the radiator core support, which is bolted to front fenders and fenderwells. All these connections create a strong integral structure that distributes load and stress from the subframe. Some Camaro owners choose to remove their inner fenderwells so they can run lowered stance and bigger front tires without having interference and scrubbing. This also eliminates a few pounds from the front end. With these benefits, some people don't pay attention to the major drawback to removing them. Without them, the front sheetmetal relies on ten 3/8-inch bolts that attach the front fenders to the firewall, and two larger bolts that attach the radiator core support to the frame. This leaves a lot to be desired in the structur-

The inner fenderwell has been removed from this car. There is a lot of flex without them, but with the support bars added to connect the frame to the bars located on the opposite side of the firewall will take car of that.

This is the body-bushing bracket for a reproduction radiator core support. When I went to install my Detroit Speed & Engineering solid body bushing, it would not fit. The bushing hole was 3/16-inch smaller diameter than my factory core support hole. Reproduction parts are rarely exact copies, so be aware.

If you want factory sheetmetal to repair your car, salvage yards have all kinds of parts available. With this extremely clean rear section, you could bring new meaning to "back-halving" your car.

108   *How to Build GM Pro-Touring Street Machines*

Body and Electrical

al-integrity department. The subframe is able to flex more than it was designed for. Cracks can start forming in places you would never imagine. The inner fenderwells not only add integrity for hard driving stresses, they also add strength to the front end if you were to ever get into an accident, keep gravel thrown up by front tires from putting outward dents in your front fenders, and they help keep your engine compartment free of dirt and gravel.

If you are going to remove a part from your car, take a good look at why it was there. If it adds strength, and you remove it, you will regret it sooner or later. Most people remove the steel inner fenderwells for tire clearance, but you can still keep them and modify them so you still have the strength and protection they provide. I've seen them trimmed in such a way as to leave a large hole at the top of the well that isn't visible from the engine compartment. You can also build your own panel to fit in the hole if you don't want to leave it open for rocks and dirt. If you still insist on removing them, at least add some support bars from the firewall that extend down to a point in front of the spindle centerline.

Custom Bodywork

Some Pro-Touring applications require modifying body parts to make your parts fit. Not all barriers can be broken by bolt-on parts. Sometimes you need to modify or fabricate parts to achieve a certain look or goal.

If you want to change your old stock door handles, you could use an old custom trick and shave (remove) the door handles. Then use electric solenoids with hidden pushbutton switches to actuate the latches. With new technology, you could even do away with the hidden pushbuttons and use an electronic remote opener on your key chain. Another custom door handle trick is to swap door handles from a newer model car or truck. If your door skin is fairly flat, you could swap in a set of door handles from a '90 Chevy truck. They fit completely flush for a clean look.

Some GM cars and trucks have fenderwell openings that hang too low or are too small for the size tire you would like to run. Without flaring the fender openings, you can modify them to look and function better for your application. For instance, if you lower the stance of your car and the fender lip hangs too low for your liking, you can cut the outer fender lip off, and reattach it a couple of inches higher to keep the factory look, but allow for better tire to fender clearance.

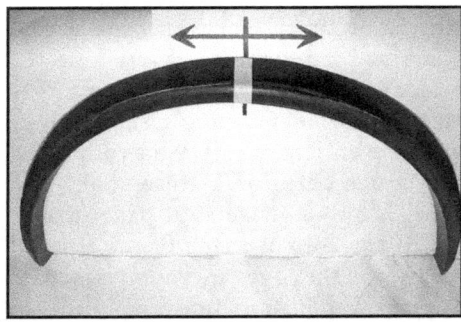

Here is what you need to do to stretch the front fender opening and retain somewhat of a stock appearance. Cut the outer edge off the fender, cut it in the center (as shown by tape on fender lip), reattach it with the necessary clearance for your tires, and then add material between the two sections of fender lip.

If you run a large tire in a front wheel opening that doesn't allow enough sweeping movement for turning and articulation while pulling in and out of driveways, you might decide you want to widen the front fender opening. You can keep the factory appearance of the wheelwell opening by cutting a couple of inches of the outer lip off the car. Cut the lip in half and reattach it to the fender with a gap between the two sections. If you need more room to turn the tires, you will need a bigger gap between the two pieces. After figuring out how much wider the opening is, you will need to fabricate another section to fill that gap.

GM and restoration parts companies don't make all the trim pieces we need to complete all of our cars. Sometimes you can't find good pieces at wrecking yards or swap meets to use on your project. Or maybe you simply want to remove the trim for a cleaner look. Some people resort to custom making their own trim pieces at a high cost. Others simply remove the trim and spend countless hours welding in new sections of steel to take the place of the original trim.

Probably the largest job in the history of removing body trim is the job of removing window trim and flush mounting windows. If it's done right, they look awesome. This gives the clean appearance we all see on new production cars. It is necessary to fabricate all new sections of steel that fill in all the

If you want to spend endless hours fabricating new window openings, you can make your car's windows flush mounted like all the new cars. It's a great look that is subtle enough to have people know something is different, but not know what it is.

The ignition coil here has been relocated to the cowl, where it will be hidden by a cover. Some people hide components so well that it can take hours just to replace an ignition box. These parts fail, so keep that in mind when hiding them.

Chapter 7

areas previously taken up by window trim. With the windows flush mounted and the trim removed, your car will be more aerodynamic, since the air won't catch under all the extra edges. People I have talked to that have accomplished this huge task say they are very happy they did it, but would not do it again.

Firewall

When you pop the hood on your ride, people see more than just the engine. The firewall stands out, especially since it is usually cluttered with electronic ignition components, and other parts people can't seem to find a better place to mount. If you are interested in removing some of the clutter in you engine compartment, you can find hidden or less obvious places to mount your ignition boxes and coils. Wherever you mount these items, make sure you can still access them within a reasonable amount of time when they fail. If and when something fails, you might end up having to spend three hours to replace or troubleshoot something that you hid too well. As I have pointed out in another section of this book, don't mount your fuel pressure regulator on your firewall, since some racetracks won't let you race if the regulator is in the path of a scattering flywheel.

If you are interested in smoothing your firewall, there are a few ways to go about it. In the 1970s, guys would take a large sheet of aluminum and rivet it right to the firewall, with total disregard to how it looked or if it actually sealed engine fumes from getting into the car. These days, builders are taking more pride in their cars, so filled and smoothed firewalls are more common.

The firewall is a high-stress area, since some GM bodies have frame mounts connected to them. If you are going to smooth your firewall with body filler, be aware that firewalls on early GMs are usually spot-welded together. If you simply fill the seams up with body filler without performing the following steps, there is high probability the filler will crack. The only way to truly get a clean weld is to remove the spot welds, remove the panels, take all the surfaces down to bare metal, and weld them back up. That is a lot of extra work, but the welds would not be contaminated by paint and 30 years of garbage that seeped between panels. Then weld a bead all the way around panels that were originally spot-welded.

Firewall Fill-Plate Install

If you have a first-generation F-body or second-generation X-body and want to remove the heater core and fill your firewall, Detroit Speed & Engineering has a product that cuts down on fabrication time. They make a panel that is meant for filling the gaping hole the heater core leaves when installing a Vintage Air air-conditioning system. It also works even if you just want to remove the heater core for a clean look. The panel is an 18-gauge steel panel that is cut to the correct shape of the firewall seams, and the edges are hammer formed for easy welding and finishing.

There are two methods to installing it. DSE's preferred method is to weld it into place. In order to do this, you must remove all the seam sealer in the body seams, strip the firewall, remove anything inside the car that can get damaged or catch on fire when welding, tack weld the panel in place, slowly weld a bead around the perimeter of the panel to keep it from warping, clean up the welds, reseal the body seams, and refinish the firewall.

These photos show the other method, which is not as strong as welding the fill plate in place, but does its job

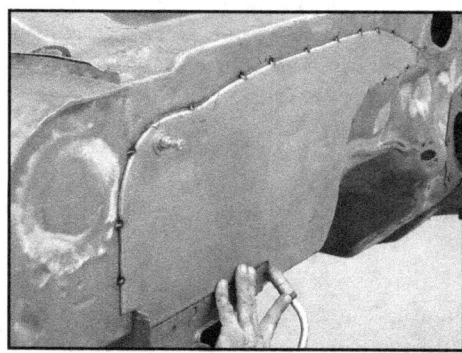

Detroit Speed & Engineering's preferred method of installing the fill plate is to weld it into place. Strip the firewall of all its paint and seam sealer, and make sure there isn't anything close to this area inside the car that will catch on fire . Do this before you start welding, and keep a fire extinguisher handy at all times. The panel is held in place with a 3/8-inch bolt (where the fender attaches to the firewall), then tacked every few inches. To keep the panel from warping, it is welded with a bead in sections around the panel until the entire perimeter is welded.

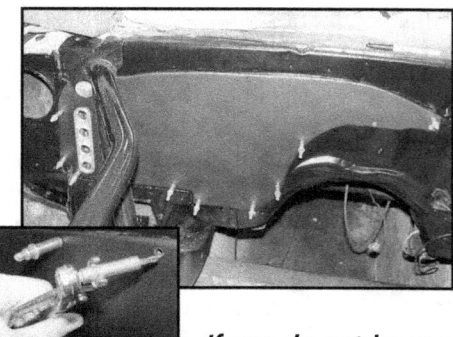

If you do not have a welder, you can use rivets. Once you have the panel held in place with a 3/8-inch bolt (seen in the first photo), lay out the marks every few inches where you want your rivets. Try to get them equally spaced if you can. I spaced mine about 4 to 6 inches apart, depending on the area and contour of the panel. Mark the spots with a felt-tip marker, and then drill the holes. I used Clecos (a kind of temporary, reusable rivet) to hold the panel in place while I drilled the holes.

After all the holes were drilled, the panel was riveted into place using stainless-steel rivets. Aluminum rivets are not as strong as stainless ones, and they are not as resistant to the elements. After the rivets are all in place, I used a little sealer to seal the center of each one from the back side. It would be better to use stainless blind rivets (with a closed end), but I couldn't find any. The panel and firewall are ready for a few more coats of paint.

Body and Electrical

of filling the firewall and takes less time and preparation to install.

Fiberglass

Fiberglass is a wonderful material. You can build just about any body or interior dress-up panel out of it. In small application it is easier to work with than steel, and it weighs much less.

Fiberglass companies are just like any other industry. Some have good quality products, and some are low quality. For instance "Brand U" might have a history of turning out 80% of its unlimited line of products with poor quality and defects. They advertise in big publications, so they get a lot of brand recognition and sell to a lot of guys trying to build their car as cheap and light as possible and may not care too much about the quality. Brand U might have horrible customer service when you call after receiving your questionable parts, to ask them about the quality. Then, for instance, there is "Brand V." They have great quality, very few defects, good customer service, but don't advertise too much. Be careful who you buy parts from. Ask around and get a few opinions before laying down you money for some parts. You are better off spending a little extra for a better product — because you get what you pay for.

A good fiberglass part will have a good gelcoat (without pin holes and air pockets), and it will fit without having to shave the edges too much. Most fiberglass is shipped with a matte finish on the external surfaces, so it's fairly hard to tell how smooth or wavy the surface of the gelcoat is without laying some glossy paint on the surface.

A few fiberglass companies offer two different constructions for each one of their products. One is a lightweight version strictly built for saving weight, so they don't have the internal bracing, and are very light. They mount as pin-on parts and don't attach like factory parts. The second type of glass is a heavy-duty street version. It weighs more than the lightweight version, because it has internal bracing and extra layers of fiberglass for strength. The weight savings over steel components is still significant, and you can run them on the street. Some street parts offer attaching points for bolting in as stock sheetmetal and even have provisions for

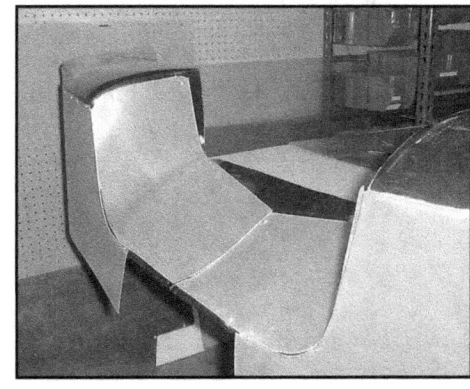

This fiberglass front bumper is getting an air dam attached to it. Flat, thin fiberglass panels are attached as a foundation for the desired shape. They help give a flat, rigid surface on which to start the project, resulting in a better finished product.

mounting factory trim and accessories. Check with the specific company before you purchase.

I've seen people running front and rear fiberglass bumpers on the street. They give the car the appearance of running a legal bumper to keep the local officials happy, unless they check to see if it's metal. They significantly reduce weight. They were designed for the purpose of reducing weight on drag cars and were never meant to be used on the street. Use them on the street at your own risk.

You should be aware that fiberglass parts save weight, but obviously are not as strong as the steel parts you replace. In an accident, the steel will have more integrity.

Before you purchase fiberglass parts, inform them of how you plan on driving the car when it's finished. That way they can better serve you in getting the strength of fiberglass parts you will need. You typically have to tell them to add extra strength if you want it. If you are going to drive with fiberglass on the street, you are better off getting glass parts that will last.

If you care about quality and the appearance of your engine compartment, U.S. Body Source offers their quality Tech Hood with a smooth gel coat on the top and underside. The appearance of this hood is a far cry from a standard fiberglass hood.

Fiberglass Hoods

A typical lightweight, competition-style fiberglass hood weighs between 12 to 20 lbs. It looks correct on the outside, has little to no internal bracing to add strength and keep it in its original shape. This hood won't have provisions for bolting to your car, it would be a pin-on style, which means you have to attach it to your car by way of quick release racing pins.

The street / heavy-duty / bolt-on fiberglass hoods are better for Pro-Touring applications. A bolt-on glass hood weighs between 25 and 50 lbs, depending on the vehicle. Since the stock steel hood weighs between 67 and 110 lbs, the weight savings is significant. They have internal bracing to add strength and offer provisions to be bolted to the original hood hinges and tabs to bolt other parts in their original locations.

One company in particular offers a third level of heavy-duty hoods. U.S. Body Source's Tech Hood line features stronger bracing and a fully finished underside for a better show appearance. If you have ever tried to clean the underside of a fiberglass hood, you would appreciate the clean, smooth finish. This typically adds about 10 pounds compared to their standard heavy-duty hoods. Compared to the weight of a metal hood, it is still a good savings.

With a bolt-on hood, you can save approximately 60 pounds. Since the front of the car weights plenty more than the rear, a 60-pound savings is a huge step in the process of equalizing the front and rear weight distribution for better handling.

Companies like VFN Fiberglass and U.S. Body Source offer fiberglass body parts and hoods in numerous configurations. They have a large line of fiberglass hoods for just about every GM car. Any fiberglass part available through VFN Fiberglass is also available in carbon fiber.

Promax Corporation is offering Fiberglass-bodied versions of Muscle Cars. This is their version of the '67 Chevy Nova, named Vennom. They changed some of the body lines, modified the wheelbase, flush mounted the windows, and more. It is much lighter than the Nova, and it will never rust. (Photo courtesy Promax Corporation)

Fiberglass Bodies

One of the fastest production cars in the U.S. is the Chevrolet Corvette. It's well known as a fiberglass-bodied car. The older Vettes are more fiberglass than the newer ones. Either way, the fiberglass construction helps GM engineers keep the weight of the car to a minimum. Nowadays, you can get reproductions of just about any popular GM body. U.S. BodySource and VFN are just two of the few companies offering complete body shells.

The Promax Corporation is offering what they call Ultimate Street Cars. They have been building serious street and race cars since 1984. They are turnkey fiberglass versions of a few 1960s cars. When I say "version," I mean they take a popular car and build an altered replica of it. For instance, their first offering is called the "Vennom." When you first look at it, you know it's a copy of a '67 Chevy Nova, but when you see GM's version next to the Vennom, you realize they are not the same. The quarter panels flow at a different angle, the nose of the car drops off a little more, the windows are all flush mounted, the fenderwell openings are different, and more. It turns out that this race-bred interpretation of the early Nova is much different. All the body and floorpanels are made of heavy-duty fiberglass. The frames are available with many options. They could be built by you or by Promax. You could adapt a full C4 suspension with an LS1 and a T-56, or just go with full C5 running gear. The beauty of all Promax's work is that they designed the Vennom to utilize most of the standard Nova trim pieces. They worked with top companies to help make the Vennom-specific parts like high-quality weather striping. The windows are all made of safety glass. One of the greatest features is the body and floorpan will never rust. The next GM body they will make a version of is the '69 Chevy Camaro.

Spoilers, Air dams, and Body Mods

There are plenty of opinions on air dams, spoilers, and ground-effects packages. Some people think they are ridiculous and are just for looks. On current production cars, they are used more for styling than for function. Coupes and family sedans are available with rear spoilers. If you take a look at all the new spoilers, you will notice a large percentage of them are very flat and neutral. Rear spoilers and air dams have not always been for looks.

The '67 Chevrolet Camaro was the first production car with a rear spoiler as a factory option. The rear spoiler and front air dam were designed by GM engineers so the Camaro would be more competitive in Trans Am racing against

The Corvette shown is built for road-course racing and uses a splitter to create extra downforce on the front of the car. The large flat surface parallel to the ground is the splitter. Air pushes down on the splitter for increased downforce, which increases cornering traction.

An adjustable rear spoiler like this one on Steve Chryssos's street fighter Camaro is not just for looks. This one could help increase downforce in the rear, resulting in better traction and faster lap times on a road course. You can adjust it to get the optimum angle. (Photo courtesy Steve Chryssos)

This VegaMods air dam is mostly for looks, but does a good job of sending the air around the outside of the car, and keeping it from getting underneath.

the Ford Mustang. The spoilers have been tested to prove their effectiveness. With the downforce of the rear spoiler, the Camaro gets more front-end lift at high speeds without the front air dam. With the front air dam and rear spoiler installed, the car gets more equalized downforce for better high-speed traction and handling. Apparently GM tested larger front air dams and experienced too much downforce in the front and too much lift in the rear at high speeds, so the engineers came to a good compromise.

Rear spoilers can play a huge part in the traction and downforce applied to the rear tires. This was proven by Jim Chaparral in the 1960s with the introduction of the huge wing on the back of his race car. Less obtrusive spoilers have been played with ever since. On a third-generation Camaro, a racer decided to install a taller sheetmetal rear spoiler. It was 6 inches tall and at about a 70-degree angle from the deck lid. He then drove it with the spoiler and without the spoiler. With the extra downforce created by the spoiler, his track times improved dramatically because he could stay on the throttle entering the corners, which equated to even faster exiting. You don't have to get too crazy on the street, but an adjustable aluminum rear spoiler might be just the ticket to increasing the fun factor when you hit the road course.

Like the GM engineers, racers have found out through testing that aerodynamics play a part in how well a car handles. Take a look at the F1 cars; they generate so much downforce with the aerodynamics of their cars that at speed, they could be driven upside down on the racetrack. The downforce would push their cars upwards to the track. There are a few ways to improve your aerodynamics for Pro-Touring cars, whether on a road course, at 160 mph in the Pony Express road race, or even on the highway at 65 mph. Air getting under the front of your car creates wind resistance, drag, and sometimes enough lift to hamper steering stability (think Corvair). A good way to limit the air getting under the car is with a front air dam. This is a good way to get the air to flow around and over the car, instead of under it. An air dam with a splitter (a protruding flat front air dam that runs parallel to the ground) increases down force in the front end, which increases tire traction. At high-speed (160+ mph), a large front air dam and splitter can create enough downforce to overwork a tire, causing it to heat up and fail. So if you are going to try modifying your aerodynamics, try modifying in moderation.

This '68 Vette was equipped with vents or gills from the factory. Racing cars and high-dollar supercars vent air from the engine compartment to keep if from getting under the car, which increases lift. These vents also allow for more speed and better cooling for the radiator.

Every car that has a radiator in the front has to let air into the engine compartment for cooling. Where does that air go after it passes through the radiator? Obviously, some of that air goes into the engine. The rest of the air builds pressure under the hood, before it flows out of the engine compartment down under the car. At high speed, if too much air gets trapped under the hood, it can cause the front end to lift a little. The air that travels under the car causes drag. If you take a look at all the high dollar super cars, and some muscle cars, you will notice engine compartment venting in the side of front fenders. These vents let air vent out the sides of the car instead of building up under the hood. This also helps keep the air flow through the engine compartment and help the engine run cooler, since the air does not stay stagnant and get heated by exhaust and engine heat. These vents have been referred to as gills (like a fish) or louvers. There are very few people putting these gills on cars that were not factory equipped with them. Front-engine Ferraris, Dodge Vipers, Corvettes, first-generation Trans Ams, and high-dollar race cars have them, so why couldn't you design and install an esthetically pleasing set of gills on an early Camaro?

Pulling air into the radiator and venting it out the hood is another way to create downforce, while keeping the air from getting trapped in the engine compartment.

Some racers simply prop the rear of the hood up with spacers. This allows the air to travel out of the engine compartment between the cowl and the rear of the hood. This seems to be effective and looks good on some cars, but it looks out of place on others. If you have a fiberglass cowl hood without bracing or an air box, the air can escape on its own. But this defeats the purpose of having a cowl hood to get cool air to the carburetor. With the big mouth/grill on early GMs, a lot of air gets forced into the engine compartment. The air pressure under the hood is higher than the air pressure that builds up at the cowl panel. All the hot air from the engine compartment tries to push past the carburetor and out the back of the scoop.

Another way to get air out from under the hood after it passes through the radiator is to vent it directly out the top of the hood. Ford's GT40, the Shelby Series 1, and some CAN AM cars use this design. This would take some serious work, since the top of the radiator would probably need to be tilted forward. A fairly generous hole would have to be cut in the hood, and ducting would have to be fabricated to vent all the air from the radiator out the top of the hood.

Chapter 7

Body kits are not just for sport-compact cars. Designing one with looks and aerodynamic function in mind takes a lot of thought. Here are two of the many designs drawn by John McBride for Tyler Beauregards '68 Camaro. (Rendering courtesy of John McBride)

Wood and metal bracing is used as a foundation for the body pieces. Then clay and composites are applied for shaping and contouring. A mold will be made from the finished product, then the parts can be made of carbon fiber or fiberglass using the mold.

With the recent popularity of body kits on import cars, some people have been apprehensive to add any sort of custom bodywork to American cars. Some builders have found there are other body modifications that can help the aerodynamics and/or help your car stand out in a sea of other cars. Some are subtle and some are not. Over the years, there have been a few builders that have changed the exterior of their cars to cheat the wind or just try to stand out. I've seen early Pro-Street Camaros with later-model Camaro-styled ground effects and side skirts.

Aerodynamics

Cars have not always been designed with aerodynamics in mind. Most were designed to be visually appealing. Only a few cars were designed to cheat the wind. Take a look at 1960s and 1970s cars. Most of them are shaped like bricks. Well, maybe not a brick, but close. Your everyday hot rodder couldn't care less about how their car cheats the wind. The guys who are finding ways to tune their bodies are the nutty guys running high-speed open-road racing, where you drive a '69 Camaro bodied car at 220 or even 160 mph. After being a part of these racing events, you will notice people making small modifications here and there to get an extra few mph on the top end

Fender flares are a good place to start. A fender flare that fits perfectly with the width and offset of your tires and wheels can make a difference in your top speed. The most aerodynamic positioning of the outside edge of the tire is as close to the outside edge of the fender lip as you can get. If the flare sticks out a couple of inches out from the tire, it will cause air turbulence around the outside of the car. The fenders can catch a lot of air that could otherwise be flowing around the car.

The grille openings in the front of the car are massive on earlier body styles. The large grille gulps a lot of air that builds up in front of the radiator. The air that gets through the radiator and into the engine compartment gets caught under the hood or travels under the car. This all slows the car down. You can add some gills (vents) in the front fenders to allow trapped air to purge out the side of the car. Take a look at some high-dollar supercars for engine-compartment venting. Mark Deshetler noticed a difference in his Chevy-powered Mustang. Since he installed gills in his car has less lift at higher speeds. There are some remedies for this explained in the body mods section earlier in this chapter. Pro-Touring cars could benefit from cheating the air a little bit.

Spoilers and air dams help cheat the wind and create downforce. They are covered earlier in this section. The headlight area is another problem area on the front of most cars. A lot of earlier cars have some sort of a pocket around the headlight. Eric Pettersen got an extra 7 mph on the 145-mph top-end charge

Body and Electrical

just by adding some lexan covers over his headlight buckets. To get that same extra 7 mph, he would need to add about 15 to 20 horsepower. Imagine the difference in the cost of engine parts to gain 15 hp compared to spending a few bucks on lexan. Take a good look at your car and see if there are some modifications you could make to cheat the wind. Even if you are not going to drive your car at 220 mph, you could make a difference in your handling and fuel mileage.

Fender Flares

When you mention fender flares, guys associate the term with the 1970s hot rod vans and bell-bottom jeans. Like bell-bottom jeans, trends come back. What about vans? I digress. Fender flares don't have to be big and gaudy. Small flares are adequate, subtle, and can look good. Fender flares need to serve one purpose. They need to allow more room for wide tires that don't quite fit in the stock fenderwell. A wider tire will give you more traction, and a wider track width will give you more cornering stability. If you tub your car and put all the rubber between stock fender lips, you are limiting the track width of your car and its stability.

When I refer to flares, I'm not talking about a seven-inch fender flare because you want to put 345/35x17 tires on the back of your '63 Chevy II (which barely fits a 235-wide tire). As with everything in life, a little moderation is good. I'm talking about flares that give you an extra inch or so of room to stick some wider tires inside the fender lips. Mini tubbing would be the first avenue you may want to pursue on the Chevy II. If you want to set yourself apart from other cars and only need an extra inch of clearance, there are different ways you could go about flaring your fenders. Some flaring techniques will be covered in this section, but not all will be covered. Of course, not all cars look great with flares of any type, and some bodies don't lend themselves easily to flaring.

Back in the late 1960s, Trans Am racers were flaring the fenders in a subtle manner. The rules would not allow the cars to have any metal added, removed,

Remove the quarter panel, leaving the edges intact. Do the same with a donor car. Stretch and form both panels. Split them directly over the center of the wheel-well opening, leaving enough material so they will be bulged out, but still meet in the center. Weld both panels in and contour them for an effective, but subtle flare.

or recontoured on the fenders. Teams resorted to heating and stretching the rear fenders within the limits of the rules, since they were only bulged, not recontoured. This can be done to Pro-Touring cars too, since part of Pro-Touring gets its roots from the historic Trans Am cars. Some shops still perform this extensive modification by removing the skin of the quarter panel around the outer perimeter of the panel to keep the perimeter body lines intact. Take another quarter panel from a donor car and stretch it and shape it. Leaving some overlapping material on both panels over the wheelwell, cut the two panels in half near the centerline of the wheelwell opening. With the panels overlapped over the center of the wheelwell, pull them and stretch them until the bulges are uniform. Then tack weld it back into place. With the quarter bulged, cut the overlapping material in the center, and butt-weld the two halves together. There will be a gap on the inner fenderwell where it meets the outer skin. A panel will need to be fabricated to fill the fenderwell gap and then tacked into place. The tack welds are followed by a stitch weld and all the finishing bodywork. The finished product is very subtle and nets about an extra inch or two of extra tire clearance.

You can flare the fenders without modifying the entire panel in a couple different ways. Some techniques work better on some cars than others. Ninety-nine percent of the time, rolling the fender lip or performing any type of fender flaring will damage the paint on the outer surface of the panel. For a small flare in the lip of the fender, you can sometimes do this with body tools if you have extensive experience. I've seen a fender-lip rolling tool utilized for rolling lips and minor flaring. Sometimes it's necessary to make a cut in the inner fenderwell near the point where it attaches to the outer panel, if hammering

Chapter 7

the fender does not get you enough space. This allows the panel to stretch a little further. Once the flare is made, don't forget to weld up any open surfaces in the fenderwell. Contour the fender lip to your liking, accentuating the original design. If the front and rear fender lips don't match, making them match might be a good idea.

Another style of flare allows you to keep some of the original bodylines, but gives a subtle accent. Use your sharp felt-tip marker to lay all your lines out on the fender before you start. Make a

This fourth-generation Camaro is running 335x17s in the rear. Since it is raced hard, the fenders need to be flared so the suspension travel doesn't cause any tire contact with the quarter panel. This flare matches the front fender and is almost invisible to the untrained eye.

Another flaring technique is moving the outer edge of the fender outward after slicing it across the top and making a few cuts for stress relief. The fender is not sliced all the way to the front or the back. A jack and some wood were used to bulge the fender. (Photo courtesy Total Control Products)

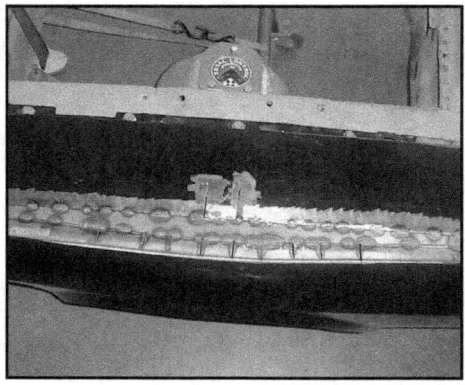

When the fender is bulged the amount you want, use a piece of posterboard to make a template of the opening you want to fill. Transfer the template to a strip of sheetmetal, and weld it in. (Photo courtesy Total Control Products)

cut in the top of fender about an inch inward from the outside edge of the fender. The cut runs almost from the doorjamb on the top of the fender nearly all the way to the headlight bezel. Small perpendicular cuts are made in the fender to allow it to flare easier. Some other relief cuts may be necessary to allow the panel to be stretched. Pull the outside panel to give yourself enough flare to clear the tire. There should be a slit open on the top of the fender. Cut a filler strip of sheetmetal to fill the gap. Tack weld every couple inches around the outside of the filler strip.

Rolling the Fender Lip

You may need to roll the fender lips to get an extra half-inch of clearance fitting a tight tire in your fenderwell. Sometimes the tire fits well in the wheelwell until you pull in and out of a driveway and the tires rub on the inside of the wheelwell or on the outside fender lip. It's also possible that the rear end (rear axle) is not centered in the body. It's typical for Chevy rear ends to be a half-inch more towards one side than the other, which sometimes causes rubbing. If you need an inch more room on the inner wheelwell, you should get some mini-tubs installed. If you need a quarter inch in one small spot, you may be able to use an air hammer with a blunt tip to add a little clearance, but this doesn't work on all cars. This section is about getting a little more clearance on the outside of the tire.

Whatever you do, do not cut the fender lip in little sections to bend them up easier or cut the fender lip off the wheel opening. You will reduce the strength of the fender and greatly increase the chance of slicing your tires. Nothing hurts more than slicing up a brand new set of 335-wide tires — well, cutting your hand on the fender lip hurts too.

This tool is the best thing since Star Wars. It is used for rolling fender lips. It is bolted to the axle, adjusted to the lip of the quarter, rolled back and forth, and then adjusted more. This process is simpler and cleaner than using a baseball bat.

Compared to the old days of sticking a baseball bat in the fenderwell and rolling the car back and forth, there are better ways to roll the fender lips. There are tools specifically designed for rolling the lip of a fender. Find a good shop that has one or buy one for yourself, and charge your friends to fix their cars and recoup the cost. That tool requires you to remove the tire and bolt the tool base flange in place of the wheel where it pivots. The tool will crack the paint on the inside of the lip. If you want to take a little extra precaution against the paint peeling all the way to the external edge of the fender lip, carefully use a razor knife to score the paint along the entire radius of the lip. It should be an 1/8-inch inward of the outside edge of the lip. Before rolling the lip, keep in mind that the roller could distort or damage the outer fender. So you could cause your-

Body and Electrical

self some extra paint and bodywork, especially if you try to roll the lip too much, or roll too much all at once.

Sweep the tool back and forth while cranking the handle, until the large roller contacts the fender lip. Sweep it around the arc of the wheelwell. Tighten the roller a little, roll the lip some more, and then repeat until the desired amount of clearance is reached. Adjusting the roller a little at a time ensures you will stretch the metal a little at a time. If you adjust it too much, you will increase the possibility of distorting the outside edge of the fender. To reduce the possibility of flaking and rusting, treat the bare metal and use a little touch-up paint on the line you scored with the razor knife when you are done.

Safety Upgrades

With all of the lawyers, laws, and safety regulations, we are all driving safer vehicles than ever before. Since Pro-Touring cars are supposed to embrace new technologies in suspension, brakes, tires, and drivetrain, we should go the next step and embrace technological advances in safety equipment.

Fire Systems

If you are reading this book, there is a good chance you have a good amount of time, money, and pride invested in your car — not to mention in your own well being. Purchasing a fire extinguisher for in your car should be high on your priority list. You can purchase fire extinguishers in hardware stores and speed shops, just make sure you purchase one for automotive use, since there are different extinguishing agents available for different types of fires. For your safety, make sure to purchase a DOT approved extinguisher. To get the best extinguisher and advice, there are companies that make and sell fire systems exclusively. Safecraft Safety Equipment offers many different hand-held extinguishers, mounting brackets, and extinguisher systems specifically designed for cars, motorsports, and just about everything else.

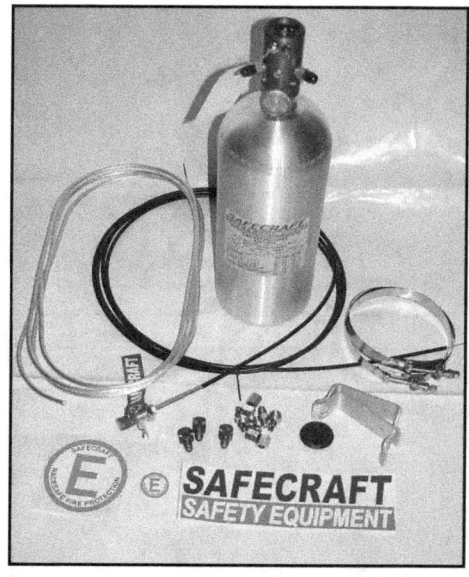

This is a Safecraft Safety Equipment RS extinguishing system with the optional 10-pound bottle. It comes with mounting brackets, T-bar clamps, hardware, pull cable, discharge tubing, and discharge outlets. The 360-degree discharge head has three outlets and provisions for mounting one push knob and two pull cables (separate cables for the driver, navigator, and safety crew).

To add some extra protection and insurance against fire, you should install an extinguisher system. Safecraft offers many options in extinguisher systems. They offer 2, 3, 5, 10, and 20 pound capacity Halon bottles. The different systems have 360-degree swiveling push, pull, and pneumatic discharge head options. Installing one of these systems is very easy. Mount the bottle out of the direct sunlight, install the activation cable, and run the discharge tubing and nozzles. Racers typically have discharge nozzles located in the engine compartment, passenger compartment near the driver, and around the fuel cell. Call Safecraft for installation suggestions and advice on which of the different types of extinguishing agents and systems are best for your application.

Side Mirrors

There are a few reasons to upgrade the side view mirrors on your car (especially on car up to the mid 1970s). The

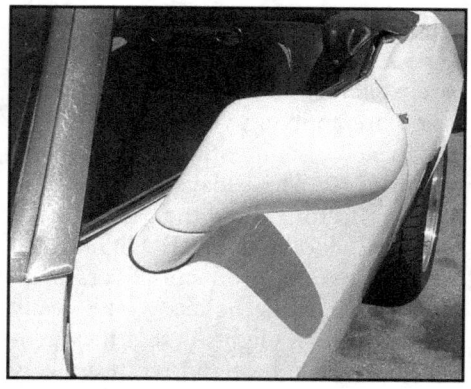

C5 Corvette mirrors look good on Doug Craft's '69 Camaro. They give almost twice the viewing area, so you can see better at a glance. They also feature a stronger mechanism to hold the mirror steady even during harsh driving.

newer mirrors are larger for safety purposes, have stronger hinge mechanisms, and they are more aerodynamic. The stock side mirrors on, for instance, a '66 Chevelle, are small diameter round units. You can't safely see out of them at a quick glance. Their pivot ball mechanism does not stand up well after a few years of normal driving with stock suspension. Add a some stiff springs and shocks into the equation and they start having a mind of their own, in fact I personally saw one commit suicide and fly off at about 140 mph. Which also brings up my next point, old chrome mirrors lack any hint of aerodynamics. Mirrors as early as late 1970s, F-body units were designed with a little aerodynamics in mind. But even they don't have the greatest hinge mechanism to keep the mirror steady. Newer C5 Corvette and '01 Dodge Viper mirrors are designed much better and have a large viewing area. Depending on the bodylines of your car, you can find a decent set of mirrors from a newer donor car that will mount and flow well. For an added bonus, if you found the right donor cars, you can add mirrors with electric movement, heaters, automatic dimming, and turn signals.

Taillights

Newer taillights are much brighter and easier to see than just about any tail-

Chapter 7

light predating 1995. Technology has come so far since the 1960s. People can barely tell if you have your blinker on or if you are applying your brakes in you '66 Chevelle, or any other GM cars built before 1970. These days, the chrome-plated reflector behind the bulb makes a single bulb look like 35 LED lights. And then, there are production cars with actual LED brake lights. What's really cool about LED lights is that they generate very little heat and require a very low amount of voltage. A brighter taillight can help save your car and all your time and labor. Their blinding brightness might catch the attention of some guy driving while talking on his cell phone, who might have otherwise rammed into your rear end.

Taking apart any new production-car light and utilizing the reflectors, bulbs, or LEDs to custom build some lights for your older car could make for some great results. Just keep in mind that light bulbs generate heat, some more than others, and installing one too close to a reflector or lens could cause a fire or at least melt the lens.

There is a company called Technostalgia that offers complete LED conversion kits that really work, and they remove the guesswork from converting to LEDs. They offer kits for at least twelve GM cars at the time this book was written.

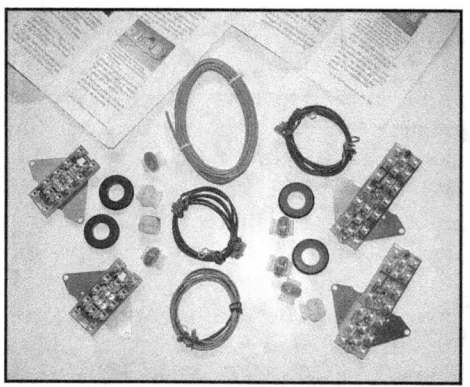

1. On the left is a turn signal and back-up LED conversion kit. On the right is the brake and tail LED conversion kit. These kits come with LED bulb panels, grommets for protecting wires, wire harnesses, custom push-style locking electrical connecters, and instructions.

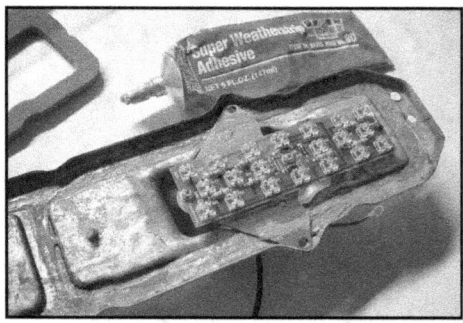

2. Install the rubber grommets in the housing to protect wires from chafing, and lay LED arrays in housing. The turn/back-up array is the same size as the housing cup, so it is easy to center it for installation. The brake/taillight array is longer than the cup in the housing. There is only one correct way to mount it. The longer end of the array is positioned toward the end of the housing (as shown).

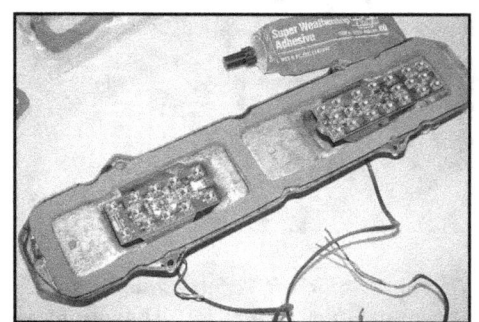

3. I spread Permatex 80 weather-strip adhesive (known as gorilla snot) around the edges of the housing on the gasket-sealing surface. This adhesive does not fully harden. To keep moisture from getting to the LED arrays, a little adhesive was placed between the array's "bat wings" and the housing. A new set of original equipment reproduction gaskets were used to seal the LED arrays.

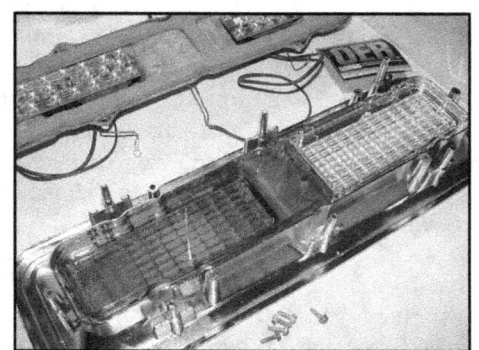

4. The finish on my original taillight bezels left much to desired, and the taillight lenses were not in the best shape either. Since I had everything apart, I decided to replace them with new OER bezels, lenses, and gaskets from Classic Industries. With the lenses in the bezels, the bulb housing is ready to bolt together.

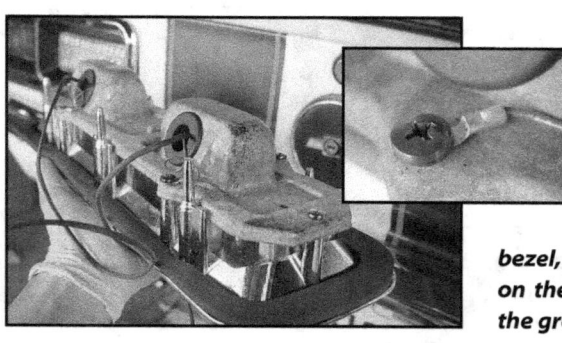

5. The LED wire harnesses each have a grounding wire. When installing the screws holding the bulb housing to the bezel, install the ground connecters under the screw (seen in inset photo). Put the bezel-to-body gasket on the bezel, and then you are ready to install it on the tail panel. The main photo shows the grommets installed correctly.

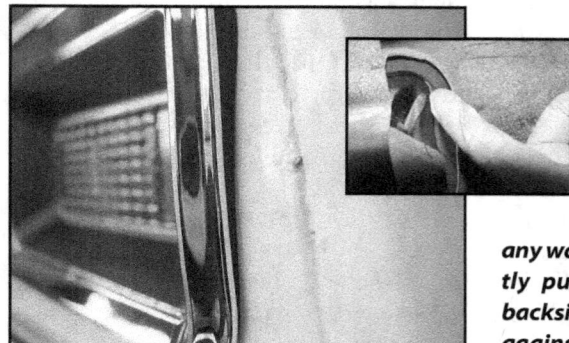

6. Correctly installing the bezel gasket is important. The gasket will not just fit correctly. As seen in this picture, the gasket pushed out at the top and sucked in at the bottom. The gasket is now so out of wack that it won't seal out any water. While tightening the bezel, gently push the gasket outward from the backside, until the gasket completely seals against the tail panel.

Body and Electrical

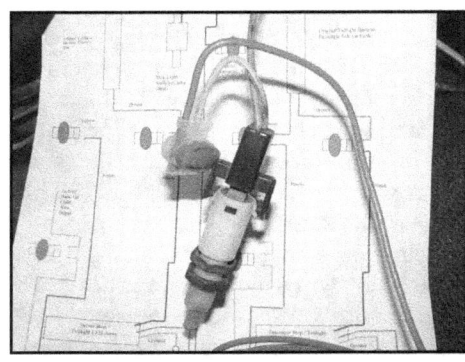

7. Installing the brake light kit by itself uses a different wiring schematic than installing it with the back-up light kit, so refer to the schematic that comes with your kit for the correct wiring connections. The back-up light kit requires running a wire from the brake light switch to the taillight LED array. Other than that, only the factory wires are necessary for connecting. Simply trim the wires as close to the original bulb sockets as possible to ensure you have enough wire to work with.

8. Reconnect your battery and test the functions of the new LED arrays on both sides of the vehicle. Notice that they are much brighter than factory units. Imagine how much safer you will feel, knowing you are protecting your investment, since now people can actually see your lights. Coupled with the Technostalgia LEDs, the OER lenses and bezels brought a whole new life to the car's tail panel.

If you want to spend extra time making your own LED brake lights, there are a few companies offering round and oval LED units designed for 18-wheelers. These come as single function brake lights, taillights, or flashers. They are also available as multi-function units with turn lights, taillights, and brake lights. Make sure you get the right lights for your application. For safety's sake, think of ways to convert to LEDs.

If you don't like LED taillights, but want to upgrade to a newer set of taillights, you can always take a look around at other production taillight lenses off new domestic or import cars. Maybe some of them can be adapted or grafted into your tail panel or bumper. I have seen C5 Corvette taillights and a custom tail panel grafted onto a '68 Camaro. With the amount of different cars on the market, the possibilities out there are almost endless.

3rd Brake Light

In addition to installing safer taillights, take a look at all the new 3rd brake lights on production cars. Most of the coolest units are the slim LED units. Some are for mounting inside the car on the rear deck, or in the headliner. Some units are for external mounting on the roofs of SUVs and sunk in the spoilers of sports cars. A few aftermarket companies offer custom 3rd brake lights in plastic and billet housings. A cool way to mount a 3rd brake light would be grafting a thin LED unit into a stock '68 Camaro, or installing one in a custom headliner on a '71 Chevelle. There are many options with the different mounting solutions, shapes, and sizes. Plus, some insurance companies offer discounts on policies if your car is equipped with a 3rd brake light.

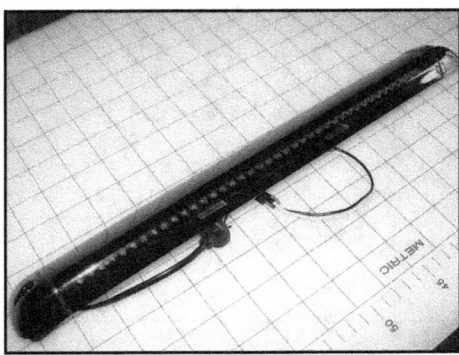

This LED 3rd brake light assembly came off a 1995 GM SUV. This and other types of 3rd brake lights can be cleanly incorporated into your car and make it more visible to cars behind you.

Headlights

Stock T3 headlights did their jobs in the past, but are not as bright or as safe as the newer halogen units. The Halogen lights are direct replacements for original standard bulbs. They plug right into the original socket. If you want brighter high-tech headlights, you can upgrade to a Bright Drivers kit available from Detroit Speed and Engineering (DSE). They offer all the late-model features like moisture-proof Gortex one-way valves and replaceable bulbs. The lightweight polycarbonate lens is safer for on-track and everyday driving, and 30 times stronger than stock glass lenses. This kit, unlike others on the market, does not require hooking up relays or modifying the headlight bucket.

This Bright Driver headlight kit is a step above standard glass halogen headlights and delivers brighter and safer driving light. These lights are a simple bolt-in upgrade (without modifications), and they are almost a pound lighter than stock lights. They are also made of materials 30 times more rock resistant than glass, have moisture proof features, and have available replaceable bulbs. (Photo Courtesy Detroit Speed & Engineering)

To go the extra mile, high-intensity discharge (HID) lights are even brighter, and they are the largest step in high-tech lighting at the time this book was written. Sylvania offers HID conversion kits for dual round, quad round, dual rectangular, quad rectangular, and a couple of other headlight combinations/applications. With some electrical wiring skills, one of their kits could be installed in an afternoon. Mounting the HID lights in the stock headlight housings is the easy part. HIDs come with a ballast resistor for each light assembly. You will need to mount those in close proximity to the lights. Then you will need to wire in the supplied wire harness and relay.

Wiper Motors

If you want to really put the "touring" in your Pro-Touring car, you will drive it anywhere, everywhere, and just about anytime (except when there is snow and salt on the roads). In some parts of the country, you can drive your car everyday, but would eventually get stuck driving in the rain. If your car was built before the 1980s, there is a high possibility your car is equipped one of those annoying windshield wiper systems. You know what I am talking about. It has three speeds: off, high, and ludicrous speed. If you are driving in a light rain or mist, you click the knob to the left and then back to off, so the wipers only sweep once. Unfortunately, you are forced to do this ritual every minute or two. Some builders have noticed the flaw in this type of system and upgraded to systems from late-model cars equipped with delay features.

Some guys don't want a wiper motor mounted on their firewall in the traditional location. For a really clean look, a few guys cut the wiper flange off the firewall and weld the flange to the firewall behind the left front fender. Then they fill the hole in the firewall where the wiper was originally. Then they install a custom extended arm on the mechanism and move the wires. This leaves the firewall with a very clean uncluttered look.

Charging System

With the addition of electrical components like electric fans, an electric water pump, fuel injection, stereo systems, etc., you will need to upgrade your charging system by installing a better battery and a higher-output alternator.

The most popular battery on the market is made by Optima. Their batteries are identified by the battery top, which is red, yellow, or blue. The red battery is good for typical street car applications where the car is driven almost everyday and doesn't have electric fans, fuel injection, and a big stereo. Yellow top batteries are best suited for Pro-Touring applications, especially if you don't drive your car for a few weeks at a time and have some power draining accessories. Blue top batteries are best suited for marine applications.

Optima batteries have a unique Spiralcell Technology that provides features standard batteries don't have. The cells have more surface area, with closer spacing, and ability to use higher purity lead. This equals out to lower resistance, quicker charge acceptance, better shelf life, and more battery power. The plates are immobilized, which translates to improved vibration resistance. This means they are much better for Pro-Touring cars than a standard battery, since they will last longer under hard driving with stiff suspensions.

Car batteries have two different types of terminals: post and side terminal. Optima batteries come in two configurations. They either have top posts, or come as dual-terminal types, with top posts and side terminals. Buying a dual-terminal battery will allow for extra connections you may need for extra accessories.

Optima Batteries can vent if they're severely overcharged or if the alternator or regulator produced more than 15 volts for extended periods. There are two safety valves that will purge excess pressure and then reseal completely. An alternator overcharge condition is very rare, and you should never experience one. On the other hand, a standard battery outgasses continuously while it

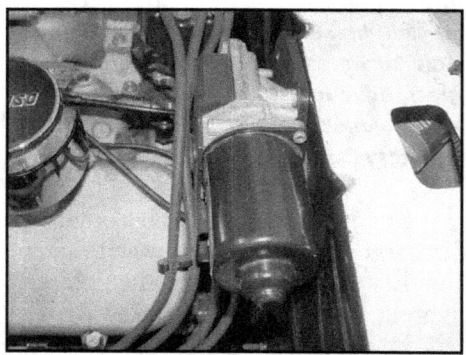

The Detroit Speed & Engineering wiper motor is available for a few different early GM cars. The motor is easy to install, has 5 delay speeds (plus a low and high setting), and is compact enough to allow easy valve cover removal.

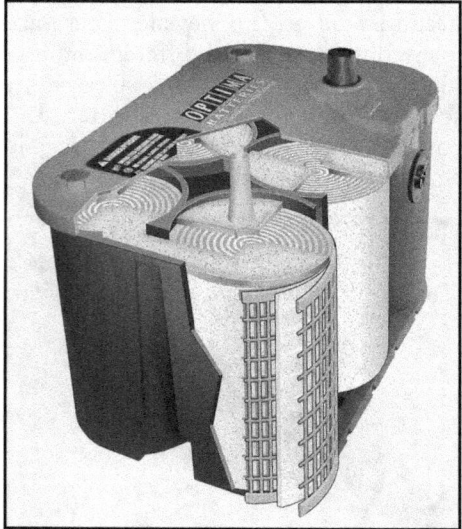

The Optima battery is constructed with the unique Spiralcell Technology. The features include more cell surface area, higher purity lead, and immobilized plates that resist damaging vibrations. (Photo credit to Optima Batteries)

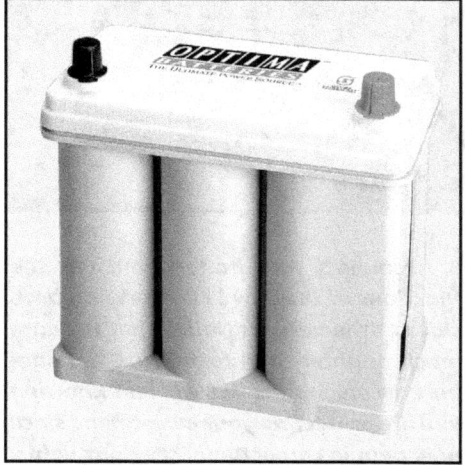

Optima added the group-51 battery to their product line. It was introduced to meet size requirements for sport compact cars, but is becoming popular with the domestic crowd, because it tips the scales at a svelte 26 pounds. That is sixteen pounds lighter than the standard group-34 yellow-top Optima battery. With 500 cold cranking amps, it exceeds almost any V-8's starting needs. (Photo credit to Optima Batteries)

Body and Electrical

charges and is prone to leaking, which causes corrosion around the battery location. Optima batteries do not leak and corrode your battery tray or surrounding area.

Mounting the battery in the trunk is a good way to move 25 to 40 pounds to the rear of the car, which is a great start in a process of balancing the weight ratio between the front and the rear. There are a few different ways to mount the battery in the trunk. You can put it in a racing-approved plastic or metal vented battery box, or you can mount it in an open-air battery mount like the ones shown in the Optima battery picture. If you are going to mount a battery in an open-air mount in the trunk, only use a sealed battery, since you don't want poisonous gasses in your trunk.

Basic Electrical and Wiring

As with any other part of Pro-Touring, or any kind of hot rodding for that matter, it's a good idea to do things the right way. The electrical system should not be treated like and afterthought. There are good and bad ways to perform every part of your project. Why do something half way, when spending a little extra time can produce something so much better. You may be asking what that has to do with the electrical system. This section will be a brief overview of wiring.

Cross-Linked

Electrical wires are available in different qualities. There is the normal wire you get at the local hardware store, and there is better quality wire. The quality wire is called "cross-linked" wire. It uses polyethylene insulation to ensure it is durable for automotive environment. Wire used on a car needs to have good abrasion resistance and the insulation needs to stand up to dirt, oil, and temperatures up to 275 degrees Fahrenheit. Cross-linked wire is resistant to getting kinked, which is a good thing for wires you pull through panels and around accessories. It would be a big headache to completely wire your project and have a gremlin in your wiring because you kinked a couple of wires during installation. Maybe your fuel injection just won't run right, and later you find that the kink caused too much resistance in a wire for your fuel injection that requires a certain signal to run correctly. Cross-linked wire is available in bulk from automotive wiring companies.

Wiring Harnesses

Not every project needs to have a completely new wire harness. Some projects need a new fuse panel in addition to the stock panel. Either way, there are a lot of aftermarket wiring companies offering different solutions. Two good companies that come to mind are American Auto Wire and Painless Performance Wiring. They offer good solutions to just about any custom wiring job. The better companies offer harnesses that have wires printed with labels, not just a stick-on label that can fall off during installation. The labels are still going to be visible years later to help troubleshoot a problem. If you want a stock wiring harness, American Auto Wire can get you what you need. They also have completely detailed wiring schematics available for just about every American automobile, which can be helpful when wiring a car.

Connections

When changing anything or adding components to your electrical system, it is a good idea to make good connections. Using crimped hardware-store butt-connectors to splice wires is alright, but splicing and using solder and heat-shrink tubing would last longer and be a little more resistant to moisture. For connecting an accessory in an area that might get any sort of moisture, there are weatherproof electrical connectors available. The best ones on the market are called Weather Pack connectors. The auto manufacturers use them to ensure electrical connections have the best possible connection in extreme environments. Weather Pack connectors have a male and female quick release male (tower) and female (shroud) connector. Inside the connectors are a male and female terminal. A seal is also installed on the wire to ensure a weather-resistant connection. The nice thing about Weather Pack is the time it can save on wiring, since they are designed to be used without solder. The terminals have a small cross-hatched pad that the wire is crimped to for a positive lock. Special wire crimpers are needed for assembling Weather Pack connectors.

Electrical Accessories

What size alternator do you think your car should have? I found a good source of information on how to pick the right starter and an alternator with the proper voltage for your application. Check out Powermaster Motorsports website www.powermastermotorsports.com. They have a chart and some questions that will point you in the right direction. Alternators come in many different shapes, sizes, and outputs. With the new technology and cramped engine compartments of today, the alternator cases and starters are getting smaller,

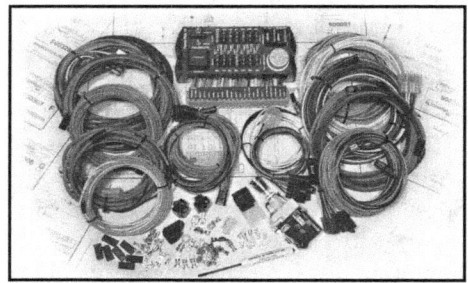

Electrical wiring harness kits like this Power Plus kit are somewhat universal. It comes complete with all the necessary plugs, connectors, wires, rubber boots, and a fuse box. (Photo courtesy American Auto Wire)

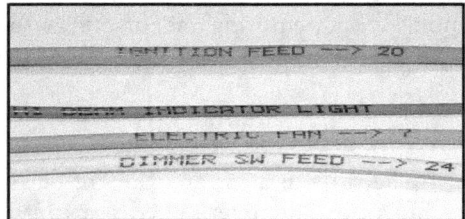

Depending on the company, some wiring kits come with easy-to-read pre-labeled wires. They make wiring easier, because you don't have to spend extra hours tracing wires (especially if you are color blind). (Photo courtesy American Auto Wire)

Chapter 7

The Weather Pack terminal utilizes a weatherproof rubber seal (in center of photo) that keeps the elements away from the terminal after plugging it into the connector. The seals come in different sizes for different gauges of wire.

which also means you can benefit on your older car too. If you need to make room for your twin turbos or just shed a few pounds, there are some small alternators and aftermarket brackets available to help. If you have any charging or starter questions, call Powermaster.

Interior

There is no limit to what you can do with the interior of a Pro-Touring car. Sometimes you only need stock equipment with a few extra gauges, but upgrading to some late-model amenities or going all out with new everything is good too. Some early factory parts are not as safe as new factory and aftermarket parts, so upgrading could save your life. There are laws and federal mandates that require auto manufacturers include certain safety features in new cars. They are constantly growing stricter every model year, requiring manufactures to upgrade their safety features.

Seats

The seats in a car are thought of as comfort item, but overlooked as a safety feature. Seat comfort is not as important as your safety. Low-back bucket seats work well and go with a stock-looking interior, but unfortunately, they are not safe in a rear-impact accident. Imagine you are stopped at a light and someone hits you doing 10 miles per hour or more. Your head will snap back. Without a headrest to limit travel, you run the risk of neck injuries. Take a look at brand new car seats; they all have adjustable headrests for safety reasons.

Seats are also a part of comfort and control. A seat with side bolsters on the back and seat bottom help support your thighs and body from moving side-to-side as you maneuver your car through corners. You can get seats with this lateral control from late-model factory cars and aftermarket companies. Factory seats are built for the average-sized person, so they are not typically as supportive as an aftermarket seat purchased for your size. You can order some aftermarket seats in different widths to fit your rear end better. Someone with wide hips would not be as comfortable in a narrow-bodied seat. Since Pro-Touring is about driving, your comfort is important.

If you have a certain type of material you want to upholster your interior and seats with, you can send it to some seat manufacturers and they will build

Seats aren't just for looks, they're for safety too. This aftermarket high-back seat gives you more control for performance driving. This seat gives good lateral support for your back. (Photo courtesy of Corbeau)

you a set of seats using your material. Good upholstery shops can reupholster any seat with your choice of fabric if you have a set of seats you want to keep. If you don't have a huge cage in your car, and still have a back seat, you can get material to cover your seat and make it match your front seats. Some rear seats out of late-model cars will fit in older cars with very little modification. If you have mini-tubbed your car, you will most likely need to narrow your rear seat, or at least modify the seat frame to better fit the larger inner wheelwells.

Center Console

If you are going to drive your car on a regular basis or drive it on long trips, like on the *Hot Rod* Power Tour, you will need some extra amenities. One item to consider is a center console with an armrest, at least two cup holders, and possibly a place to put your cell phone or other electronic devices. Only high-optioned early cars had consoles. Those consoles have a small compartment for vehicle registration and tickets, a little room for a gauge or two, and a place to rest your seat belt buckle when it isn't in use. Nowadays they have extra accessory ports for laptop converters and cell phone chargers, cup holders, CD holders, hidden compartments, and adjustable arm rests. If you do some research and modifications, you can fit a late-model console in your early-model Pro-Touring car. Getting a late-model console to fit usually requires modifying the console, mounting the brackets on the floorpan and transmission tunnel, and sometimes modifying the dash.

If you are going to build a console, make is as useful as possible. Integrate some cup holders from a late-model car, truck, or van. Adding at least one cup holder will be very useful. It doesn't get much worse than stopping for a bite to eat and not having a place to set your vat of soda. If there are no cup holders, it usually ends up resting between your legs. If you are unlucky, you will end up wearing the soda or spilling it in your car. I have heard that some areas of the U.S. have laws against driving with a drink resting between your thighs.

Body and Electrical

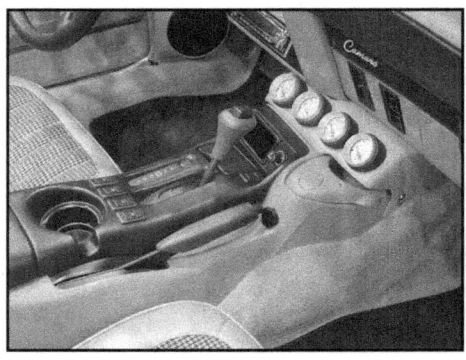

Adapting a late-model console or building a custom console for your car is a nice touch. This is a '98 Z28 console in a '69 Camaro. The floorpan was modified to fit the width, the shifter and E-brake handle were adapted, and a custom gauge console was built. (Photo courtesy Year One)

Chris Kerr says his cup holder is one of the most used items in his car. When driving on the Hot Rod *Power Tour, he constantly had a drink to keep himself hydrated. It also holds his CDs and cell phone, so they are not just floating around the car.* (Chris Kerr)

Pedals

A good set of pedal pads can look racy and actually give your more grip and control with your feet. A stock rubber pedal pad might allow your shoes to get better traction on the pedal, but make sure it is attached well. If a pad were to slide off while driving, it could be dangerous. Once you get used to the feel and size of your pedals, a change could affect your driving and foot positioning.

A dead pedal is very useful for the driver. It gives you a place to support and control your body weight during hard cornering. It also gives you a place to rest your foot, instead of on your brake or

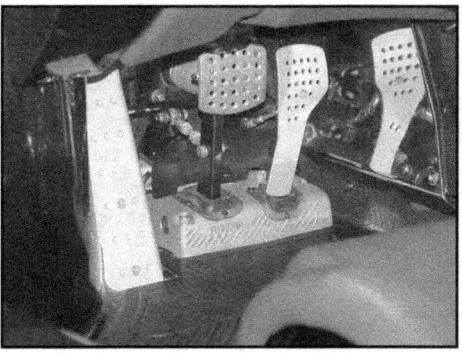

Styling cues can be picked up from looking at other cars. This is the pedal setup in a Ferrari. Along with the aluminum pedal pads, it is equipped with a big dead pedal. It gives you a place to rest your foot and support your body weight.

clutch pedal. They are starting to become standard equipment on new sports cars.

Some cars have their seats so far from the firewall, that the passenger can't comfortably (if at all) reach it with their feet to help support their weight while you throw your car through the corners. Installing a stationary or adjustable foot plate would show that you take more than yourself into consideration when building your Pro-Touring car.

Dashboard and Gauges

Customizing a dashboard is nothing new to any type of hot rodding, but the trends have become more elaborate and more detailed than before. A few years ago, guys would just remove the gauge pod, replace it with a little aluminum insert, and squeeze in a few extra gauges. Nowadays builders are going the extra mile to cleanly replace large sections of the dash or replace the entire thing.

Replacing the factory gauges with aftermarket units brings a whole new step to modifying the dash. Most of them have the turn signal indicators, emergency brake warning light, and high-beam indicator as an integral part of the gauge face. For safety reasons, you should find the wires connecting to these indicators and wire them into some small LED lights on the new dash. That way you will have indicators. The LEDs are available in different colors and sizes.

Stock GM gauges typically have indicator lights integrated into the bezel. When upgrading to custom gauges, indicators should be retained. These little LED lights from DSE are perfect for the job. (Photo courtesy Detroit Speed & Engineering)

This interior is all business. Cam Douglass decided to remove the entire stock dash and replace it with a contoured aluminum open-road race-inspired version. The important gauges can be seen by either the driver or the navigator. (Cam Douglass)

The '69 Camaro dashboard has never been easy to add big gauges to. Detroit Speed & Engineering came up with a design to replace the complete cluster with a hand-fabricated steel dash insert. Now you can fit a huge array of gauges and accessories. They sell it with and without bosses for the factory headlight switch, wiper switch, and the stock factory heater control unit.

The typical street car has a speedometer, tachometer, oil pressure gauge, volt gauge, fuel level gauge, and coolant temperature gauge. That setup is great until you get out on a road course or go to an open-road racing event. Once you start driving your car harder, you better start monitoring oil temperature and transmission temperature (for automatics). The engine and transmission temps can soar when you are racing. If you don't monitor them, you might have serious failure without realizing there were problems.

Along with keeping track of the vital signs of your engine, gauge should placement should be taken into consideration. Each application may have a better placement for gauges. The old trick for racing cars is to rotate all the gauges, so at average operating speed and conditions, the needles would point in the same direction. That way if all the needles were pointing straight up, the drive would know the car is operating normally, at a quick glance. The last thing you want to do is pull your eyes off the road for any length of time at high speeds. For that same reason, placing your gauges up on the dash closer to eye level is better if you plan on racing your car. Placing gauges on the console was an easy and cheap way for GM to add factory special-option instruments. Taking your eyes off the road to down at your console-mounted gauges can be dangerous. The closer you mount your instruments to your line of sight, the safer and more convenient they will be.

Air Conditioning

Not every Pro-Touring car on the planet needs air conditioning. Some Pro-Touring cars are set up for more of an all-out performance experience, and some cars are built with a little more comfort in mind. Some cars are equipped with air conditioning from the factory, and some didn't have air conditioning to start with. If you want air conditioning in your car and don't want to use the original factory system, you can install an aftermarket system.

Air-conditioning systems are comprised of a few key components. I will briefly go over the parts, so if you have questions after reading this, give Vintage Air, Inc. a call.

The evaporator is the largest of the components. It typically fits behind or under the dashboard. Air is cooled or heated in the evaporator and then blown out of the unit by the integrated blower fan motor. The compressor is basically a pump driven by the engine crankshaft that, when engaged, circulates refrigerant through the system. It pulls refrigerant in a vaporous state from the evaporator, pressurizes it, and pumps it through the condenser. The condenser is the large component that resembles a radiator. It's purpose to dissipate the heat absorbed from inside the car by condensing the high-pressure gas into a liquid state. The refrigerant then flows through the receiver / drier, which filters out any particles, and removes any moisture from the refrigerant. The refrigerant then flows through the expansion valve into the evaporator where it evaporates into a gas and absorbs heat to complete the cycle.

Vintage Air

The most popular aftermarket air conditioning manufacturer is Vintage Air. Not only do they offer air conditioning kits, you can assemble your own kit from parts to tailor to your own needs, they also offer everything you will need to install the system in your car. Vintage Air offers custom accessory brackets for separate components and a complete engine accessory drive system in a compact unit named The Front Runner. As of the publishing date of this book, Vintage Air was offering Front Runner systems for the small-block and big-block Chevys.

Vintage Air sells Sure Fit systems for many older GM cars and trucks. These kits take the guesswork out of installing aftermarket air conditioning. They come with all the parts you will need for installation, and are designed as complete bolt-in kits for specific applications.

Vintage Air also offers all the components separately for people who want a custom-fit kit that may fit in custom locations better, perform better because you want a bigger evaporator, and may look better because you can get upgraded: controls, fittings, hoses, dash vents, and compressors. Kyle Tucker of DSE has taken Vintage Air installations to a whole new level. He has installed enough custom-tailored systems that his company offers custom brackets to easily mount the largest and most powerful evaporator under specific dashboards.

There is an involved process of installing the Vintage Air Sure Fit kit or a custom-tailored kit. The three major processes to installing the air conditioner are the refrigerant/air conditioning system, the electrical system (for operating controls, safety system, and thermostatic system), and the engine coolant system (where the heat comes from). Some of the processes of installing a custom-tailored kit in a '68 Camaro are covered in the following series of photographs. I do not have enough space to show all of the steps in the process, so any additional questions could be answered by the knowledgeable technicians at Vintage Air or by the folks at DSE.

1. This is not a system you can order as one part number. Working closely with Kyle Tucker of Detroit Speed & Engineering, I was able to order all the Vintage Air parts to piece together a kit that would be more powerful than Vintage Air's Sure Fit kit. It meant extra install time, but it was well worth it. The parts necessary for the install were: Gen II Compac evaporator, drier with trinary compressor safety switch, compressor, bulkhead fitting, condenser, block off plate (not shown), hose kit, and control panel. The Gen II Series features fully electronic, servomotor operation that eliminates reliance on engine vacuum or original control cables. The Gen II also utilizes an adjustable heater control valve to give you "just right" temperatures year round.

Body and Electrical

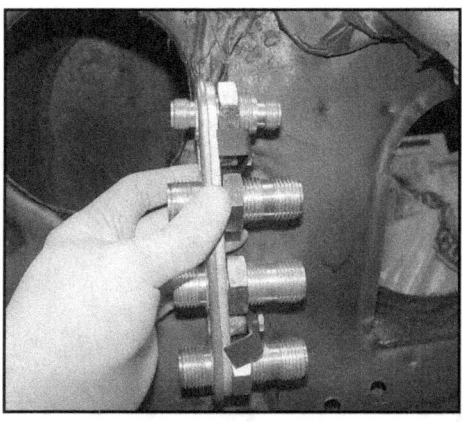

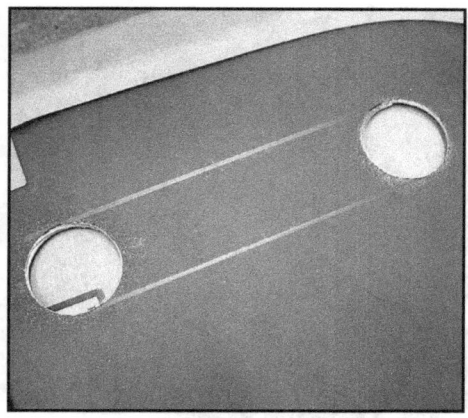

2. To run the coolant hoses and the air conditioner lines through the firewall, I chose to use the Pro Cast four-way inline bulkhead fitting. I decided not to use the more compact standard four-way setup, since the inline version allows more wrench access for removing or installing hoses. I also decided to fill the gaping hole in the firewall with a Detroit Speed & Engineering firewall fill plate also mentioned on page 110.

3. From the inside of the car, measurements were made to ensure the fitting would protrude through the firewall into the passenger compartment, not into the fresh air duct (further towards the outside of the car). With these measurements, I transferred marks to the Detroit Speed & Engineering fill plate. A mark showing the centerline of the bottom hole was made and then center-punched and drilled using a hole saw the exact size of the "step" on the backside of the bulkhead plate. If the hole is too big, the plate will fall through.

4. After one hole was made, the bulkhead plate was used to ensure the top bulkhead centerline was laid out on the fill plate. The distance is important, but if you want it to look good, make sure your top hole is located so that the bulkhead plate will be straight up and down. Failure to do this will result in a crooked bulkhead. Once the centerline of the top hole is laid out, make the second hole. Take a straightedge and mark lines that connect the two holes, then cut out the material between the holes.

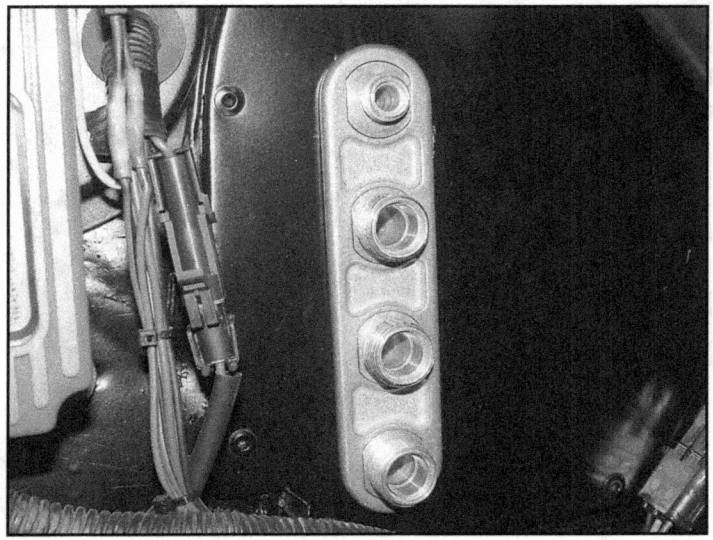

5. With the slot cut in the Detroit Speed & Engineering fill plate, the panel is set up against the firewall. Using the fill plate as template, the firewall is marked with a scribe. The hole saw was used to cut the two holes, and then we brought out the air shears to cut out the material between them. Since the fill plate and firewall have the same size holes, the bulkhead plate was a tight fit, but that's what you want.

6. The fill plate was painted after it was installed. Install all the bulkhead fittings before installing the bulkhead plate. Then install the bulkhead plate using the nuts and mounting straps on the inside of the interior.

How to Build GM Pro-Touring Street Machines

Chapter 7

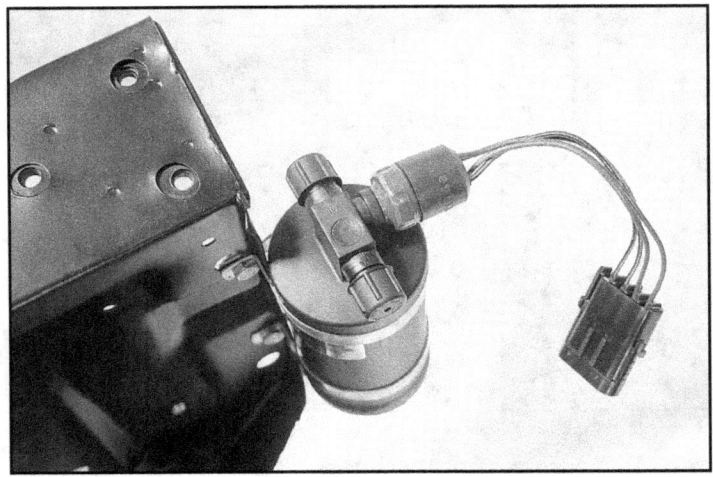

7. The standard drier with trinary switch was chosen. Two small holes were drilled in the end of the radiator support (behind the passenger-side headlight). It was easy to mount the drier by sandwiching the core support between the clamps' ends, using the straps supplied with the drier. The wires come without any connectors, so a Weather-Pak connector was installed for a clean, protected connection. The drier is mounted between the evaporator and the condenser. The side marked "IN" is the side coming from the condenser.

8. Vintage Air sells brackets to place the pump in many locations. I decided to do things the hard way. I wanted the to fit the 508 compressor between the engine block and the frame where the mechanical fuel pump normally mounts, but it had to clear the sway bar. I notched the frame for clearance, then I nestled the compressor on some objects to mock up the bracket. The angle on the crankshaft pulley was matched to the compressor pulley to ensure that the V-belts would line up.

9. Once the compressor was exactly where I wanted it (with access to the compressor fittings), a piece of cardboard from a cereal box was fitted into place as a template. The template was cut to match the diameter of the compressor body. I used the two bosses on the front of the big block and the mounting ears on the front and back of the compressor as points to attach the bracket to. Mounting the bracket solidly is very important.

10. The compressor bracket is nearly completed. From the cardboard template, two flat brackets were made from 1/4-inch steel plate. Aluminum spacers were machined from aluminum bar stock to fit between the brackets, and to space the compressor to line up with the V-grooves on the crankshaft pulley. I didn't know which pulley groove I would use, but I could space the compressor forward or backward by just swapping in different spacers. Since the bracket is non-adjustable, an idler pulley will need to be fabricated for belt adjustment.

Body and Electrical

11. Vintage Air offers a few different air conditioning controllers. I could have used the stock control panel, but decided I wanted the controls mounted elsewhere. For this job, the standard four-lever horizontal controller was chosen. Select the best location for your controller, then cut the mounting hole using the template supplied with the controller. The corners of the hole must be rounded. If you cut the hole with square corners, they will show after the control panel faceplate is mounted. Don't forget to follow the wiring diagram included with your controller.

12. The Gen II System also has heater and defroster functions. It requires hot water to run through the heater core located in the evaporator. The hot water has to come from the high-pressure side of the engine's cooling system. The water usually comes from a fitting located in the intake manifold under the thermostat, or in this case, a fitting from the high-pressure jacket at the rear of the engine on the intake manifold. The return (suction) side coming from the heater core would hook up to the water pump.

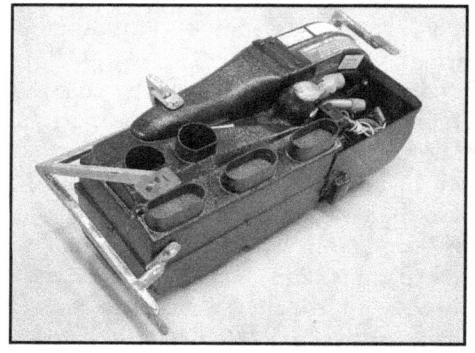

13. Mounting the evaporator is probably the toughest part of installing a universal kit, as opposed to using a Vintage Air Sure Fit kit designed specifically for a certain application. Detroit Speed & Engineering is taking the hassle out of installing the Gen II evaporator under a few different dashboards. The bracket mounts the unit up as high as it will go, but still allows space for the hoses and ducts. The bracket is worth the price of knowing your evaporator will fit without having to lie on your back for hours under the dash, trying to make your own bracket.

14. Once all of the tubes, hoses, and electrical connections are made, install the evaporator in its location under the dashboard. You will need to connect some of the shorter ducts, since the evaporator is in a raised position. Be careful to not kink or crush any of the ducts, hoses, or electrical wires. Double-check all hoses, mounts, and electrical connections. Once everything is in good working order, you are ready to get the system evacuated, checked for leaks, and charged with 134a refrigerant.

15. The latest in compact brackets for small blocks and big blocks is the Vintage Air FrontRunner system. The system is well engineered and has all of the best parts. (Photo courtesy Larry Callahan)

Chapter 7

MAD Chevelle
The Desmond Brothers '65 Malibu SS

MAD Ink made this concept rendering before spending any money on their '65 Malibu SS. It gave them an idea of how it might look when it was done, using the same color, stance, and chosen parts. ((Photo courtesy MAD Ink)

What do you do, when you are thinking you want to build a car, or just make some modifications, but you don't know what it will look like? Do you pour a ton of money into the project and hope it will look good? What if you get done, and your $30,000 (or more) project car looks totally wrong? There is a more cost-effective route. You can enlist an artist like Mike Desmond from MAD Ink, to make a rendering of your idea. That way you get a clue to the possible outcome before spending a ton of hard-earned cash on something less than what you want.

MAD designed the wheels. Bonspeed worked with MAD to build the custom wheels from their design. You can see the Baer Brakes caliper peaking through the opening in the wheel. (Photo courtesy MAD Ink)

MAD Ink took it upon themselves to use that same philosophy. They were going to build up a '65 Chevrolet Chevelle, but wanted to know what it would look before starting the project, so their MAD skills were put to use, and a rendering was born. They liked the looks, so they put the project in motion.

To start off, the car is powered by a behemoth big-block Chevy 502 assembled by Craig Christansen. To give it some extra power, they chose a Crane Cams Hydraulic roller cam with .640-inch lift and 295 degrees of duration, Crane Cams stud girdle, Brodix aluminum heads, custom Moroso oil pan, and 2-inch custom Hooker Super Comp headers. A custom twin 3-inch air intake system designed by MAD with K&N filters mounted in front of the radiator support feeds a programmable tuned-port fuel-injection setup. An Airdyne electric fuel pump and filter help get fuel to the beast from the 23-gallon Fuel Safe fuel cell with bladder. A Be Cool aluminum radiator and some electric fans keep it cool. To harness the power and increase driveability, they chose a Jet 4L80E 4-speed overdrive transmission with a 10-inch 2800-rpm converter built by Joe Rivera at ProTorque. The power is put to a narrowed Fab 9 rear end stuffed with a 4.88:1 gears and a Detroit Locker. Hovering over the rear axle is a Chassisworks rear subframe with four-link, tubs, and Koni coil-overs. Front suspension consists of stock parts mixed with Superior 2-inch dropped spindles, Hotchkis springs, and fat sway bar. An MP Brakes master cylinder gives whiplash braking power to the Baer Brakes system with 13.5-inch front and 12-inch rear rotors. The MAD Chevelle is wearing MAD Delta-Vee 18x7-inch front wheels with 4.5-inch backspacing and 20x11-inch rear wheels with 5-inches of backspacing. The front tires are 225/40ZR18 Nitto NT555 Extreme ZRs, and the rears are 305/50/R20 Nitto NT404 Extreme Force tires.

The engine was lowered 1 inch and moved into the passenger compartment 1.5 inches, so a custom firewall and trans tunnel were fabbed. Other body mods include: the rocker trim, a custom frenched rear deck SS emblem, the rear wheelwells were stretched 1 inch, and fenderwell trim was removed. The body was colored 2001 Dimont BC 151 silver. The body was completed by Team X and MAD Ink. The interior was not left unattended. The dash pad was removed, a

Body and Electrical

MAD Chevelle
The Desmond Brothers '65 Malibu SS (Continued)

The finished product looks very close to the way MAD envisioned it; in fact, I would say they nailed it. It's a well-executed project. (Photo courtesy MAD Ink)

custom gauge panel by MAD was installed with AutoMeter Pro-Comp series gauges inset, and a custom cover was made for the B&M shifter. Recaro seats were re-covered in black leather. MidValley Sound did the sound system and tinted the windows. Ward Interiors stitched the upholstery. Restoration parts came from Original Parts group. An eight-point roll cage accompanies the black and charcoal interior.

The Chevelle was built by the Desmond Brothers, Brian Bullard, and Harry Hendrix. MAD Ink would like to thank Jet Performance, Original Parts Group, Pro-Torque, Team X, Bonspeed, Baer Brakes, and Performance Auto. They should actually thank themselves, without the original rendering they could have spent a lot of money and time building the MAD Chevelle into something a lot less MAD.

The tuned-port-injected 502 breathes through a MAD designed 3-inch twin air intake system. The silver/aluminum theme was carried out throughout the car. The engine was lowered and moved back for a little better weight distribution. (Photo courtesy MAD Ink)

How to Build GM Pro-Touring Street Machines

Chapter 7

Jim Sheldon's '56 Oldsmobile 88

Most of us remember a car we once sold, and wish we could have it back. Jim Sheldon remembers having a '56 Olds 88 when he and his wife Eleanor got married in 1961. To relive some old times, Jim bought another 88 in '02 and had Detroit Speed & Engineering make some updates. (Photo courtesy DSE)

The original engine was discarded for a more powerful and reliable 385 Fast-Burn GM crate engine. DSE removed a large section of the frame and grafted a section from a first generation Camaro frame in its place. (Photo courtesy DSE)

With every year that passes, certain memories grow fonder. Sometimes the memories get a little more magnificent as time goes on. Not necessarily because we are lying to ourselves, but because we don't always think the present day is as good as it could be. Jim Sheldon remembers how he enjoyed the '56 Oldsmobile 88 he owned back in 1961 when he and his wife Eleanor got married.

In 2002, Jim decided to relive some early memories by purchasing a restored '56 Olds 88. It had the 324-ci engine, 4-wheel drum brakes, and 1956 suspension technology, just like when it rolled off the assembly line. Jim decided to upgrade the car for better all-around performance, so he could drive in style and have a little fun at the same time. He enlisted the help of Detroit Speed & Engineering (DSE) in Brighton, Michigan.

A section of the frame was removed, and a section of a first generation F-body subframe was grafted in its place. It was installed five inches higher than the original frame so the car would have a lowered stance without oil-pan clearance issues. DSE installed one of their coil-over kits, a pair of their tubular upper control arms, and a slough of other DSE steering components. A Baer Brakes 13-inch Track kit with polished calipers was installed in the front. In the rear, there is a Ford 9-inch rear end equipped with a Baer Brakes 12-inch Track kit with polished calipers. To keep the engine compartment clean, an 8-inch Master Power Brakes booster was installed under the drivers seat, actuated by a Kugel brake-pedal assembly. The tire and wheel combination consists of 17-inch Budnik wheels, with 245s in the front and 285s in the rear.

The engine is a GM 385-hp Fast-Burn crate engine, coupled with a 4L60 overdrive transmission. A complete Vintage Air Front-Runner system was installed to keep the drive comfortable on those not-so-cool days.

Most of the interior was kept stock. Since the engine and transmission were higher than the original equipment, the floor panels were modified, and new carpet was necessary. DSE installed new Dynamat, and had Jerry Stewart from All American Upholstery installed a layer of jute to act as a heat and sound barrier. Then he installed all new carpet to compliment the stock interior panels. The body was left stock, but DSE added a custom firewall panel with a bead rolled in it that was inspired by the grill opening. It's a nice touch to use one feature and carry it out on custom parts elsewhere on a car. DSE also built some custom panels and brackets in the engine compartment and modified the inner fenderwells to a factory-look to finish off the job.

Who knew you could have good memories, live them again 42 years later, and have the ability to make even fonder ones. Jim and Eleanor's Oldsmobile is faster, better looking, and much more comfortable they remember or ever imagined.

The car handles like a dream, with the addition of properly selected coil-overs and improved suspension geometry. Compared to the 4-wheel drum brakes, the new Baer Brakes actually stop the car. Photo courtesy DSE)

CHAPTER 8

BUYING PARTS AND FINDING INFORMATION

Purchasing Parts

When you are building a car, you will need many parts. Some parts might be used, but some will need to be new. There are many different sources for parts these days. More manufacturers are making parts than ever before. You can save some money by buying from mail-order warehouses. To support your local economy and get expert advice, you can buy from your local speed shop. Automotive swap meets are a great place to get a good deal on hard-to-find parts. With the Internet growing, options for purchasing what you want or need has increased. Most of the parts you need are available from one or more sources.

Mail-Order Warehouses

Everyone is familiar with mail-order warehouses. They send you catalogs with ridiculously low prices on all the parts you need for your car. They can off these low prices because they buy their parts in bulk. They may buy 250 small-block Chevy billet distributors at one time. The manufacturers cut them deals because of the volume of parts they purchase. Mail-order companies make their money from volume sales and shipping and handling charges.

There is a drawback to ordering your parts through mail-order warehouses. They don't offer the customer service that you can get at a local speed shop. Maybe you want a new carburetor, but don't realize you need other parts like return springs, gaskets, carburetor studs, air cleaner stud, hose, fittings, etc. Maybe you don't know the exact size carburetor you need for your engine. You may need a little tuning help once you receive the carburetor. It might show up damaged from shipping, and you need to return it. If you order from a mail order warehouse, these issues are not as easy to deal with as they would be if you paid a little more for the carburetor from your local speed shop.

Speed Shops

Your local speed shop is a great place to buy new parts. If they do not have what you want in stock, they can usually order it for you. The parts may be more expensive than mail-order warehouses, but they offer services mail-order companies cannot. Maybe you are not sure

If you have a local speed shop, support them. They can't always beat the prices advertised by mail-order companies, but they do have the parts in stock when you need them.

How to Build GM Pro-Touring Street Machines

Chapter 8

When you need help finding the parts that are right for you, or some qualified advice, your local speed shop can help. If you have a problem with your purchase, you don't have to deal with shipping it back. Support local businesses.

which part is best for your application. Maybe you want to actually compare the part to a similar one from a different manufacturer. If you buy a part that turns out to be defective, you can drive back to the speed shop and swap it for a good part. What if you have a question about installing your part? There are always a few employees with knowledge to assist you. Mail-order warehouses can offer lower prices, but they cannot compete when it comes to customer service. If you spend your money at your local speed shop, you will be putting money back into your local economy. Speed shops cannot compete with mail-order warehouses in terms of pricing. Some people actually spend hours at the speed shop asking for help. Then they go home and order the parts from a mail-order warehouse. Sure, they save a few bucks, but they did not support the shop with the service. Speed shops cannot survive without support from customers. If you have a good local speed shop, support them by buying your parts there. That way they will still be in business the next time you need a little help with your project.

Swap Meets

There are not too many places you can get great prices on new and used parts. Swap meets offer a large selection of new and used parts. Maybe you are looking for a good deal on a fiberglass hood or some vintage valve covers. There are many good deals available at swap meets. For the most part, guys get up extremely early and set out their parts, hoping to get rid of everything. Not all their parts will sell, but they may be willing to come down on their price so they do not have to pack it all back up.

Wrecking Yards

Maybe your project calls for some stock parts. Maybe you need an interior panel that is not available from original equipment manufacturers or re-manufacturers. In this case, you may have to check some wrecking yards. A wrecking yard can be a goldmine. Sometimes they have everything you need. If nothing at all, they are a good source for simple small parts like bolts and washers. You may need a complete roof section or a complete firewall and cowl section. These parts are not available from reproduction companies. As time goes on, it is getting harder to find some parts. If you search yards off the beaten path, you may find what you are looking for.

Some wrecking yards have wrecked cars of all makes and models. Some are specific to antique cars. Some are specific to trucks. Others are specific to

Planning on upgrading to a new fuel-injected engine and 6-speed transmission? Some salvage yards like GM Sports Salvage in San Jose, California, have engine and transmission combos fresh out of cars and waiting for you. They typically include computers, harnesses, and sensors.

If you need a body panel or an interior part that is not reproduced, you will most likely find it here. An average wrecking yard might have two Camaros at all times if you are lucky. This salvage yard specializes in GM cars. Because of their popularity, this yard keeps plenty F-bodies in stock at all times.

Buying Parts and Finding Information

manufactures. These specialty wrecking or salvage yards help increase your chances of finding a specific part that you are searching for.

Salvage yards have complete engines out of new Camaros and Corvettes with transmissions and wiring harnesses. Some of these might even have high-performance parts already installed. For instance, an LT1 engine might have headers, cam, performance injectors, and ported heads. People have been known to find full-tilt racing transmissions, engines, and rear axles in wrecking yards. Maybe you will find a set of re-upholstered sport seats or a new aftermarket shifter. You never know what treasures lurk at your local wrecking yard.

Wrecking yards offer more than just the ability to purchase used parts. They are a great place to get reference information. Maybe you need to know how a part was installed. This might be necessary because you are doing a custom installation on your project and need to see how a part is installed from the factory on a car. You can see how a cup holder or a door panel is installed on a car or truck. A lot can be learned by removing interior panels on a newer car. You will get to see how the factory installs its parts. There are many new engineering ideas waiting for you to soak them up on newer model cars. Attention to these details will give you valuable information you can use when building your car.

Maybe you need to measure the frame width or the width of a 12-bolt rear end for a '69 Camaro. You may be installing suspension for a different vehicle, and you can get measurements from donor cars. Keep your eyes and your mind open to new ideas next time you stop by a wrecking yard. Bring a pen and some paper to jot down information. You can try bringing a camera, but most wrecking yards don't allow them for insurance reasons. Check with the management.

Internet

Before the 1990s there were less places to buy parts for your car. With the Internet growing as it has in the last ten years, your options for purchasing

This ZL-1 Camaro clone was built into a Pro-Touring car of epic proportions. It has a Wayne Due subframe, a T-5 transmission, an engine producing over 1000 hp with an all-aluminum Arias block. It has been seen for sale on E-Bay. (Charley Lillard)

what you want or need have increased. Now, from the comfort of your home, you can access parts manufacturers, warehouses, wrecking yards, distributors, builders, and other automotive related businesses.

Internet auctions are also a growing source for finding the parts you need or want. With the Internet auctions like E-Bay, you can buy parts from someone on the opposite coast. It is like having a wrecking yard or speed shop the size of the planet, but accessible from your home. The seller posts his new or used part on the website. You can log in and bid on it. If you are the highest bidder, you win the auction. People sell small parts you would not think twice about throwing into your garbage can. They also sell complete 1000-hp Arias blown big-block Pro-Touring '69 Camaros.

Other less-formal Internet sites have message boards with good car parts for sale. These message boards are not monitored or controlled by a secondary source to promote honesty. Most of the online buyers and sellers are honest, but you take your chances with any online purchasing, even with monitored purchasing.

Purchasing Cars

You may need to start your Pro-Touring project by purchasing a car. There are many items to take into consideration before purchasing a car.

Unfinished Projects

Check around, you will find good bargains. I saw an article once that stated that over 70 percent of "frame-off" projects are sold before they are finished, or never finished. After being in the automotive enthusiast hobby for almost twenty years, I believe in that figure. There are many reasons big car projects are sold before they are finished. The reasons range from loss of interest, lack of funds, life changes, and changes in overall planning. Most of the reasons can be traced to one problem. That reason is the lack of an original plan, or the ability to stick to it. Either way, you can benefit from purchasing a project car that has tons of money and hours poured into it. These cars are usually sold for less than half the money and time invested. This is a good way to save some money.

Chapter 8

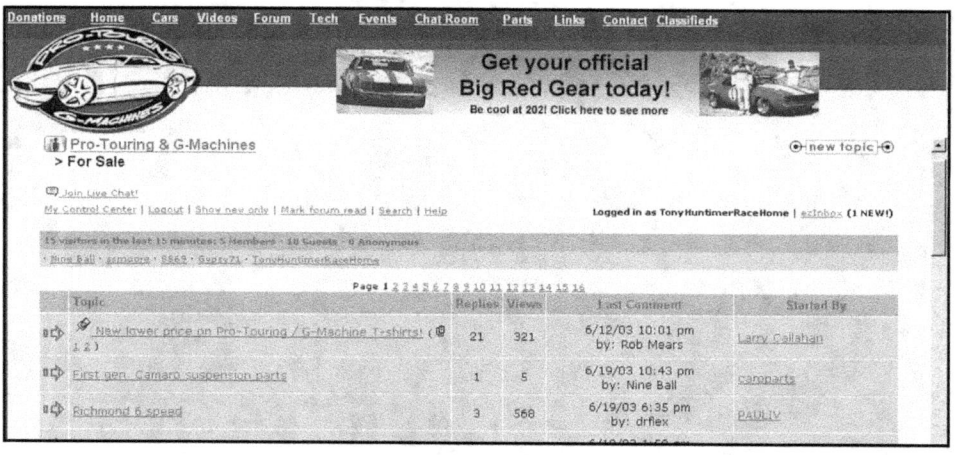

E-Bay isn't the only place on the Internet to find new and used parts for a bargain. www.pro-touring.com has a "For Sale" section on the message board. (Image courtesy www.pro-touring.com)

Purchasing an unfinished project car can also be a bad thing. It's possible the builder found a flaw in his plan or found some serious hidden rust or damage. An unfinished project might be slapped together with shoddy bodywork or inferior parts. If the car has a roll cage or heavily fabricated framework, inquire about the type and thickness of the tubing used. Bring a tape measure and check some of the measurements for symmetry and straightness. If you don't have experience surveying a car for possible problems, have an experienced person inspect the car before purchasing it.

If you have a good idea of what you are looking for before you start looking, you might not make a bad choice. For instance, if you are making a Pro-Touring car, you may want to stay away from some unfinished Pro-Street projects. Some Pro-Streeters are easily converted, but don't forget, they are set up for straight-line racing. It could cost more money than it's worth to get the car modified for Pro-Touring duties.

Clean Title

One hidden gremlin is paperwork. If you are building a Pro-Touring car, you will be driving it on the street, so make sure the title is clear. If the title is not clear, you may spend months getting it straightened out. You could spend an eternity at your local department of motor vehicles with little headway. Soaking long hours and a lot of money into a car that can't be registered for driving on the street would be heartbreaking. Do a little research on the status of the title of a car before you fork over your cash.

When I purchased my '68 Chevy Camaro from a tow yard, I had big plans. It was a rolling shell. I started pursuing registration right away. When I went down to DMV, I learned the car had been purchased by seven different parties within a six-year period. I spent months tracking the previous owners and had many unhappy visits to the DMV.

Every time I went to the DMV, I got a different story as to the path I had to traverse. Every teller had their own

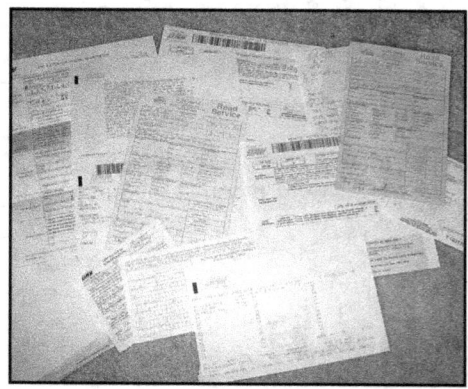

Here is a pile of paperwork and letters I have left over from the 7-month process I had to endure when I tried to register a car without a "clear" title.

interpretation of the registration process. After a few visits, I made sure to request the same teller. I had to attempt to contact all the previous owners, to make sure they would not contest my purchase of the car. I had to send registered letters to each party asking permission to register the Camaro in my name. One of the seven parties was living at the address on the paperwork. The fastest way to get the paperwork straightened out was to come to an agreement that he would refuse my registered letter as if he did not live there. Once I had all the returned registered letters, I went back to DMV. Now I was able to transfer ownership to myself. Since my car was not running, I had to register it as Non-Operational. The process was time consuming and frustrating. If you are not an easy-going person, like myself, don't attempt this at home. Once the Camaro was registered in my name, I started laboring on it. The last thing I wanted was to find out the car could not be registered, and have all my work done for nothing.

Vehicle Condition

You might think purchasing a rusted hulk of a body would make a good start for a Pro-Touring project, since you won't be ripping up a good car. Some think purchasing a completely restored car with the intent of turning it Pro-Touring would be a mistake or downright wrong. If you spend more money in the beginning for a straight body, you will be saving more money in the long run. Body and paint is typically the most expensive part of building any hot rod. Pro-Touring cars are no exception, so buying a car that does not need two new quarter panels and a floorpan is a good investment. You can find rust almost anywhere under a vinyl top, especially at the base of the rear window.

Sometimes sellers are pretty good about making a badly damaged car look very good. A friend once bought a car with the entire trunk area attached with two-by-fours, drywall screws, and a ton of body filler. If she had known to look at the inside of the quarter panels from inside the trunk, she would have seen the

Buying Parts and Finding Information

Be careful when purchasing cars and parts. Close inspection of this '68 Camaro shows evidence of a replacement quarter panel — from a '68 Pontiac Firebird. You can see the Bondo seeping through the emblem holes, and only the Firebird has these specific emblems. (Photo courtesy Bob Leveque)

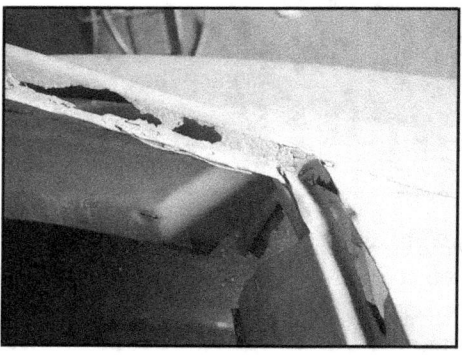

This is a common sight for owners of 1960s and 1970s GM cars. The rear window channel area is prone to severe rust. Repair will require cutting out areas and welding in patch panels.

Some earlier GMs have a high risk of rusted metal dashboards, especially towards the front where it meets the windshield. Rust never sleeps, so repair is important, and expensive.

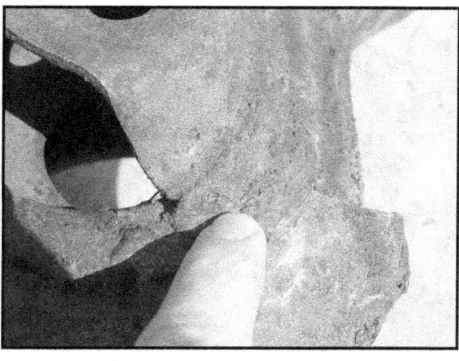

This is an upper shock mount on a '68 Camaro subframe. After inspecting a few frames, this hairline crack appears to be common. Cracks like this travel fast once they start.

Look under a car before you buy it. This first-generation Camaro frame has obviously seen some serious trauma. The opening in the frame is supposed to be a square shape. There is a good chance the frame is no longer square.

horrible work. The trunk section fell off when she was in an accident. The moral of this story is: Check the inside of body panels. Use a flashlight if necessary. Ask the seller if he or she would mind taking the car to a shop and putting it up on a lift for further inspection, before purchasing a car. Check the bottom seam of the quarter panel from behind the rear tire to the tail panel. Check the bottom seam of the tail panel. These areas are often overlooked when a panel is replaced or when rust is repaired. Floorpanel replacement is hard to detect without putting the car up on a rack. Some body shops don't spend a lot of time making floorpanels look perfect, since most people won't see them from underneath. Sometimes they leave the old rusty floorpan in place and put the panel right over the top. This allows rust to multiply fast, since moisture gets between panels.

If you are buying a 30-year-old car from just about any state, you should inspect the car for rust damage. Even some California-coast cars have excessive rust from damp coastal weather. When it comes to the structures of cars, there are many problem areas.

Getting Information

Information comes in many forms. It can be technical data. It can be a picture. It can also be advice. There are quite a few sources to pick up this information. Books, people, and hands-on experience are a few places to get this information. There are many other places to get ideas and reference material. Keep your eyes peeled and your mind open.

Books and Magazines

Since this is a book, I want to promote using books for information gathering first. There are many "How-To" books on the market. They have proven to be a good source of information and reference. I personally would not have been able to write this book if it were not for all the information available in my bookcase. In most cases, information written in books has been checked and is correct. As with anything in life, it is a good idea to double (and triple) check information before starting any project.

Performance automotive magazines are also a good place to pick up new ideas. Some magazines try to keep up on the latest trends, and some try to keep more low-buck, with cheap ways to modify your car. Cheap is good, but a line needs to be drawn somewhere. An engine rebuilt with a fifteen dollars and some duct tape will not last you very long. Most hot rod magazines try to be leading edge, by printing current products. Some products are not even available for public consumption at the time of print. You may see a new dashboard setup you think would look good in your car, or you might get to read about the addition of the current Detroit powerplant between the fenders of a '69 Camaro. Either way, there are many tips, tricks, and modifications waiting to be soaked up on the newsstands.

People

Manufacturer technical staff, speed shop personnel, friends, family, and other people can be great places to get information. Be careful. Get a second or third opinion before starting a project or buying a part.

Obviously, the manufacturers' technical personnel are the most qualified to give you information on what you need for your application or how to install a part they sell. They know the limitations of their products better than anyone. Be aware that you have to ask them the correct questions to get the correct answers. Some tech personnel want to sell you their parts and might not supply the all the information you may want. This depends on the company. If you are going to buy a transmission, and you have a 600-hp big-block Chevy, you might ask how long their transmission would last on a road course. Before you buy parts, make sure you let them know exactly how and where you plan to drive your car.

Checking with a competing manufacturer is a good idea. It will give you an idea about what is available and what may work best for you. Before buying parts, make sure you are making the correct decision. Impulse buying does not usually pay off.

Speed shops typically have at least one knowledgeable person who can usually offer great technical advice. Some speed shops are fully staffed with knowledgeable personnel. They can tell you which parts might be best for your application based on good and bad experiences they have had.

Friends and family members can be a good source of information, if they know what they are talking about. You will need to make your own decisions on which friends you use as a resource of information. For instance, when I was 18, I had a friend named Chris Fogarty. He had already graduated from a

There are many technical how-to books available from CarTech to assist you on building engines, chassis, and other parts of your car. Even if you don't do your own work, you can educate yourself and tell someone else exactly what you want.

Enthusiast magazines can also be a good source of information and inspiration. Most of the time, magazines include a healthy mix of technical articles, product installs, and car features. There are a variety of magazines available, and at least one of them is sure to catch your eye.

Buying Parts and Finding Information

technical school. He constantly distributed qualified advice, which proved to be correct. I knew the advice from my goof-ball 16-year old friend was not always correct. Even advice from my dad was not as qualified or as good. Picking whom you gather information and advice from can be important to your car and even your life.

Internet

The Internet is a great source of information. It can also be a great source of bad information. Getting information from the Internet is much like getting information from your friends. Some Websites have message boards and chat rooms. Be careful, a small percentage of people and Websites post bad or erroneous information. On the other hand, most Websites offer great information and reference material.

Pro-Touring.com is one Website in particular that is well put together. The message board is filled with good information about every aspect of Pro-Touring. Knowledgeable people frequent the site to dispense good information about build-ups. Some of the people have finished a project that you may be starting. They might be able to offer advice on what works and what does not work.

Pro-Touring.com also has good reference material. It has a message board with builders trading advice and experiences. The owners of the cars posted on this Website are friendly and willing to share technical information on how their cars were built or tips on how to get better performance out of your next upgrade.

The Internet is useful in other ways too. Just the other day, I needed to buy a transmission dipstick for a customer's LT1 and 4L60E install in a '69 Camaro. I didn't want to install a flashy chrome or aluminum dipstick that may detract from the overall look of the engine install. I was looking for a functional factory assembly. I jumped online and went to my favorite search engine, and typed in "LT1" and "Camaro." I found many pictures of Camaros with 4L60E transmissions. The dipsticks were way too long to look good in the customer's

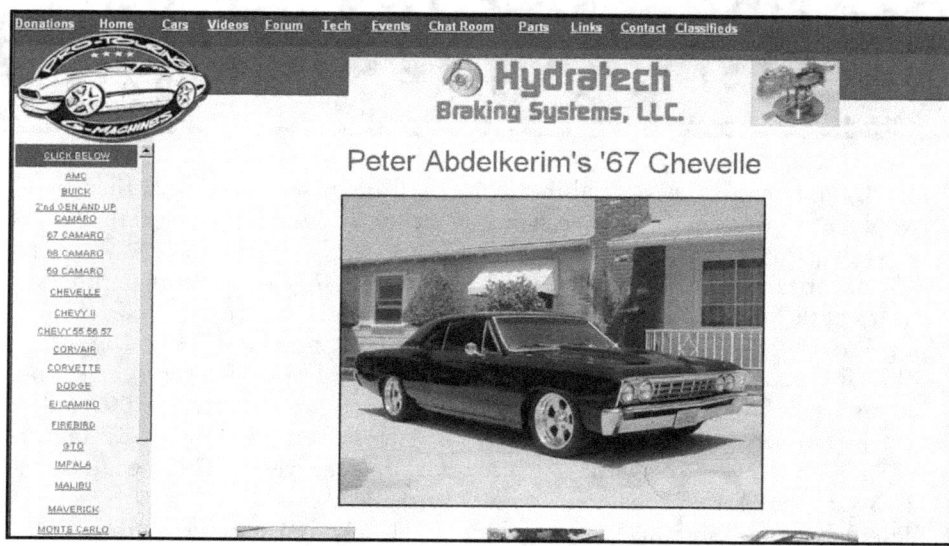

www.pro-touring.com is one of many great websites. It has good reference material, and a message board with builders trading advice and experiences. The owners of the cars posted on this website are friendly and willing to share technical information on how their cars were built. They also have plenty of tips on how to get better performance out of your next upgrade. (Courtesy of Larry Callahan and Peter Abdelkerim)

application. After typing in many other combinations in the search engine, I typed in "4L60E" and "Impala." I found a '95 Chevrolet Impala with an LT1 and a 4L60E transmission. I found a few high-resolution images of the engine compartment. The factory dipstick looked like it was the right length and configuration I needed for the application. I called the Chevrolet dealer and ordered the dipstick, dipstick tube, and tube seal. Once it showed up, it was the perfect shape and length. We only had to change the mount due to space constraints, but other than that, the Internet was a great tool to get what I needed without leaving the office.

New Car Dealers

Just like the wrecking yard, you can get new ideas on how to install parts and the latest cool parts available from the factory. Maybe you will see a new cup holder or a third brake light that would be perfect for your car. Look under the hood of a new car. You will notice the trend of dress-up covers that hide necessary wires and hoses. The automotive manufacturers have found better ideas for wiring new vehicles. If you take a good look at wiring bulkheads and fuse boxes, you will notice better components than those of a technologically challenged 1960s Chevrolet wiring system. Take a good look at the fit and finish of the interior and external panels. Manufacturers have advanced in this area in the last 15 years. Taking a little more time and attention to fit and finish detail on your Pro-Touring project makes a big difference.

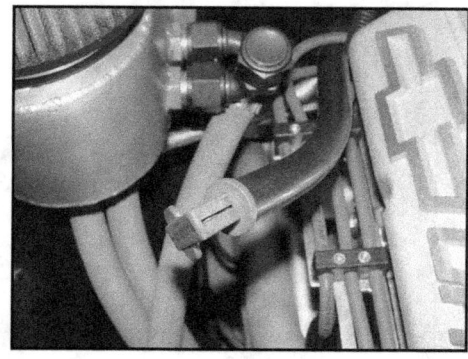

Instead of spending hours looking through magazines or going to the dealership to look through parts books to find a dipstick that would fit with the accessories on this engine, I turned to the Internet. Within minutes, I found the exact part I needed, so I called my local GM dealership and ordered the right part.

Chapter 8

Cam Douglass' '71 Camaro Z28

Cam Douglass is a dyed-in-the-wool performance nut with high status at a company called Optima Batteries. The batteries are powerful players in all forms of the automotive world, including Pro-Touring. Cam wouldn't think of relying on any other battery to power his heavy-hitting '71 Camaro Z28. He has driven it in two Silver State Classic Challenge races without issue. This is impressive considering the desert heat and sustained torture of averaging 135+mph for over 30 minutes at a time. If he didn't trust the products he sells, he wouldn't think of running them in his car.

Cam drove the car to a first place victory two years in a row at the Silver State race. His navigator was writer/photographer Scott Parkhurst, who wielded a trusty Radio Shack hand-held stopwatch. He drives the car on road courses every chance he gets, and has put over 10,000 miles worth of street miles on the car in just a couple of years. This beauty gets used and abused.

The body is stock with the exception of the Harwood cowl hood. MASCAR covered everything with the original color, PPG Citrus Green Metallic, and white stripes. The Z-28 is powered by an original numbers matching, 1971 4-bolt LT1 block. It was assembled with a GM steel crank, Bowtie rods, JE 10.5:1 pistons, Jesel Belt-drive, Crane mechanical roller cam and rockers, AFR 210/64cc aluminum heads, Edelbrock Victor Jr. intake, and a Holley 750 double pumper. The engine is topped off with a K&N air filter and K&N carbon fiber valve covers. The cooling chores are accomplished with a Meziere electric water pump and a Ron Davis aluminum radiator with electric fans.

A Centerforce Light Metal billet aluminum clutch and flywheel is the

Cam Douglass built this heavy-hitting '71 Z28 Camaro for all-around performance. That's what Pro-Touring is all about. He and Scott Parkhurst have taken 2 consecutive first place finishes in the Silver State Classic Challenge. (Photo by Scott Parkhurst)

Buying Parts and Finding Information

Cam Douglass' '71 Camaro Z28 (Continued)

grabbing force that turns the Richmond 6-speed trans, aluminum driveshaft, and 12-bolt with 3.08:1 Richmond gears. Rolling stock consists of American Racing 17x9.5-inch and 17x11-inch wheels wrapped with Goodyear GSC 275/40x17 and 315/35x17 tires. The braking is accomplished by Baer Brakes Track and Touring brake kits. Hotchkis Suspension is responsible for the Race-tuned spring and sway-bar package. Some welded subframe connectors help reduce chassis flex, but Cam didn't stop there. He had Fast Eddies Race Cars install a 6-point roll cage and do some other chassis fabrication. To continue the race-bred interior, he installed some Cobra carbon fiber race bucket seats, Crow harnesses, Tiki-built door panels, and AutoMeter gauges installed in a custom aluminum dash built by Tiki.

When Cam is getting ready for a race, he has Art and Mike Chrisman "race-prep" the Z28 to be sure everything is in good working order. Cam's racing enthusiasm and Optima Batteries have been great together. Who knows what great ventures are on the horizon.

Looking at the rear of the Camaro, you see it is all business. The 315's on 17x11-inch American Racing wheels fill up the rear wheelwells. The 6-point cage is just a subtle hint of performance potential. (Photo by Scott Parkhurst)

The interior is simple and to the point. Its Cobra carbon fiber seats, Tiki-built door and dash panels, AutoMeter gauges, and roll cage say it's not your average street car. The paper in the middle of the dash helps Scott Parkhurst navigate when he and Cam road race the car. (Photo courtesy Cam Douglass)

The block is an original numbers matching LT1. It's equipped with all the go-fast hard parts. The Optima battery mounted in the trunk and the Powermaster alternator help keep electrical accessories like the Meziere water pump running strong. (Photo courtesy Cam Douglass)

How to Build GM Pro-Touring Street Machines

APPENDIX A

Pro-Touring Source Guide

A. O. Engineering
19523 Delaware Cir.
Boca Raton, FL 33434
(561) 483-2984

Aeromotive, Inc.
5400 Merriam Drive
Merriam, KS 66203
(913) 647-7300
www.aeromotiveinc.com

AGR Performance
4920 Rondo Dr.
Fort Worth, TX 76106
(817) 626-9006
www.agrsteering.com

American Auto Wire
150 Heller Place, #17W
Bellmawr, NJ 08031-2555
(856)933-0801
www.americanautowire.com

American Touring Specialties
7207 W. Mesa Vista Ave
Las Vegas, NV 89113
www.t56kit.com

Art Morrison Enterprises
5301 8th St E
Fife WA 98424
(800) 929-7188
www.artmorrison.com

Baer Brakes Inc
3108 W. Thomas Rd, Suite 1201
Phoenix, AZ 85017-5306
(602) 233-1411
www.baer.com

Bonspeed
3544 E. Enterprise Dr.
Anaheim, CA 92807
(714) 666-1999
www.bonspeed.com

BRP Hot Rods
5849 Rogers Rd.
Cumming, GA 30040
(770) 751-0687
www.brphotrods.com

Cadillac Hot Rod Fabricators
(760) 451-8796
www.chrfab.com

Campbell Auto Restoration
260 Cristich Lane, Unit A-1
Campbell, CA 95008
(408) 371-5522

Classic Industries
18460 Gothard Street
Huntington Beach, CA 92648
(800) 854-1280
www.classicindustries.com

Corbeau USA
(801) 255-3737
www.corbeau.com

Detroit Speed & Engineering
185 McKenzie Road
Mooresville, NC, 28115
(704) 662-3272
www.detroitspeed.com

Dynotech Engineering
1635 Northwood
Troy, MI 48084
(800) 633-5559
www.dynotechengineering.com

FuelSafe
63257 Nels Anderson Road
Bend, OR 97701
(800) 433-6524
www.fuelsafe.com

Fuel System Solutions
www.dynowest.com

General Motors
www.gm.com

Global West
1455 North Linden Ave.
Rialto CA 92376
(877) 470-2975
www.globalwest.net

Pro-Touring Source Guide

Hotchkis Performance
12035 Burke St. Suite 13
Santa Fe Springs, CA 90670
(877) 466-7655
www.hotchkis.net

Hotrods to Hell, Inc.
100 East Prospect Blvd.
Burbank, CA 91502
(818) 842-4360
www.hotrodstohell.net

Hydratech Braking Systems
26642 Haverhill Dr.
Warren, MI 48091
(586) 427-6970
www.hydroboost.com

Jags That Run
P.O. Box 66
Livermore, CA 94551
(925) 462-3619
www.jagsthatrun.com

Johns Fuel Systems
2535 West Winton Ave
Hayward, CA 94545
(510) 786-2505

Katech Inc.
24324 Sorrentino Ct.
Clinton Twp., MI 48035
(586) 791-4120
www.katechengines.com

Keisler Automotive Engineering
2216-B W. Gov. John Sevier Highway
Knoxville, TN 37920
(865) 609-8187
www.keislerauto.com

Koni North America
1961 International Way
Hebron, KY 41048
(859) 586-4100
www.koni.com

KRC Power Streering
2115 Barrett Park Drive
Kennesaw, GA 30144
(770) 422-5135
www.krcpower.com

Mad Ink
P.O. Box 2626
Marysville, CA 95901
www.madmachines.com

Martz Chassis
PO Box 538
646 Imlerton Rd
Bedford, PA 15522
(814) 623-9501
www.martzchassis.net

Metal Works Performance Engineering
12540 West Cedar Drive
Lakewood, CO 80228
(303) 980-4700
www.metalworksperformance.com

Meziere
220 S. Hale Ave.
Escondido, CA 92029
(760) 746-3273
www.meziere.com

Milodon Inc
20716 Plummer Street
Chatsworth, CA 91311
(818) 407-1211

OER
18460 Gothard Street
Huntington Beach, CA 92648
(800) 955-1511
www.oerparts.com

Optima Batteries
Johnson Controls Inc.
(888) 867-8462
www.optimabatteries.com

Painless Performance Products
9505 Santa Paula Drive
Fort Worth, TX 76116-5929
(800) 423-9696
www.painlesswiring.com

Performance Stainless Steel, Inc.
PO Box 67266
Scotts Valley CA 95067
(831) 335-7901
www.performancesst.com

Phoenix Transmissions
1304 Mineral Wells Hwy.
Weatherford, TX 76086
(817) 599-7680
www.phoenixtrans.com

Pole Position Racing Products
2021 E. 74th Avenue, Unit J
Denver, CO 80229
(888) 303-8555
www.polepositionrp.com

Precision Brakes Company
476 Applegate Way
Ashland, OR 97520
(541) 488-2604
www.precisionbrakes.com

Promax Corporation
207 J.D. Yarnell Ind. Pkwy
P.O. Box 960
Clinton, TN 37717-0960
(865) 457-7605
www.vennom.com

Prothane
3560 Cadillac Ave
Costa Mesa, CA 92626
(714) 979-4990
www.prothane.com

Pro-Touring.com
www.pro-touring.com
www.g-machines.com

RaceHome.com
P.O. Box 8232
San Jose, CA 95155-8232
www.racehome.com

Robert Gumm
8605A Michigan Ct.
Clovis, NM 88101
www.v8monza.com

Safecraft Safety Equipment
5165-C Commercial Circle
Concord, CA 94520
(800) 400-2259
www.safecraft.com

Saldana Racing Products
3800 N. State Road 267, Unit B
Brownsburg, IN 46112
(317) 852-4193
www.saldanaracingproducts.com

Appenix A

Setrab Oil Coolers
P.O. Box 419
3958 North SR3,
Sunbury, OH 43074
www.setrab.com

Speed Direct
1901 S. FM 129
Santo, TX 76472
(888) 425-2776
www.speeddirect.com

Speed Merchant
345 Lincoln Ave
San Jose, CA 95126
(408) 295-0930
www.speedmerchant.com

Technostalgia
1889 E Telegraph Hill Rd
Madison IN 47250
(812) 265-0062
www.cool-leds.com

Total Control Products, LLC
9901 Kent Street, Suite 1
Elk Grove, CA 95624
(916) 405-8200
www.totalcontrolproducts.com

Tuned Port Induction Specialties
4255 Creek rd.
Chaska, MN 55318
(952) 448 6021
www.tpis.com

U.S. Bodysource
9009 South East C.R. 325
Hampton, FL 32044
(352) 468-2203
www.usbody.com

VegaMods
(714)-449-2800
Vegamods@aol.com

Vintage Air
18865 Goll St.
San Antonio, TX 78266
(800) 862-6658
www.vintageair.com

Wayne Due
14003 Smokey Pt. Blvd.
Marysville, WA 98271
(360) 657-4810
www.waynedue.com

Weir Hot Rod Products
(707) 647-0513
www.weirhotrodproducts.com

XRP
5630 Imperial Hwy.
South Gate, CA 90280
(562) 861-4765
www.xrp.com

Year One
P. O. Box 521
Braselton, GA 30517
(800) 932-7633
www.yearone.com

This HTH equipped 1966 Chevelle, owned by Geoff Chandler, is designated as an A-body. (Photo courtesy Geoff Chandler)

Appendix B

General Motors Body Designations

The following is a list of General Motors body/frame letter designations. The early GM cars were not actually designated as body types, so some of the cars are matched up with the body designation of the years following the adoption of the body designation. For instance, the early Corvettes were not originally considered Y-bodies, but since the Y-body designation was given to them in 1972, the 1953 through 1971 Corvettes are listed in the Y-body group.

This 1969 Camaro is considered a first generation F-body. It was built by Metal Works Performance Engineering for J. R. Osborne. (Photo courtesy Kip Valdez)

of the cars change body designation when they change from a 2-door to a 4-door. For instance, a 1973 Olds Cutlass 2-door was an A-body, but it used a G-body frame for its 4-door versions. There is not enough space for every body/frame type or car model, and some are not currently popular for Pro-Touring build-ups. For instance, the following bodies are not listed: C, D, E, J, K, N, T, P, and W. There are quite a few GM cars not listed because they were released before body designations were adopted.

This 1962 Impala, built by Jesse Greening of Greening Auto Company, might not be Pro-Touring with its air-bag suspension, but it's beautiful and it's a B-body.

Most cars models of each body are not represented in the body listing due to space constraints. For instance, Buick Regals are listed, but I didn't list all of the models: Grand National, T-type, GNX, LeSabre Grand National, and Sport Coupe, Turbo-T, and WH1. Some

Stan Davis's 1987 heavily modified Buick T-Type is a good example of a G-body. (Photo courtesy Joe Pettitt)

High-Performance Car Stereo

Appendix B

In addition, the cars below are not all designed the same from the first year to the last year. For Instance, the F-body Camaro was completely redesigned four times between 1967 and 2002, and it had a redesigned frame (without a complete redesign of the body) between 1970-1/2 to 1981. Due to references in the book the F-body and X-body are broken down into generations.

A-bodies
1964-1987 Chevy Chevelle
1964-1987 Chevy El Camino
1964-1981 Buick Skylark
1964-1981 Olds Cutlass
1964-1973 Pontiac GTO
1973-1981 Chevy Monte Carlo

B-bodies
1958-1985 & 1991-1996 Chevy Impala
1959-1960 Chevy El Camino
1962-1968 Pontiac Grand Prix
1972-1992 Cadillac Fleetwood

F-bodies
First Generation 1967 through 1969
Second Generation 1970-1/2 through 1981
Third Generation 1982 through 1992
Fourth Generation 1993 through 2002
1967 through 2002 Chevy Camaro
1967 through 2002 Pontiac Firebird

Britt Guerlain's 1976 Vega is one of the many H-body cars GM produced. These cars are light and make great Pro-Touring candidates. (Photo courtesy Britt Guerlain)

G-bodies
1969-1987 Pontiac Grand Prix
1978-1988 Chevy El Camino
1978-1987 Buick Regal
1978-1988 Olds Cutlass
1982-1988 Chevy Monte Carlo

H-bodies
1971-1977 Vega
1971-1977 Pontiac Astre
1975-1980 Chevy Monza
1975-1980 Buick Skyhawk
1975-1980 Olds Starfire
1976-1980 Pontiac Sunbird

Y-bodies
1953-1982 Corvette
1984-2004 Corvette

X-bodies
First Generation 1962 through 1967
Second Generation 1968 through 1974
Third Generation 1975 through 1979
1962-1979 Chevy Nova and Chevy II
1971-1977 Pontiac Ventura
1973-1975 Buick Apollo
1973-1979 Olds Omega
1974 Pontiac GTO
1976-1979 Buick Skylark

This 1967 Nova is considered a first generation X-body. (Photo Courtesy Geoff Chandler)

Dave Morin's mid-60s Corvette isn't technically a Y-body because GM didn't assign the designation until 1972, but most enthusiasts now refer to these cars as early Y-bodies.

More great titles available from CarTech®...

S-A DESIGN

Super Tuning & Modifying Holley Carburetors — Perf, street and off-road applications. *(SA08)*

Custom Painting — Gives you an overview of the broad spectrum of custom painting types and techniques. *(SA10)*

Street Supercharging, A Complete Guide to — Bolt-on buying, installing and tuning blowers. *(SA17)*

Engine Blueprinting — Using tools, block selection & prep, crank mods, pistons, heads, cams & more! *(SA21)*

David Vizard's How to Build Horsepower — Building horsepower in any engine. *(SA24)*

Chevrolet Small-Block Parts Interchange Manual — Selecting & swapping high-perf. small-block parts. *(SA55)*

High-Performance Ford Engine Parts Interchange — Selecting & swapping big- and small-block Ford parts. *(SA56)*

How To Build Max Perf Chevy Small-Blocks on a Budget — Would you believe 600 hp for $3000? *(SA57)*

How To Build Max Performance Ford V-8s on a Budget — Dyno-tested engine builds for big- & small-blocks. *(SA69)*

How To Build Max-Perf Pontiac V8s — Mild perf apps to all-out performance build-ups. *(SA78)*

How To Build High-Performance Ignition Systems — Guide to understanding auto ignition systems. *(SA79)*

How To Build Max Perf 4.6 Liter Ford Engines — Building & modifying Ford's 2- & 4-valve 4.6/5.4 liter engines. *(SA82)*

How To Build Big-Inch Ford Small-Blocks — Add cubic inches without the hassle of switching to a big-block. *(SA85)*

How To Build High-Perf Chevy LS1/LS6 Engines — Modifying and tuning Gen-III engines for GM cars and trucks. *(SA86)*

How To Build Big-Inch Chevy Small-Blocks — Get the additional torque & horsepower of a big-block. *(SA87)*

Honda Engine Swaps — Step-by-step instructions for all major tasks involved in engine swapping. *(SA93)*

How to Build High-Performance Chevy Small — Block Cams/Valvetrains — Camshaft & valvetrain function, selection, performance, and design. *(SA105)*

High-Performance Jeep Cherokee XJ Builder's Guide 1984-2001 — Build a useful, Cherokee for mountains, the mud, the desert, the street, and more. *(SA109)*

How to Build and Modify Rochester Quadrajet Carburetors — Selecting, rebuilding, and modifying the Quadrajet Carburetors. *(SA113)*

Rebuilding the Small-Block Chevy: Step-by-Step Videobook — 160-pg book plus 2-hour DVD show you how to build a street or racing small-block Chevy. *(SA116)*

How to Paint Your Car on a Budget — Everything you need to know to get a great-looking coat of paint and save money. *(SA117)*

How to Drift: The Art of Oversteer — This comprehensive guide to drifting covers both driving techniques and car setup. *(SA118)*

Turbo: Real World High-Performance Turbocharger Systems — *Turbo* is the most practical book for enthusiasts who want to make more horsepower. Foreword by Gale Banks. *(SA123)*

High-Performance Chevy Small-Block Cylinder Heads — Learn how to make the most power with this popular modification on your small-block Chevy. *(SA125)*

High Performance Brake Systems — Design, selection, and installation of brake systems for Musclecars, Hot Rods, Imports, Modern Era cars and more. *(SA126)*

High Performance C5 Corvette Builder's Guide — Improve the looks, handling and performance of your Corvette C5. *(SA127)*

High Performance Diesel Builder's Guide — The definitive guide to getting maximum performance out of your diesel engine. *(SA129)*

How to Rebuild & Modify Carter/Edelbrock Carbs — The only source for information on rebuilding and tuning these popular carburetors. *(SA130)*

Building Honda K-Series Engine Performance — The first book on the market dedicated exclusively to the Honda K series engine. *(SA134)*

Engine Management-Advanced Tuning — Take your fuel injection and tuning knowledge to the next level. *(SA135)*

How to Drag Race — Car setup, beginning and advanced techniques for bracket racing and pro classes, and racing science and math, and more. *(SA136)*

4x4 Suspension Handbook — Includes suspension basics & theory, advanced/high-performance suspension and lift systems, axles, how-to installations, and more. *(SA137)*

GM Automatic Overdrive Transmission Builder's and Swapper's Guide — Learn to build a bulletproof tranny and how to swap it into an older chassis as well. *(SA140)*

High-Performance Subaru Builder's Guide — Subarus are the hottest compacts on the street. Make yours even hotter. *(SA141)*

How to Build Max-Performance Mitsubishi 4G63t Engines — Covers every system and component of the engine, including a complete history. *(SA148)*

How to Swap GM LS-Series Engines Into Almost Anything — Includes a historical review and detailed information so you can select and fit the best LS engine. *(SA156)*

How to Autocross — Covers basic to more advanced modifications that go beyond the stock classes. *(SA158)*

Designing & Tuning High-Performance Fuel Injection Systems — Complete guide to tuning aftermarket stand-alone systems. *(SA161)*

Design & Install In Car Entertainment Systems — The latest and greatest electronic systems, both audio and video. *(SA163)*

How to Build Max-Performance Hemi Engines — Build the biggest baddest vintage Hemi. *(SA164)*

How to Digitally Photograph Cars — Learn all the modern techniques and post processing too. *(SA168)*

High-Performance Differentials, Axles, & Drivelines — Must have book for anyone thinking about setting up a performance differential. *(SA170)*

How To Build Max-Performance Mopar Big Blocks — Build the baddest wedge Mopar on the block. *(SA171)*

How to Build Max-Performance Oldsmobile V-8s — Make your Oldsmobile keep up with the pack. *(SA172)*

How to Make Your Muscle Car Handle — Upgrade your musclecar suspension to modern standards. *(SA175)*

Full-Size Fords 1955-1970 — A complete color history of full sized fords. *(SA176)*

Rebuilding Any Automotive Engine: Step-by-Step Videobook — Rebuild any engine with this book DVD combo. DVD is over 3 hours long! *(SA179)*

How to Supercharge & Turbocharge GM LS-Series Engines — Boost the power of todays most popular engine. *(SA180)*

The New MINI Performance Handbook — All the performance tricks for your new MINI. *(SA182)*

How to Build Max-Performance Ford FE Engines — Finally, performance tricks for the FE junkie. *(SA183)*

How to Build Altered Wheelbase Cars — Build a wild altered car. Complete history too! *(SA189)*

How to Build Period Correct Hot Rods — Build a hot rod true to your favorite period. *(SA192)*

How to Rebuild and Modify AMC V-8 Engine — Build an AMC beast! *(SA193)*

Automotive Sheet Metal Forming & Fabrication — Create and fabricate your own metalwork. *(SA196)*

How to Build Max-Performance Chevy Big Block on a Budget — Great new Big Block from the master, David Vizard. *(SA198)*

Chevy/GMC Pickup Performance Projects 1967-72 — Great new projects for Chevy's most popular truck. *(SA201)*

Performance Automotive Engine Math — All the formulas and facts you will ever need. *(SA204)*

S-A DESIGN RESTORATION SERIES

How to Restore Your Mustang 1964 1/2-1973 — Step by step restoration for your classic Mustang. *(SA165)*

Muscle Car Interior Restoration Guide — Make your interior look and smell new again. Includes dash restoration. *(SA167)*

How to Restore Your Camaro 1967-1969 — Step by step restoration of your 1st gen Camaro. *(SA178)*

S-A DESIGN WORKBENCH® SERIES

Workbench® Series books feature step by step instruction with hundreds of color photos for stock rebuilds and automotive repair.

How To Rebuild the Small-Block Chevrolet — *(SA26)*
How to Rebuild the Small-Block Ford — *(SA102)*
How to Rebuild & Modify High-Performance Manual Transmissions — *(SA103)*
How to Rebuild the Big-Block Chevrolet — *(SA142)*
How to Rebuild the Small-Block Mopar — *(SA143)*
How to Rebuild GM LS-Series Engines — *(SA147)*
How to Rebuild Any Automotive Engine — *(SA151)*
How to Rebuild Honda B-Series Engines — *(SA154)*
How to Rebuild the 4.6/5.4 Liter Ford — *(SA155)*
Automotive Welding: A Practical Guide — *(SA159)*
Automotive Wiring and Electrical Systems — *(SA160)*
How to Rebuild Big-Block Ford Engines — *(SA162)*
Automotive Bodywork & Rust Repair — *(SA166)*
How to Rebuild Pontiac V-8s — *(SA200)*

HISTORIES AND PERSONALITIES

Quarter-Mile Chaos — Rare & stunning photos of terrifying fires, explosions, and crashes in drag racing's golden age. *(CT425)*

Fuelies: Fuel Injected Corvettes 1957-1965 — The first Corvette book to focus specifically on the fuel injected cars, which are among the most collectible. *(CT452)*

Slingshot Spectacular: Front-Engine Dragster Era — Relive the golden age of front engine dragsters in this photo packed trip down memory lane. *(CT464)*

Chrysler Concept Cars 1940-1970 — Fascinating look at the concept cars created by Chrysler during this golden age of the automotive industry. *(CT470)*

Fuel Altereds Forever — Includes more than 250 photos of the most popular drivers and racecars from the Fuel Altered class. *(CT475)*

Yenko — Complete and thorough of the man, his business and his legendary cars. *(CT485)*

Lost Hot Rods — Great Hot Rods from the past rediscovered. *(CT487)*

Grumpy's Toys — A collection of Grumpy's greats. *(CT489)*

Woodward Avenue: Cruising the Legendary — Revisit the glory days of Woodward! *(CT491)*

Rusted Muscle — A collection of junkyard muscle cars. *(CT492)*

America's Coolest Station Wagons — Wagons are cooler than they ever have been. *(CT493)*

Super Stock — A paperback version of a classic best seller. *(CT495)*

Jerry Heasley's Rare Finds — Great collection of Heasley's best finds. *(CT497)*

Ed 'Big Daddy' Roth — Paperback reprint of a classic best seller. *(CT500)*

Visit us online at www.cartechbooks.com for more info!

More Information for Your Project ...

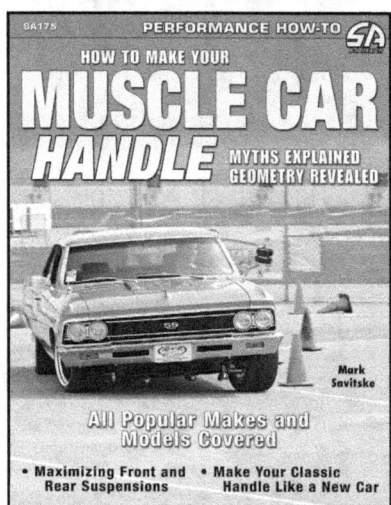

HOW TO MAKE YOUR MUSCLE CAR HANDLE by Mark Savitski. How to Make Your Muscle Car Handle defines, explores, and reviews the complete suspension system, and teaches you how to best choose your upgrades for maximum effectiveness. Cornering and handling is becoming a critical part of any performance car, and the great American muscle machines have the potential to do so on par with many modern sports cars. Softbound, 8.5 x 11 inches, 144 pages, 400 photos. *Item# SA175*

HOW TO SWAP GM LS-SERIES ENGINES INTO ALMOST ANYTHING by Jefferson Bryant. This book shows how to fit these powerhouse engines into popular GM F-Body cars, such as the Camaro and Firebird, but also how to install them into non-GM muscle cars, sports cars, trucks, and of course, hot rods. This book includes a historical review, complete specs, and detailed information so you can select and fit the best LS engine for a particular vehicle and application. The book also shows you how to perform necessary oil-pan modifications and adapt accessory drivers as well as choose the most suitable fuel pump, exhaust system, wiring harness, and electronic control module. Softbound, 8.5 x 11 inches, 144 pgs, 375 color photos. *Item# SA156*

HOW TO SUPERCHARGE & TURBOCHARGE GM LS-SERIES ENGINES by Barry Kluczyk. In How to Supercharge and Turbocharge GM LS Series Engines, supercharger and turbocharger design and operation are covered in detail, so the reader has a solid understanding of each system and can select the best system for their particular budget, engine, and application. Also covered in detail are the installation challenges, necessary tools, and the time required to do the job. Once the system has been installed, the book covers tuning, maintenance, and how to avoid detonation so the engine stays healthy. Softbound, 8.5 x 11 inches, 144 pages, 391 photos. *Item# SA180*

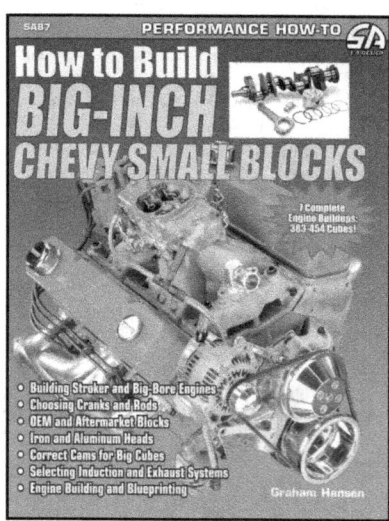

HOW TO BUILD BIG-INCH CHEVY SMALL-BLOCKS (COLOR EDITION) by Graham Hansen. By building a big-cube small block, you can have all the additional torque and horsepower of a big block, without all the extra weight, expense, and effort. In this all-new color edition, Graham Hansen takes a step-by-step approach to selecting the best OEM or aftermarket block, crank, rods, and pistons to construct your big-inch short block. Edition is a new color update. Softbound, 8.5 x 11 inches, 144 pages, 328 photos. *Item# SA87*

AUTOMOTIVE WELDING: A Practical Guide by Jeffrey Zurschmeide with Russell Nyberg. Automotive Welding: A Practical Guide covers the kinds of welding and metalworking available or commonly used, the tools required to perform welding tasks, the different types of welders available, basic welding techniques, grinding and cutting, various forms of sheetmetal work, frame repair and reinforcement, filling body holes and rust repair, tube-steel projects, and more. Automotive Welding: A Practical Guide is a practical book packed with useful information on the types of projects that a self-trained welder can complete and that a typical automotive enthusiast would want to undertake. Softbound, 8.5 x 11 inches, 144 pgs, approx. 400 color photos. *Item# SA159*

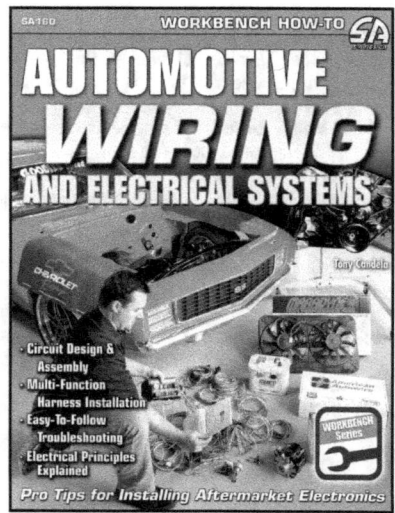

AUTOMOTIVE WIRING AND ELECTRICAL SYSTEMS by Tony Candela. Automotive Wiring and Electrical Systems is the perfect book to unshroud the mysteries of automotive electrics and electronic systems. The basics of electrical principles, including voltage, amperage, resistance, and Ohm's law, are revealed in clear and concise detail, so the enthusiast understands what these mean in the construction and repair of automotive electrical circuits. All the tools and the proper equipment required for automotive electrical tasks are covered. Softbound, 8.5 x 11 inches, approx. 350 color photos. *Item# SA160*

www.cartechbooks.com or 1-800-551-4754

www.ingramcontent.com/pod-product-compliance
Lightning Source LLC
Chambersburg PA
CBHW051412070526
44584CB00023B/3398